CONVICTION
AT ANY COST

PROSECUTORIAL MISCONDUCT AND THE PURSUIT OF MICHAEL SEGAL

CONVICTION
AT ANY COST

PROSECUTORIAL MISCONDUCT AND THE
PURSUIT OF MICHAEL SEGAL

"You'll wear a wire on anyone we tell you to, you
know everybody in this town."
– FBI AGENT PATRICK MURPHY

Maurice Possley

For information about this title or to order other books
and/or electronic media, contact the publisher:

McDonough & Green Publishing
10 S. Riverside Plaza, Suite 1450
Chicago, IL 60606
https://convictionatanycost.com/

ISBNs
978-1-7331554-0-3 (hardcover)
978-1-7331554-2-7 (paperback)
978-1-7331554-1-0 (ebook)

Library of Congress Control Number: 2019915029

Printed in the United States of America

Cover and Interior design: Van-garde Imagery, Inc.

Contents

Dedication

THIS BOOK IS DEDICATED TO all of members of Michael Segal's family, business associates and friends whose support was an inspiration and a pillar of strength, as well as those who unselfishly contributed to Michael's legal defense at the risk of possible ridicule. In particular, this book is dedicated to four men who were very special to Michael and who have passed on. George Dunne was a mentor and role model. His character, standards of decency and support provided Michael with the skills to succeed in the insurance business as well as in life. Harvey Silets was Michael's attorney and friend who fought so hard for him. Jerry Solovy was a close friend whose legal guidance Michael will always cherish. And especially, Uncle Marvin Leibowitz, who uniquely helped support Michael's family.

Introduction

WHEN MICHAEL SEGAL FIRST REACHED out to ask me to help him write a book about his federal prosecution, he was still in prison. I told him I wasn't interested. He said he wanted me because of my expertise as a journalist writing about prosecutorial misconduct in Chicago and in California. I still said no.

What possibly could be interesting about the case of a man who had been convicted and sentenced to prison for—according to the charges—looting about $30 million from his Chicago company, Near North Insurance Brokerage? It was, it seemed to me, just another case of financial fraud in a city that seems to churn out financial frauds quite regularly.

I couldn't have been more wrong.

Over time, Michael began sending me documents from the case that were enticing and began to spell out a tale of prosecutorial misconduct that had gone unchecked and unpunished despite layer upon layer of proof to the contrary.

The trickle of documents and court records began as a trickle and ultimately turned into a torrent. And I was hooked.

What emerged is the story you are about to read. It is the story of how federal prosecutors attempted to force Michael to wear a concealed recording device to try to entrap his friends and others—virtually anyone that the FBI told him to record—and the consequences of his refusal to do so. It a story about how Segal and his lawyers uncovered evidence he was a victim of cyberspying and the covert taping of his own lawyer.

It was a decision that cost him his company, the fifth largest insurance brokerage in the United States, and cost him his liberty for eight years. Close to 1,000 people lost their jobs.

This story, based on transcripts and court records, could be the basis for a spy novel, except that it is true. It is a story of how prosecutors ran roughshod over a man to destroy him and the company he spent a lifetime building and nurturing.

And in the end, there were no victims, there was no fraudulent intent, and the company that had supposedly been bilked suffered no losses.

How does this happen? It was a question Michael and his lawyers had been asking for years. This book is an in-depth look at what did happen—the playbook of the prosecution—and sheds some light on why it happened.

What happened here is not unique just to Michael. Over the last decade, cases of prosecutorial misconduct increasingly have surfaced across the United States and have affected the lives of a wide range of people—from the man on the street to corporate titans to elected officials, including a U.S. senator.

Michael has been adamant that his case should present a lesson that others may see and learn, particularly in the insurance world that he successfully inhabited for four decades. As a consequence, there will be discussions of the law and accounting and insurance from which lawyers, accountants, insurance professionals, and the public in general can profit.

So, what was Michael Segal's crime?

Hopefully, this book will help the public set aside preconceived notions and judge for themselves—and reach their own conclusions. And along the way, perhaps readers will become more objective in their judgment of facts and seriously concerned as to whether the system of checks and balances that is supposed to operate under the U.S. Constitution can and does fail.

Through the prism of court documents, trial transcripts, and the personal recollections and insights of Michael Segal emerges a story quite unlike any other in Chicago history.

~ Maurice Possley

Chapter 1

The Arrest of Michael Segal

ON AVERAGE, CHICAGO EXPERIENCES FEWER than 100 days of full sunshine a year. Most of the 265 other days are overcast and many of these occur during the winter months, when the wind off Lake Michigan gusts down through the canyon of high-rise buildings on Michigan Avenue.

Saturday, January 26, 2002, was uncharacteristically sunny. Shortly before 8 a.m., as Michael Segal strolled into the lobby of the Westin Hotel, the thermometer was pushing toward 50 degrees, inspiring hope for an early spring. And, beyond the weather, Segal had another reason for optimism. He was packed and ready to fly to London in just a few hours to nail down a lucrative insurance deal with the Sony Corporation. Weeks of extensive negotiation were about to pay off in a multi-million-dollar transaction for Segal's company, Near North Insurance Brokerage. Segal came to the hotel at the request of Tim Gallagher, a former employee who had asked to meet for coffee. Gallagher was one of a group of former Near North employees—whom Segal had branded the Takeover Group—who had unsuccessfully tried to force Segal to hand over control of Near North about eighteen months earlier. Segal had quelled the insurrection and the employees all departed Near North.

Six days before the breakfast meeting, Near North filed a lawsuit in Cook County Circuit Court against Gallagher and his fellow Takeover Group members: Matthew Walsh, Dana Berry, and Jeff Ludwig. The lawsuit had been a bold move by Segal, but he had spent his life making bold moves. It accused Walsh and the others of attempting to destroy Segal's company by stealing trade secrets, tortious interference and, in flagrant violation of their non-compete agreements, trying to shift tens of millions-worth of insurance business to Aon Corporation—a politically connected Fortune 500 company and bitter rival of Near North. Aon, one of Near North's most aggressive competitors, had welcomed Walsh, Gallagher, and Berry with open arms and signing bonuses, $250,000 salary packages, and options for thousands of shares of Aon stock. Berry's direct supervisor was initially Pat Ryan, the head of Aon. In the insurance industry, this was viewed as highly unorthodox. Now, it seemed to Segal, perhaps Gallagher was attempting to distance himself from the group's ringleaders, Berry and Walsh. Although Segal wondered how Gallagher knew he was leaving town, he brushed that off for the moment. He would discover months later how Gallagher actually knew. What Segal also didn't know was that the breakfast meeting was a trap.

As Segal entered the hotel lobby, he spotted Gallagher standing at the far end of the room and picked up his pace. As he approached, Gallagher thrust out his right arm and extended his middle finger. Before Segal could react, two men appeared at his side.

One introduced himself as Patrick Murphy, an agent with the FBI. "I would like to speak with you about a confidential matter," Murphy said. "Please come with me."

Astounded and trying to gather his wits, Segal replied, "I'm not coming with you. I don't talk to the FBI. You can talk to my lawyer."

Murphy's voice hardened. "I have authority to place you under arrest, Mr. Segal. But we don't have to do it that way. You can come with me to hear what the government has to say." Segal had no way of knowing it at the time, but Murphy had no warrant or any authority to arrest him. This was the first of many misrepresentations Murphy would make.

At that moment, Segal suppressed what the lawyer in him had been trained to say, and instead followed the instincts bred in him through years of salesmanship. He relented and accompanied Murphy to the bank of elevators. Silently, they rode to the ninth floor, where Murphy directed him to a suite. There, he was introduced to Dean Polales, a prosecutor in the U.S. Attorney's Office in Chicago.

"What is this about?" Segal demanded, suspecting that it was connected to the Takeover Group. "Is this about what Walsh and those others are saying about violations of the Premium Fund Trust Account?"

"We'll get to that," Polales said.

This was the same response that Polales would give whenever Segal asked about calling his attorney. A career prosecutor with nearly twenty years of experience, Polales had his speech ready. He began pulling out files relating to insurance contracts for Homer Ryan, son of Illinois Governor George Ryan (no relation to Aon's Pat Ryan) and John Daley, brother of Mayor Richard Daley. Segal quickly realized that these documents had somehow been surreptitiously removed from Near North—that is, stolen—and provided to the prosecutor.

"Mr. Segal, we are investigating you and your insurance business for fraud. Our investigation shows that you have violated Illinois Department of Insurance regulations that require that client funds be kept in a trust account. We have evidence that this has gone on for years. You are facing serious charges that can send you to prison for many, many years—probably for the rest of your life."

Segal attempted to interrupt Polales, but Murphy intervened. "Wait until he's finished," Murphy insisted. "Hear what he has to say."

Polales went straight to the point. "We want you to cooperate with us," he said. "We want your help."

"Now can I talk?" Segal asked, naively thinking that he could explain the extent of the plot against him. But before he could continue, Murphy jumped in.

"This is your chance to cooperate. If you don't, we have forty agents prepared to execute search warrants at your condo, your home on the North Shore, your office, and your storage spaces. Cooperating means telling the truth. Do you understand?"

Segal drew a breath. "I want to reserve the right to talk to my attorneys about this," he said. "I'm an attorney myself and I probably shouldn't be saying anything, but there are some things you've got wrong."

Polales then said that while the government didn't think Segal had done much of anything wrong, he would be required to help the prosecution and plead guilty to a felony. Polales went on to cite a supposed case as precedent—Segal believed it to be fictitious—that implied he had to accept a felony charge, which he realized would help the Takeover Group destroy Near North.

Suppressing his shock over the day's events, Segal deduced that the Takeover Group had surreptitiously obtained the stolen documents that Polales had thrust at him to try to leverage his cooperation. These documents must have been used to entice the government to buy into what appeared to be a continuing effort by the Takeover Group to wrest control of Near North from Segal.

In fact, Segal later learned, Walsh and the others had peddled a tale of financial mismanagement at Near North to the U.S. Attorney's Office.

On September 4, 2001, when Patrick Fitzgerald took over as interim U.S. Attorney in Chicago after being nominated by Illinois Republican Senator Peter Fitzgerald (the two men were not related), it was not lost on Segal that one of the senator's biggest campaign contributors was none other than Aon's Pat Ryan. Segal understood very well that nothing would please Pat Ryan more than the annihilation of Segal and Near North.

"I've committed no crime," Segal said to Polales. "You are being told a bunch of lies by some of my former employees, who are trying to destroy me and my business. They have no credibility."

Polales cut him off. "You are going to have to take a felony," he repeated. "Or it can be worse."

As Segal was led into another room of the suite to consider his situation, he wondered what could be worse than a felony. He had no idea that "worse" could mean a wide-ranging indictment with the potential to destroy his company.

While Segal was waiting, other members of the prosecution were appearing before U.S. Magistrate Morton Denlow and obtaining search warrants for the offices of Near North, as well as Segal's Lake Shore Drive condominium and his home in the northern suburb of Highland Park. They also obtained a warrant for Segal's arrest, which was highly unusual. It is extremely rare for federal agents to arrest any suspects except in crimes of violence.

Nearly an hour later, Murphy and Polales returned and Murphy was adamant.

"I have fifty agents standing by," he said this time, increasing the number from forty. "They are ready to go to your house. They are ready to go to your office. You need to work with us."

"I have been sitting here without a lawyer for forty-five minutes," Segal retorted, "and I've answered your questions. I've told you the truth."

"You need to work with us," Murphy repeated.

"I don't like corruption," Segal said. "What do you want me to do?"

"Wear a wire," Murphy said.

"What? Wear a wire on who?" Segal asked.

"Anyone we tell you to," Murphy replied. "You know everyone in this town."

"I won't wear a wire for anyone, on anyone, at any time," Segal declared.

What happened next would have seemed almost comical, if it weren't so serious. Two agents who had been hiding behind a set of floor-to-ceiling curtains emerged and moved toward Segal.

"Michael Segal, you're under arrest," Murphy declared, as the two agents grabbed the 59-year-old Segal by each arm. Meanwhile, just as Murphy had threatened, FBI agents were converging on Segal's home in Highland Park, as well as his Lake Shore Drive condominium. They had arrived at Near North's offices and were tearing it apart. Nearly a dozen blue-jacketed FBI agents rushed into the lobby of Segal's condominium and crammed into the elevator. The agents were accompanied by Assistant U.S. Attorney Virginia Kendall. Her personal participation was unusual; prosecutors rarely accompany agents executing search warrants.

In the apartment, Segal's wife, Joy, a Ph.D. and certified family life educator, was holding a pro bono group therapy session. The agents abruptly informed her that the session was over and that her husband was under arrest. Joy was told she might not see him again for a long time, except through the glass window of a prison visiting room.

The agents presented a copy of a search warrant, along with an affidavit, apparently based on the claims of the Takeover Group, alleging that Near North's Premium Fund Trust Account (PFTA) had a deficit of as much as $22 million. This was the start of the misrepresentation that the regulations did not provide for a traditional trust account and any alleged deficit would not a cash deficit. That allegation, according to the affidavit, was made by two former Near North executives identified only as Cooperating Individual No. 1 and Cooperating Individual No. 2. (Not surprisingly, they would turn out to be Berry and Walsh.)

When Joy asked to leave the condominium to attend to her daughter, Robin, who suffered from lupus, she was confined to a room for four hours—even though she was not under arrest—and was denied permission to leave, though no legal basis for detaining her was ever articulated. Joy had been expecting her daughter to come over and she asked if she could telephone her and tell her not to come. She didn't want her to come in and be confronted by the FBI. But Joy was not allowed to make any calls. She was not even allowed to go to the bathroom alone—a female FBI agent accompanied her. She later said that she considered her treatment to be outright bullying by Kendall and the FBI agents. Whether it was legal or not, it served to preclude her from contacting an attorney. Segal himself wasn't permitted to contact a lawyer until 3 p.m. that afternoon. Mysteriously, the FBI later revealed photographs of numerous white envelopes arranged on a bed in the condo, which the agents said had contained thousands of dollars in cash. Joy was aware of having just a few envelopes with cash—money that she had been saving over a period of time. Segal later concluded that the photographs were staged.

Meanwhile, Murphy had gone to Segal's offices on Michigan Avenue, where he was directing the seizure of records. This seizure, Segal's lawyers later asserted, violated Segal's attorney-client privileges as well as U.S. Department of Justice and FBI guidelines. In addition to documents, the agents seized Segal's desktop and laptop computers.

To be clear, law enforcement agents routinely seize electronic records during the investigation of white-collar crimes. Laptop and desktop computer hard drives may very well contain records of events and communications that relate to the investigation. But because these devices hold significant amounts of information created over a long period of time, they may also contain information about unrelated matters that are protected by attorney-client or other privileges. When such records are seized during a search, or sought by subpoena, the government requires that a "taint team"—consisting of agents and prosecutors not involved in the investigation—be established to review them. This team is supposed to identify any files that the prosecutors handling the investigation should *not* be permitted to see. The idea is to shield the government from a defense motion to suppress electronic record evidence based on an argument that the prosecution and investigating team was "tainted" by viewing records it had no right to see.

Even when this procedure is followed to the letter, there is no guarantee that prosecutors will be shielded from all privileged, confidential, and irrelevant information.

In Segal's case, there was no taint team at all.

Directing the search was not all that Murphy was doing that day. Telephone records later revealed that he used a Near North telephone to give directions to the FBI agents carrying out the searches of Segal's house and condominium. Near North's security cameras recorded Murphy sitting in the lobby using a Near North telephone, apparently because he could not get service on his FBI-issued cell phone.

The records showed that Murphy made multiple calls to Walsh and Berry, who in turn began calling the media in every city where Near North had an office to report Segal's arrest. Berry also placed a call to the president of Aon.

As a result, someone at Aon contacted Sony officials in London to break the news that Segal was under arrest and would not be arriving as scheduled. Then they began *their* pitch to acquire the business for Aon. Within minutes of Segal's arrest, Takeover Group member Jeff Ludwig, who was now working for insurance giant USI, began calling Near North employees to tell them that Segal was in federal custody and this was their chance to leap from a sinking ship.

The rest of the day was a blur for Segal. He was taken to the Dirksen Federal Building where he was fingerprinted, photographed, and put into a holding cell, pending an appearance in court.

The prosecutors attempted to delay Segal's bond hearing, but U.S. Magistrate Morton Denlow, who had authorized the search warrants that morning, came back to court (though it was his birthday) and allowed Segal to be freed on a $750,000 bond secured by his signature. His release ended any government hope that by keeping him behind bars, Segal would change his mind and agree to cooperate.

There was no doubt that the entire day had been coordinated to do as much damage as possible to Segal, his company and his family. In fact, the Takeover Group leaked Segal's arrest to the media before the U.S. Attorney's Office issued a press release announcing it.

This was just the beginning of what would become a massive campaign of leaks to the media designed to smear Segal prior to his trial and to influence customers to panic and leave Near North. The ultimate extent of the damage would not be known for quite a while, but the infiltration of Near North by the Takeover Group—whose members were acting essentially as a stalking horse for the federal government—was deep.

Very deep.

Chapter 2

Hidden Agenda

"Someone must have slandered Josef K., for one morning, without having done anything truly wrong, he was arrested."

— *Franz Kafka,* The Trial

PEOPLE DEAL WITH SHOCK IN different ways. Segal had long ago been diagnosed with Attention Deficit Disorder (ADD), but rather than consider it a liability, he devoted his life to making the condition work in his favor to remain cool and rational in stressful situations. This was critical right now because this was the most stressful situation of his life. Segal already had concluded that the leaders of the Takeover Group—Berry, Walsh, and Gallagher—had been stealing records from his company. What Segal didn't know and couldn't have predicted was that federal prosecutors would become allies and protectors of the Takeover Group.

Still, the heavy-handed treatment at the Westin Hotel was baffling to someone with a law degree and four decades of experience running a respected insurance brokerage. The insurance industry is regulated by state law, under the McCarran-Ferguson Act, which is a congressional mandate. In all his years in the business, it had never occurred to

Segal that the federal government would—or could—get involved in an insurance matter. Near North had never been named in a regulatory complaint in its four decades of existence and Segal himself had never received so much as a traffic violation.

If Near North's Premium Fund Trust Account (PFTA) was out of balance under account reconciliation, as prosecutor Polales claimed, then the matter should be a civil one that would properly be dealt with by the Illinois Department of Insurance, which was empowered to issue a citation or impose a fine. Wasn't this out of the federal government's jurisdiction?

Segal huddled with Jim Meyer, a twenty-year Near North veteran and managing director who oversaw employee benefits. Meyer was puzzled. "There hasn't been a policyholder who didn't get insurance or an insurance company that hasn't been paid on time," he said to Segal.

Months earlier, when the Takeover Group first made the unsupported claim that the PFTA was out of balance in their attempt to force Segal to give them control of the company, Segal, out of an abundance of caution, had utilized the self-reporting option provided by the Illinois Department of Insurance.

Despite his exercise of caution, Segal now faced scrutiny from an Assistant U.S. Attorney, who was pressuring him to plead guilty to a federal crime and wear a wire to incriminate others. "These are the tactics they use for street criminals, not upstanding citizens engaged in a business regulated by the state," Segal seethed. "Fifty agents swooping down on my business and my home? This is all part of a hidden agenda—to make me buckle."

Still, he attempted to remain calm and to begin sorting out the day's events. At the same time, his wife Joy, who had never even worked for Near North, was reeling.

"They rang from downstairs and said there's somebody down here to speak to you from the FBI," Joy told Segal after he was released.

"About 15 agents came up and demanded the combination to our home safe. I tried to ask them what it was about, but they just started firing questions at me. I think I did everything wrong…but they never said I didn't have to answer their questions."

She recounted how the agents and prosecutor Virginia Kendall kept her confined to a room for four hours while they searched the apartment and prevented her from calling the family attorney, Harvey Silets, or their daughter. "It was humiliating," she said. "Why stage this? I can understand if it was Bin Laden. This is Kafkaesque…it just doesn't add up."

What they didn't know was that they were about to face off with one of the most powerful juggernauts in the nation—the federal government. And as they sat there that night, they were unaware that a former Near North computer consultant already had stolen hundreds of confidential emails and shared them with the Takeover Group who were working with the FBI. Proof of this extensive hacking later was found on the server of Aon Corporation where Walsh, Gallagher, and Berry now worked. These stolen emails had given the Takeover Group and the FBI an almost daily window into what Segal was doing, including the initiation of the self-reporting process to the Illinois Department of Insurance.

The timing of Segal's arrest was no accident. If Segal agreed to plead guilty to a felony and wear a wire, his civil lawsuit would disappear before it could expose misconduct by prosecutors and agents collaborating with the Takeover Group.

Segal later concluded that the date of his arrest was the preference of Dana Berry, the leader of the Takeover Group, because Berry had promised his new boss at Aon that he would secure the Sony Account and Segal's arrest prevented him from going to London.

His arrest was the product of enormous planning. A virtual army of agents and prosecutors worked through the weekend preceding the confrontation at the Westin. The son of a friend of Segal who worked in the U.S. Attorney's Office later confided that he had never seen so many prosecutors and agents in the office at one time. Records later showed that Takeover Group leaders working at Aon were in regular communication with the FBI just prior to the arrest.

Segal and Silets tried to puzzle out what was going on. One target of the raid appeared to be Near North General Counsel Sherri Stanton, whose office was searched even though her files contained extensive lawyer-client privileged documents.

Why Stanton? Segal believed that the government was looking for evidence that Stanton had advised him that his actions were legal, which would have made a prosecution of him more difficult—although neither Stanton nor Segal could have anticipated federal involvement. Seizing Stanton's files also provided cover for the fact that the federal government had already obtained privileged information through other questionable means, including the theft of his emails.

Segal knew that there was no evidence that the PFTA was out of balance, since the new CFO Tom McNichols—who had been brought in by the Takeover Group in the effort to take over Near North—never performed the necessary accounting analysis, despite Segal's urgings, that would show the state of the account. And up until his arrest, Segal had no reason to doubt that he would have the time and the opportunity to work with the Department of Insurance to get an accurate, reconciled accounting of the PFTA.

Ultimately, Segal and his lawyers concluded that the prosecution knew little about him and Near North and that Polales's ploy had been a calculated risk.

"Polales didn't do his homework," Segal told the lawyers. "He was sold a false story by these guys. And the FBI apparently has bought it." Indeed, years later, some former members of the U.S. Attorney's Office characterized Segal's arrest as a gambit by Polales to revive a career that was beginning to sputter after twenty years. A successful high- profile prosecution not only is a status booster, it can help secure a white-collar criminal defense position at a major law firm.

Segal had been surprised by the actions of the Takeover Group. He had long been known as someone who would hire people if they were ambitious and willing to work hard and learn, even if they did not have a college degree. Segal enjoyed educating them about the business and guiding them as they rose in stature at Near North. He was demanding, but well liked. Otherwise, how else could he have built a four-person operation into the country's fifth-largest independent broker, with nearly a thousand employees?

Before they became the Takeover Group, Segal had groomed his employees for leadership and gave them personal attention. When some of them expressed concern about the fact that Segal was nearing the age of sixty, and expressed interest in owning stock in the company, Segal commissioned an employee stock ownership plan that widely benefitted employees.

Now, as he looked back, Segal began to realize that at the same time he was immersing himself in trying to expand the services and reach of Near North and its subsidiaries, the Takeover Group was working to undermine and sabotage him.

Segal wasn't the only one caught off guard.

Lee McDonald, who, during an eighteen-year career at Near North, had become vice president of marketing, later recalled, "We were a tight community. We worked together, and after work we met and socialized. Matt Walsh and I worked in the same department, while Dana Berry and Tim Gallagher worked in sales. Mike bent over backwards and put a lot of faith, trust, and power in their hands. They were favored, so it was kind of shocking when they betrayed him. When Dana Berry was ill, Segal called doctors across the country to get him the best medical care. Mike treated Berry with kindness when he had cancer, so it was doubly shocking when Mike was betrayed."

The betrayal went beyond the four corners of Near North. After Segal beat back their takeover, they intensified their efforts to sabotage Near North by repeatedly delaying action on requests for accounting information and spreading stories to outsiders that the firm was on the verge of collapse, even though the company had $38 million in retained earnings. Phone records later showed that as early as February 2001, nearly a year before Segal's arrest, Berry, Walsh, and Gallagher had begun making numerous calls to Aon President and Chairman Pat Ryan. Berry even called the unlisted number of Ryan's vacation home in Lake Geneva.[1]

Segal and his lawyers agreed that Polales had miscalculated. With no underlying crime, the prosecutor had no leverage. The question that remained, however, was whether the unexpected alliance of prosecutors and Takeover Group members would be a serious challenge to Segal's efforts to protect the company he had spent his life building and what tactics prosecutors would engage in going forward.

There was a lot riding on the case for U.S. Attorney Patrick Fitzgerald, who took office a few days before Segal's investigation began. A flurry of favorable publicity had portrayed Fitzgerald as a white knight prosecutor from New York City who came from a modest background. Fitzgerald was a hard-charging prosecutor like his former boss Rudy Guiliani, whose flair for publicity and the dramatic had attracted enormous media attention and paved the way for his election as New York mayor in 1994.

Media coverage of Fitzgerald, who was officially sworn in as U.S. Attorney in October 2001, noted that he was sponsored by outgoing U.S. Senator Peter Fitzgerald, but later on, when the Segal case was in the headlines, the media did not touch the relationship between Senator Fitzgerald and Pat Ryan, the head of Aon.

Before coming to Chicago as the chief federal prosecutor, Fitzgerald

---

1   Phone records show Takeover Group had more than 250 calls with Aon and FBI.

had spent only one day in the city—to attend a wedding in 1982. He scarcely knew the players, yet now he had greenlighted a high-profile arrest and FBI searches. Because this was his first major case, it was a case Fitzgerald could ill afford to lose.

He had a staggering array of criminal statutes to pick and choose from.

Beginning in the 1970's, federal prosecutors had expanded their quiver of laws by the score. By 2001, the number of criminal statutes had run up into the thousands with hundreds of thousands of regulations in place to implement those laws.

Alan M. Dershowitz, a renowned criminal defense attorney, noted, while writing about the explosion of criminal laws and resulting prosecutions:

"Our system of checks and balances depends on a vigorous judiciary and legislature serving as a brake on excessive prosecutorial zeal. It also depends on an alert private citizenry willing to exercise its constitutional right, indeed obligation, to petition the government for a redress of grievances. But when the executive branch, through its politically appointed prosecutors, has the power to criminalize ordinary conduct through accordion-like criminal statutes, the system of checks and balances breaks down."

In 2015, Michael B. Mukasey, former U.S. Attorney General, writing for The Heritage Foundation, said, "Overcriminalization is a serious problem and needs to be remedied before it further worsens the plight of the people tripped up by it and further injures the public interest... The Congressional Research Service reportedly has been unable to come up with a definitive total of federal criminal laws; the nearest they could come was to say they number in the thousands...The result is that there are more criminal laws than anyone could know."

But beyond the proliferation of laws and the resulting morass of confusion was an even more alarming development—an increase in prosecutorial misconduct in state and federal courts.

While the majority of prosecutors follow the precept that their function is not to get convictions but to see that justice is done, the number of cases where prosecutors have committed misconduct without being punished or sanctioned in any way has increased. In fact, prosecutors who engage in misconduct at times usually are promoted, not punished. Many become judges or are elected to public office.

Fitzgerald came under harsh criticism for his actions in the prosecutions of Lewis "Scooter" Libby, the chief of staff of Vice President Dick Cheney, and Conrad Black, a Canadian newspaper publisher.

Black, whose convictions—all but two counts—were overturned on appeal (and who in 2019 was the beneficiary of a Presidential pardon on the remaining two counts), said: "Fitzgerald's underlings in the U.S. Attorney's Office in Chicago, sometimes under his direct supervision in person in court, were caught red-handed in lies and misrepresented evidence many times, never with any serious rebuke from the judge or supplementary advice to the jury to treat prosecution allegations with caution. It was clear that the entire case against me was a fraud, from the launch of the prosecution by Fitzgerald, in a blaze of accusatory publicity designed by him to poison the well of the jurors, following the *ex parte* seizure of the proceeds of the sale of my condo in New York on a false affidavit that the proceeds were 'ill-gotten gains,' all to deny me the money to pay counsel's retainer, which he knew from illegal telephone intercepts to be my intention. Fitzgerald's stooges ended by calling their chief cooperating witness a perjurer, as if anyone but Fitzgerald extorted and suborned the perjury and granted immunity for it."

"Patrick Fitzgerald was a rotten apple infesting the Chicago courthouse," Black wrote, "even by the subterranean norms of official ethics in Chicago and the almost totalitarian standards of a prosecution service that dwells in a world foreign to the Bill of Rights and secures convictions on 99.5 percent of prosecutions, 97 percent of those without trial. In any other serious common-law jurisdiction, Fitzgerald and his ilk would be disbarred."

These reports of the use of false evidence, false affidavits, and illegal eavesdropping were not news to Segal. In fact, they would be mere echoes of his prosecution.

After Segal was released on bond, his criminal defense attorney, Harvey Silets, filed a motion for a preliminary hearing. When it was granted, Silets issued subpoenas for Takeover Group members Walsh, Berry and Gallagher. But the hearing was not held because the prosecution—rather than allow the Takeover Group members to face interrogation under oath—dismissed the complaint. The investigation continued and on February 14, 2002, the prosecution began in earnest when a federal grand jury indicted Segal on one count of insurance fraud.

The indictment accused Segal of filing a materially false statement to the Illinois Department of Insurance. Fitzgerald said that an application for a renewal of Segal's insurance producer license "falsely declared that he properly maintained premiums in a premium trust fund account, when, in truth, he knew that he failed to properly maintain premiums in such an account as required by state law, and that the fund was millions of dollars deficient."

Silets noted that the charge was not the same charge that Segal had been arrested for on January 26 at the Westin Hotel.

"If they had evidence of the wrongdoing he was arrested for, we would have had those charges," said Silets. "My guess is that they are going to try to get that evidence while this indictment is in effect." He said the prosecution had the case "backwards"—obtaining an indictment before they had the evidence.

Chapter 3

Starting Small, Growing Big

MICHAEL SEGAL WAS RAISED IN Chicago's West Rogers Park neighborhood on the city's northwest side. He was the son of Ben Segal, who, before his death in 1991, operated a fur salon in downtown Chicago. For more than a half century, much of it on Michigan Avenue—known as Chicago's Gold Coast—Ben Segal catered to an array of customers, including celebrities, minor and major. To a large extent, Segal took on the manner and mien of his father, who was often described as "a regular guy who had a lot of friends."

Michael was ambitious. He earned a degree in accounting from Loyola University of Chicago, passed the CPA exam and worked full-time for an accounting firm while attending DePaul University Law School. At DePaul, Segal made some of his most important life connections. Several of his fellow law students would go on to a life in Chicago politics, including Mayor Richard M. Daley, the son of Mayor Richard J. Daley; and future alderman Edward Burke, whose wife Anne would become a justice of the Illinois Supreme Court. Although law school provided Segal an opportunity to form deep and lasting friendships, he did not foresee a law practice as generating his livelihood. And while some of his new friends chose to move into the world of politics after graduation, Segal believed that accounting was his path to success.

Fortuitously, one of his first jobs as an outside accountant—even before he'd graduated from law school—came in 1964, when he was asked to perform some basic accounting work for Near North Insurance Brokerage. Near North was a fledgling insurance company owned by George Dunne, who hoped to pass it on to his son. By 1964, a year after he'd opened his insurance business, Dunne was on his way to becoming a political kingmaker. Aligned with former Mayor Richard J. Daley, he would become chairman of the Cook County Board in 1969. As Segal rose through the ranks, the increasingly prominent Dunne was on track to create an insurance powerhouse. Dunne did not have an office at Near North, nor did he have an active role in building the business. He'd gained confidence in Segal and hoped he'd be instrumental in expanding Near North's prospects. Over the years, Segal watched Dunne closely and took to heart his kind and gregarious manner. As they strolled together from the insurance office to the Cook County government building where Dunne maintained an office, Segal noted how Dunne shook hands, exchanged jokes with colleagues, and commented on the political stories of the day. It was not lost on Segal that Dunne was highly regarded. He was considered fair and honest, as well as modest and self-effacing. A Roman Catholic of deep faith, Dunne did not bow to the rich and powerful, nor did he treat the poor and powerless with contempt or disdain. He lived simply on the second floor of a three-flat building that housed his insurance business on the first floor.

This combination of attributes enabled Dunne to oversee the Cook County Board for 21 years, the longest term in history. His power grew exponentially after 1976 in the aftermath of the death of Mayor Daley. Dunne was elected chairman of the Cook County Democratic Party, one of the most powerful political organizations in the nation.

As Dunne oversaw his political empire, Segal was busy creating his insurance empire, drawing from the experience of watching his father sell fur coats, and from rubbing shoulders with his law school pals as well as Dunne. Ultimately, Segal adopted Dunne's approach to life:

Help everyone you can without regard for whether they will ever be able to help you in return.

As he advanced, Segal made political donations regularly and wisely and was a generous supporter of numerous charities. In fact, his charitable contributions amounted to five times what he donated to politicians. He co-developed one thousand much-needed senior-citizen housing units on the Near North Side and enlisted his partners' approval to donate a $10 million building to the Moody Bible Institute.

Segal made a point of attending political fund-raisers and parties and he frequently entertained. And though he was not a hearty-hand shake sort of fellow, Segal positioned himself near the wealthy and powerful without ever stepping on their toes.

Over time, Segal became more involved with the company. Dunne's son expressed no interest in the business and ultimately moved to California to become an actor. Segal made himself invaluable to Dunne by handling the accounting for Dunne's brokerage accounts, mostly local bars that needed dram shop insurance. The accounts produced a modest revenue of $600,000 for the firm, but Segal believed that Dunne should entertain a larger vision for the company, and he told him so. He urged Dunne to hire a business manager and begin placing advertisements in the newspapers. Dunne demurred, however. The turning point came one evening when Joy and Segal were in their one-bedroom apartment with their new baby. The telephone rang and Segal picked it up.

Dunne was direct, if nothing else. "Mike, I think I found a business manager," Dunne said.

"Oh, yeah?" Segal replied cautiously.

"It's you!" Dunne declared.

For once, Segal was caught up short. "Er, uh, I'll get back to you. Can I get back to you? Tomorrow?"

"Sure thing," Dunne said. "But I know what your answer will be."

He was chuckling as he hung up the phone.

Segal sat still for a moment.

"What was that about?" Joy asked.

"That was George," Segal said. "He wants me to be the business manager."

"That's great," Joy gushed.

"Well, I don't think I know enough about the insurance business to take this on," Segal said. "This is not something for an amateur."

Joy would have none of it. "You can learn," she said.

And with that, Segal walked over the bookshelves, reached up and pulled the letter "I" volume of the encyclopedia off the shelf and began his self-education on insurance. Years later, amid merriment at a birthday celebration, Segal was presented with a replica of that fateful book. It was an enduring symbol of a turning point in his life.

Segal proved to be a determined student of the insurance business, with a gift for salesmanship and an eye for business opportunities and specialized niche services. His promotion turned out to be advantageous and it was a good deal for both men.

Eventually, Segal purchased the business from Dunne and by 2001, he had increased revenues to $113 million, with more than $1 billion in premiums. The company had become the largest independent insurance broker in Chicago and the fifth largest in the United States. Nearly one thousand employees worked in eleven offices in seven states and the United Kingdom.

Near North and its associates created unique insurance programs and service commitments that allowed them to obtain the market share in the areas of construction, wrap-up, entertainment, surety, aviation, management liability, and real estate. The company had become the largest guarantor of motion picture production in the country and was providing an array of niche specialties for major companies, including General Electric, Walgreens, Sears, Sony, McDonald's, General Dynamics, Comcast, Aramark, Verizon, and BP Amoco.

The firm—a total of fifteen companies—had emerged as one of the largest fine arts insurance brokers, one of the largest corporate surety brokers, and a top broker in gaming and riverboats. Its settlement planning subsidiary was one of the fastest-growing structured settlement brokers in the nation, and its facultative insurance brokerage, recognized for its exemplary work, had many large insurance companies as clients.

Segal was particularly proud of engineering a joint venture between Near North and Fireman's Fund Allianz to ensure the completion and the cost of motion picture productions worldwide. This insurance facility was developed to provide guarantees to financial institutions who loaned money to motion picture production companies. The company underwrote multiple Academy Award-winners, including *Four Weddings and a Funeral, Braveheart, Million Dollar Baby,* and the *Lord of the Rings* trilogy. Unfortunately, the time Segal spent in California getting this venture up and running distracted him from recognizing and dealing with the efforts of the Takeover Group to undermine all that he had built.

Near North pointed to its ninety-five percent renewal rate as proof of outstanding service to its customers. The company developed proprietary technology to enhance business processes and began marketing its technology and software to customers, insurers, and other retail brokers. As sole owner, Segal became a multi-millionaire. He bought a seventeen-acre estate directly on Lake Michigan with a home designed by architect Howard Van Doren Shaw that featured a coach house, greenhouse, and swimming pool. The grounds had been designed by landscape architect Jens Jensen for the previous owners. Segal purchased the home on an installment contract over ten years during a real estate recession, and created a foundation to restore the property, thus retaining its national landmark status for its landscape design. Under Segal's care, the grounds were restored to their former state as one of the best early twentieth-century landscapes in the Midwest.

Segal could have coasted, but that was not his style. He maintained a hands-on grasp of daily operations—some thought perhaps a little too hands-on—but he was a micro-manager who didn't like being countermanded. As chairman and chief executive officer, Segal was well aware of what he had accomplished in elevating Dunne's enterprise from a small business with fewer than a dozen employees to an insurance giant.

"From the time I walked through the door in 1986, Mike encouraged us to visit our clients frequently and support their businesses," recalled McDonald. "His goal was always to provide the broadest coverage for the best price."

Segal was willing to lose some money if it meant gaining clients because he was all about building the business. He was proud of his company's reputation for elevating women to executive positions; hiring young, relatively inexperienced workers; and attempting to reshape the industry image from stodgy and conservative to innovative and creative. In fact, the company had come to be on the cutting edge when it came to adopting new technology and Internet initiatives.

Over the years, the company had won numerous high-profile government contracts in Chicago—most of them publicly bid. But the inevitable fallout of success is the creation of friction. Sometimes that friction is with competitors; in Chicago that meant Aon and its chief executive officer, Pat Ryan. Headquartered in Chicago, Aon was the second-largest insurance brokerage in the world.

Despite the corporate size difference, a rivalry between Ryan and Segal developed and persisted.[2] One of Ryan's executives confided to Segal that Ryan became very anxious when one of his sales people informed him that they'd lost a prospect to Segal, viewing it as a challenge to his power and ego.

In one instance, Ryan, a long-time benefactor to the Chicago Art Institute, personally called a top museum official after the museum

---

2   Dueling Moguls: Aon vs. Near North, Crains, April 1, 2002.

tapped Near North to provide insurance on an exhibition of French Impressionist paintings. Although the amount—about $100,000—was relatively insignificant, Ryan tried and failed to secure a rebidding of the contract. Apparently, it wasn't the money, but Near North and Segal winning the bid that rankled Ryan. A *Crain's Chicago Business* reporter told Segal that after Near North's bid was accepted over Aon's, Ryan, who was a major contributor to the Art Institute, sought to have the official in charge of the decision fired.

On another occasion, Ryan discovered that Aon was going to be outbid for a contract to provide insurance to the Chicago Transit Authority. He called Valerie Jarrett (who would become a top advisor to President Barack Obama) to request that the time to submit bids be extended. Although Ryan's entreaty was rejected, Segal saw his actions as indicative of the lengths to which Ryan was willing to go to secure business.

Once, a corporate client of Near North sought to buy a piece of property owned by Aon, but was rebuffed. The top executive of the company later related to Segal that his rejection came only after Ryan learned that the executive was a customer of Near North—his animus extended that far.

In yet another instance, Ryan attended a meeting at which investors for a new technology company were being sought. When Segal's name surfaced as a possible investor, Ryan publicly declared that he would not take part if Segal were involved.

The only time Ryan and Segal had been in close physical proximity occurred when the host of a society dinner seated the two rivals together. Segal recalled that Ryan left halfway through the evening. "I really never could understand his hostility," Segal said. "There were many things I admired about his business acumen and while my company won some accounts in competition with Aon, we were no threat to him. Comparatively, Near North was a peanut and Aon was a peanut factory."

Nearly a decade later, when *Chicago Tribune* columnist John Kass was writing about Chicago's bid to host the 2016 Olympic Games, he interviewed Ryan, who was the chairman of the Chicago Olympic committee. Kass noted, "Ryan may be many things, but dumb isn't one of them. He's a realist, worth a gazillion dollars. His former archrival, Near North Insurance boss Mickey Segal, is a broken man, sitting in federal prison, probably going stir-crazy."[3] Kass's words were all the proof Segal needed to believe that Ryan took personal credit for Segal's conviction and the destruction of Near North.

---

3   John Kass column September 30, 2009.

Chapter 4

Insurrection at Near North

THE FINANCIAL SUCCESS AT NEAR North during the 1990's was accompanied by some serious growing pains. A new computer system was implemented in 1998 to attempt to clear up accounting problems and prepare for Y2K, but within a year, the conversion to a new accounting system was a disaster. Segal had thrown money and consultants at the problem, but it seemed to only get worse. It appeared there was no technology available that could fulfill his vision of integrating the accounting and insurance services processing.

In late 1999, as part of this attempt to fix the accounting morass, Segal hired Tom McNichols. He'd been recommended by Michael Mackey, a managing director at Near North who later became a behind-the-scenes Takeover Group member. McNichols was a CPA who had worked as a staff auditor and handled accounting-related functions at PACE, the suburban bus division of the Regional Transportation Authority. That is, until 1998, when he and two other PACE executives—Executive Director Joseph DiJohn and Deputy Executive Director Terrance Brannon—resigned following a published report that PACE officials were investigating them for visiting a suburban strip club and betting parlors during working hours.

Mackey brought McNichols to Near North without disclosing any of these facts to Segal or that McNichols was a close friend of Mackey's and a regular on area gambling boats. Mackey pretended to be Segal's ally while becoming the link between McNichols and the Takeover Group. By the time Segal found out about McNichols's background and the reasons for his departure from PACE, it was too late—McNichols was already involved with the Takeover Group. Years later, when Segal's defense lawyers subpoenaed McNichols's personnel files from PACE, the records were reported to be missing. Segal was later told by a source at PACE that in fact the records were withheld.

Although McNichols had been hired as a consultant to try to sort out the accounting and computer problems, the Takeover Group ended up naming him Chief Financial Officer just a few months later without a corporate resolution and soon McNichols was an integral part of the Takeover Group.

The Takeover Group then engineered the dismissal of Greg Lauer, the only senior accountant who had extensive experience in insurance accounting. McNichols testified at Segal's trial that Segal had fired Lauer, but on cross-examination he admitted that, in fact, he and Jeff Ludwig, another member of the Takeover Group, had actually ousted Lauer. This was but one example of false testimony by McNichols in his role as a key prosecution witness.

With Lauer gone, McNichols essentially controlled the accounting department and drummed up the primary misleading and false evidence used in the Takeover Group's attempt to take control of Near North. At Segal's trial, the prosecution's primary accounting evidence would be based on McNichols's testimony.

At the time of McNichols's hiring, Segal hoped that he and other members of Near North's top management—Dana Berry, Matthew Walsh, Jeff Ludwig, Michael Mackey, and Devra Gerber—would be able to reorganize the company's accounting departments and straighten out the computer conversion issues. The problems Segal hoped to solve primarily involved the system's inability, due to computer language issues, to integrate prior billing records of Near North's sixty-five thousand insurance accounts as well as details relating to the insurance payables to hundreds of carriers. Illinois insurance accounting regulations proscribe that an insurance brokerage maintain a designated bank account into which premiums collected from customers are deposited until they are passed along to the companies that provide the insurance policies. The purpose of the regulation is to provide an audit trail and avoid disputes, especially in the event of the bankruptcy or demise of an insurance agency. The state regulation does not require a conventional trust account, but permits a commingled bank account. This insurance regulation exists in only half of the states in the country. There are no criminal penalties under state statutes if there is no loss of money, even if there is an improper reconciliation of the account. The reconciliation is an accounting use reconciliation and cannot conclude taking or using of cash unauthorized.

McNichols and the others promoted the unverified (and later discredited) idea that Near North's PFTA was underfunded by millions of dollars and that the company was on the verge of collapse. Despite substantial cash and net-worth accounting balances—$38 million in retained income and a company value of $250 million—McNichols and the others began complaining to Segal about this supposed PFTA reconciliation deficit.

Segal responded there could not be an accurate picture until the accounting situation was resolved. But even so, all premiums were being paid and all customers were getting their insurance. So, it was a mathematical impossibility that there was a negative PFTA reconciliation and non-payment to insurance companies because the policies would be unilaterally cancelled within forty-five days if payment did not occur. In addition, the company's profits were increasing on a monthly basis. Segal later learned that McNichols inflated the estimated reconciliation by tens of millions of dollars by adding old insurance policies that had been paid or cancelled or rebilled.

Segal was aware that a majority of insurance brokers have PFTA accounting reconciliation issues for a wide variety of reasons. Some states do not have a PFTA regulation at all and some exclude brokers who exceed $1 million in premiums. He was also aware that never in the history of the Illinois Department of Insurance had any broker been criminally prosecuted for a PFTA violation. Later, an FBI report would show that a Near North competitor had informed the prosecution that PFTA reconciliation issues were not uncommon in the industry.

Segal continued requesting financial information, but it was not forthcoming. Computer accounting delays were blamed. On one occasion, when Segal asked McNichols directly for the information, McNichols asked the Takeover Group for advice and was told: Provide nothing or turn over incomplete and inaccurate records that reflected nothing close to a proper estimate of the state of the PFTA.

In 2000, the behind-the-scenes maneuvering by the Takeover Group boiled to the surface. On a summer morning, Segal was in his office when Berry and Walsh barged in unannounced, slammed the door and sat down. Walsh launched into a tirade, complaining that the company was in precarious financial condition, primarily because the PFTA was seriously out of balance. Walsh threatened to quit. The vehemence was such that Segal concluded it was time to look for executive candidates to replace them. However, he put it off because he was deeply engaged in expanding a portion of his business and was not comfortable with confrontation. Segal would ever blame himself for what eventually transpired.

There came a day when Berry insisted on meeting Segal for breakfast in the Westin hotel across from Near North's office in the Hancock Building—the same place to which Gallagher would lure him on the day of his arrest the following year. Although the day was exceedingly hot—approaching 100 degrees—Berry arrived wearing a wool sport coat. Segal was in shirtsleeves. Berry asked a series of pointed questions about the PFTA that Segal was unable to answer. A subsequent analysis of Berry's emails showed that at that time, Berry and Gallagher were investigating surveillance equipment at a downtown business called the Spy Shop. Segal later came to believe that Berry had been wearing a concealed recorder in an unsuccessful attempt to entrap him into making incriminating statements. The Illinois eavesdropping law prohibits single-party recordings.

Berry was so cocky that on September 21, 2000, he emailed McNichols, Ludwig, Gerber, Walsh, and Gallagher a message containing a parody of the lyrics to the 1978 Village People song "*YMCA*" that replaced YMCA with PFTA. The refrain went, in part: "It's fun to play with the P-F-T-A/It's fun to play with the P-F-T-A."[4]

This email's inclusion of McNichols as a recipient confirmed his involvement in the Takeover Group as well as the fact that these men were trying to use the PFTA as leverage to extort or destroy Segal.

In October, Walsh and Berry made good on their threat. Both resigned and were immediately hired by Aon. But curiously, Mackey came to Segal just days later and told him that Berry and Walsh wanted to come back to Near North. Segal would subsequently learn that, although offices had been set up for Berry and Walsh at Aon, Walsh didn't show up and Berry came to work for only a couple of days. Both returned to Near North saying they had made a mistake. However, their return turned out to be a ruse—they began accumulating proprietary information, which they ultimately took to Aon.

On November 15, 2000, Berry emailed Walsh, Gallagher, Ludwig and Gerber about his plan to take over Near North. "I was just going to do this on my own, but I have decided to cut you guys in if you are interested," he wrote.

Berry's plan was laid out in detail in a document found on his computer,

---

4   PFTA to YMCA theme.

labeled "Takeover.doc."[5] The point was to put control of the company in the hands of Walsh, Berry, Ludwig, Mackey, Gerber, and Gallagher.

These plotters proposed to assume control of Near North's Chicago operations and sell the company for $150 million. Under the plan, "Segal walks away with $120,000,000. Each of us walks with $5,000,000."

Later that same November day, Berry emailed a copy of the Takeover plan to Walsh, Gallagher, Ludwig, and Gerber. Ludwig sent an email of his own saying he had sought advice from an attorney. According to Ludwig, the attorney—whose law partner (funded by Aon) later represented Walsh, Berry, and others being sued by Segal—was "very familiar with the angles and strategies (beyond simple lying, cheating, and extortion) that other companies rely on to protect themselves in employment contracts."

Walsh emailed back: "I would not discount the tactics listed in the parentheses."

As an added insult, Ludwig, without authorization, arranged for Near North to pay his lawyer for the consultation.

On November 22, 2000, Segal sent an email to McNichols complaining that he was not getting accurate accounts payable, receivable, billing, and other financial information.

In January 2001, Segal began working on creating a stock grant plan to compensate, retain, and attract high-quality employees. He engaged lawyers to recapitalize Near North and create a plan that would benefit as many as sixty of the company's top executives. But while some employees relished the idea, some did not.

Berry and Walsh questioned Segal about his motivation for conferring stock on employees. Walsh was petulant, suggesting that some of the covered employees—Michelle Levin and Monica Lang, in particular—didn't deserve as much stock as he and Berry did. Segal, who was offended by their inflated and undeserved opinions of themselves,

---

5   Takeover document and email directory.

replied, "People work hard for this company. I want to reward them. I want them to appreciate working for this company."

The two men continued to insist that they were being short-changed, no doubt thinking they had their takeover plan in their back pocket.

They demanded more.

"That's not going to happen," Segal replied.

That could well have been the end of things, but in fact, it was not. Soon after, Segal had dinner with Walsh and Berry and both demanded more active roles. Segal asked them what they specifically would do to improve the company. Berry responded, "I have someone who might want to buy the company."

"Not a chance," Segal said. "It's not for sale. Under any circumstance." The Takeover Group didn't take no for answer.

In February 2001, McNichols drafted a new stock plan far more limited than the one Segal had proposed that would involve only a small number of top executives—basically, the Takeover Group. This stock plan was inserted into a document labeled "remediation" and was virtually unchanged from the original Takeover document, except that it was presented in the form of a corporate resolution designed to cede operational control to an executive committee—the Takeover Group.

The corporate resolution was left on Segal's desk with no explanation. Walsh, Gallagher, Berry, Ludwig and Gerber then demanded that Segal sign it. When no signature was forthcoming, Berry told Segal that if he did not sign, Berry and a large group of employees, including Diane Brinson, would walk out. (Brinson later said she'd never agreed to any such thing and she subsequently took over Near North's California operation worth millions of dollars.) Segal still refused to sign the resolution.

A month later, when they were already negotiating and inking deals to defect to Aon and another Near North competitor, Walsh, Berry, Gerber, and Ludwig demanded that they be paid large bonuses.

Otherwise, they said, they would quit. They knew that it was a critical time for Near North as several major accounts were up for renewal and the company was involved in negotiations to expand its operations. Although Segal considered the demands to be a shakedown, he worried that their departure would damage the company. So, he ordered the bonus checks issued. Two weeks later, Ludwig returned his $40,000 check, saying he didn't want to be part of what was going on. It was a noble gesture except that several weeks later, after Ludwig told the accounting department he had lost it, the check was reissued without Segal's knowledge.

They began dropping hints to fellow employees, insurance carriers and key clients that Near North was financially unstable. Even the president of Aon heard it and brought it up to a senior officer of Fireman's Fund, who in turn relayed the conversation to Segal. The Takeover Group began speaking about their plans openly and giving advice about job opportunities to other employees of Near North in an attempt to get them to leave. Walsh was so emboldened that at a risk managers' convention he approached Near North's brokerage representative in Germany and warned that he should not be dealing with Near North.

Walsh and Berry met with Joseph Messina and Russell DeLuca, top officials at DMI, a Near North affiliate, and said they were planning to coerce Segal into relinquishing control of Near North by threatening to report to federal and state authorities that the PFTA was millions of dollars in deficit.

Messina promptly informed Segal, who then sent emails to Near North in-house counsel Sherri Stanton, and Thomas Rakowski, Near North's outside counsel. Days later, Walsh confronted Messina and DeLuca, accusing them of telling Segal what he said.

How did Walsh know? That was a mystery—a mystery that would be solved but not before untold damage had been inflicted on Near North.

Walsh told Messina and DeLuca that it was time to pick a side and that if they chose Segal, things would get nasty. The message was so ominous that Messina moved out of his home for a week. Later, Walsh confronted DeLuca at a youth basketball game, telling him that when they were done taking down Segal, DeLuca would be next.

Walsh and Berry also reached out to Rich DiClemente, president of another Near North affiliate, THB Intermediaries, to try to enlist him in their takeover plan. They told him they planned to report financial irregularities and that they were scaring off other Near North employees as well. Even if their plan did not succeed, they said they intended to create such serious client problems for Near North that the company would be destroyed or sold. Devra Gerber made a trip of her own to Marc Roth, president of Home Warranty, another Near North affiliate. She told Roth that she and the others were planning to wrest control away from Segal and she asked him to join their team.

Meanwhile, on March 7, 2001, Segal emailed McNichols again to say that he was still not receiving timely and accurate accounting reporting. He added that if Near North were not in compliance with state accounting regulations, he would take steps to replace the executive team if that's what it took to ensure accurate financial reporting.

Around the end of March, Segal walked into Carton's, a Greek restaurant a block away from Near North's offices, for a solitary lunch. He immediately spotted Berry, Walsh, Mackey, and Gerber. With a smile, he sat down in an empty chair at their table—but instead of the friendly welcome he expected, the conversation came to a halt and his colleagues' faces froze. Segal began to recount recent successes and the lunch ended on a cordial note. But he later learned that the group had been meeting regularly there—a place he rarely visited—and concluded that this where they plotted and schemed.

McNichols, Walsh, and Ludwig drafted a letter, dated April 20, 2001, addressed to Segal to "express our very deep concern over our short- and long-term financial condition." The letter—which Segal concluded was orchestrated to generate evidence against him—stated that the company was suffering a severe cash shortage and a "substantial deficit" in the PFTA.

"In addition to the financial issues which we feel are the results of decades of questionable management and financial practices, we feel there is a fundamental weakness in the management structure of our company.... We feel we have reached a level of urgency that requires decisive and immediate actions in order to act in the best interests of our clients, associates, and insurance company partners."

The letter said a deficit in the PFTA was a violation of Illinois law, and accused Segal of the "misappropriation of many millions of insurance company and client dollars." They suggested several operational recommendations, but emphasized that the ultimate solution was for Segal to transfer control of the company to them so they could "fix" its financial issues within eighteen months, without a new infusion of capital.

But Segal never received the letter. Had he received it, it would have set off major alarm bells and he would have discussed it immediately with corporate counsel. Yet, McNichols later testified under oath that he had sent the letter to Segal. It wouldn't be the only time that McNichols would claim that he'd physically sent something to Segal that had not been sent at all. A forensic analysis of his email would show that there were three prior versions on Ludwig's computer hard drive, one of them dated as early as March 21, 2001. They were in Word document format, inconsistent with Near North's systems.

This letter would become a cornerstone of the prosecution's case against Segal, with one prosecutor calling it "a written summary of the evidence in this case."

Telephone records showed that, as far back as February 21, 2001, Walsh, Gallagher, and Berry were calling Aon. Gerber, who did not sign the letter, and in fact was the first Takeover Group member to leave, came to Segal's home. After first saying she wanted to take some time off, she broke down in tears. She said she really wanted to get out before the "dirty stuff" started. Nonetheless, Gerber ultimately went to Aon.

The forensic analysis of emails showed that on April 19, 2001, Walsh sent Berry an email outlining many of the same issues that were contained in the April 20 letter and written in similar language. Some of it was written in the third person—odd, since Walsh and Berry lived on the same block and drove to work together. One sentence read, "Dana and I resigned from this company due to these very problems." Segal concluded that this email, along with others, was part of the Takeover Group's creation of a false electronic record meant to be "discovered" at a later date in order to buttress their assertions.

There would never be evidence that Segal received the April 20 letter or discussed it or reacted to it, even though it requested a meeting "the first thing Monday morning, April 23, to discuss your reaction to this communication and the steps we need to bring our company into compliance."

No such meeting was ever held—and the prosecution would eventually concede that fact—though members of the Takeover Group created false records in an attempt to show that it did. Ludwig, for example, made an entry in his Lotus Notes calendar memorializing a 5 p.m. meeting with Segal regarding "Premium Trust Communication." A week later, Ludwig emailed himself a copy of a letter of resignation from Near North that again referenced such a meeting. In fact, Ludwig already had been fired by the time his resignation letter arrived.

A forensic analysis of McNichols's computer showed that about this time he began modifying email messages long after their creation. For example, an April 26 email from McNichols to Segal with the subject "Cash position" was not sent to Segal; it remained in his draft folder and was modified on May 23, nearly a month later. The analysis showed the email was changed to add the last line: "Given to MS, 4/26/01 11:15/AM, left message with secretary asking MS to call me."

These unsent messages were designed to create the false impression that Segal had been provided with updates to the April 20 letter. Unfortunately, exposure of the letter as fraudulent would not come until much later—too late to save Near North or Segal.

Chapter 5

Takeover Group's Revenge

NEWS ORGANIZATIONS SOMETIMES PLAY AN important role in cases of miscarriage of justice. In 2006, three members of the Duke University lacrosse team were charged with raping a young black woman they had hired as a stripper at a party. District Attorney Mike Nifong, who brought the charges, was running for reelection at the time. Before his team had presented any proof of the crime, the case received massive publicity in local and national media outlets. In the words of Daniel Okrent, the former public editor of the *New York Times*, the story was widely accepted by journalists because it had all of the preferred narratives: "White over black, rich over poor...all the things that we know happen in the world, coming together in one place." The university and the community demanded punishment of the three athletes and changes in university policy. The lacrosse team coach was fired and the championship team's season abruptly was cancelled.

The prosecution's case eventually unraveled, thanks to the intervention of the North Carolina Attorney General and the disclosure of exculpatory DNA evidence that Nifong had attempted to conceal.

Like Nifong, the Takeover Group embraced the media to help their effort to take Segal down and ingratiate themselves with Aon. Having been thwarted by Segal, the group embarked on a campaign of media sabotage designed to embarrass and damage him publicly. Perhaps then he would capitulate. Telephone records later obtained by Segal's lawyers showed

Gallagher called *Chicago Tribune* columnist John Kass and made a total of four calls to the *Tribune* in late April and May 2001, while still working at Near North. The pattern continued beyond the time of Segal's arrest.

Segal later learned that members of the Takeover Group met with Kass at the Billy Goat Tavern, the colorful watering hole under Michigan Avenue, directly across from the newspaper's offices.

The results were almost immediate.

On May 29, 2001, the *Tribune* published the first of three consecutive daily columns by Kass on the topic of Segal's low real estate property taxes. As a columnist, Kass was free to make snide comments and he did. He portrayed Segal as "high powered and politically favored," adding that his connections generated "oodles of government contracts. Segal has many friends in the political world." Clearly, he viewed Segal as a man living a privileged life at the expense of taxpayers. He cast Segal as a "magical, mystical figure in Illinois politics" without presenting any supporting evidence. Such are the liberties that columnists enjoy. "Segal owns a huge Highland Park estate on the lakeshore," Kass wrote. "A big wrought-iron gate keeps the peasants out." (It was a gate that was never used by Segal or anyone else, but it made a great visual for Kass.) Still, despite all of the innuendo, Kass had to admit, "Everything he's done with the 17 acres so far appears to be perfectly legal."

In fact, under Illinois law, if a property owner maintains 10 or more acres as open space, the property taxes on the land are negligible. Segal had gone a step further for the public good, creating a foundation to preserve the land since it was one of the last works of the famous Midwest landscape architect Jens Jensen. With its historic significance in mind, Segal had hired landscape expert Steven Christy to oversee the restoration of the property based on the original blueprints. Segal allowed visitors and students to come and study the restoration, and he and Christy received awards for their efforts. The property had been added to the National Registry of Historic Landmarks.

Of course, Kass reported none of this, nor did he mention that the house on the property was taxed at the conventional rate—to the tune of $60,000 per year.

Over three days—as if exposing the details of a mass murder— Kass repeatedly ridiculed Segal and suggested to the public that he was a man of "awesome power." At no time did the columnist call Segal to get his perspective. Considering the time-worn admonition against picking a fight with someone who buys ink by the barrel, Segal held his tongue. It seemed to him no coincidence, however, that Patrick Ryan was on the *Tribune* board of directors.

The Takeover Group must have had Kass and the *Tribune* on speed-dial. According to phone records, over the next several months, Gallagher called Kass forty-seven times; Matt Walsh called twice; and Dana Berry called twice as well. And that was just from their personal phones. Who knows how many more calls they might have made from other phones? This was during the period when Walsh, Gallagher, Berry, Ludwig, Gerber, and (Segal believed) Mackey were pressing other employees to join in their plan to sabotage and devalue Near North.

Despite these efforts, Segal stood strong. Ironically, despite the Takeover Group's constant complaint about the state of the PFTA, they appeared perfectly content to go forward with their plan to take over the company without any apparent concern as to the PFTA reconciliation balances. As Segal's lawyer, Daniel Reidy, would tell the jury, "They were perfectly happy to do that so long as at the end, they got millions of dollars. So, their outrage didn't extend to staying in the company and operating as if they were going to get a big piece of it."

In the midst of all this, Segal invoked an "insurance compliance self-evaluative privilege," which, under Illinois law, is a "safe harbor" provision to encourage insurance companies and other regulated persons to voluntarily and internally audit regulatory compliance issues and remediate regulatory violations. Information and documents disclosed under this provision are confidential and cannot be used in criminal, civil or administrative proceedings. Segal filed a report with the Illinois Department of Insurance to exercise this privilege in an attempt to protect Near North from the Takeover Group. Segal reported that the balance reconciliation issue with the PFTA would be cleared up once the computer conversion was complete and an accurate internal analysis could be performed.

The accounting problems, along with McNichols's confounding of any efforts to rectify them, had made it impossible to determine the true status of the PFTA. By self-reporting a "potential" violation, if there was in fact a problem, it could be remediated under the privilege.

The filing was handled by attorney Zack Stamp and two insurance regulatory consultants, both ex-deputy insurance department commissioners, one of whom had helped draft the original PFTA regulations in Illinois.

McNichols convinced Stamp that the filing should include a PFTA analysis by the accounting firm of McGladrey & Pullen, dated October 19, 1999—although that analysis could not possibly have been accurate. Near North's computer system was down for the week prior to its generation and the report was not prepared according to the methodology specified by Illinois statute and regulation. In addition, there were no working papers supporting it.

A few days after the filing, one of the former deputy directors who prepared the filing, Robert Hartsock, told Segal over lunch that he didn't think there was any violation at all.

Segal later came to understand there was only one explanation for McNichols's insistence on the inclusion of the document: As a member of the Takeover Group, McNichols was doing his utmost to pollute and interfere with the proper analysis of Near North's regulatory compliance. Near North's regulatory lawyer unaware of McNichols being the engineer of the takeover plot, inserted the false and impossible one-page accounting document and false on its face, when the lawyers were filing with the Department of Insurance. Almost immediately, *Crain's Chicago Business* got wind of Segal's actions. It didn't take a genius to figure out how that happened. Telephone records later showed that Gallagher telephoned the Department of Insurance twice—on September 14, 2001, and October 12, 2001— once for sixteen minutes and again for eight minutes. Soon after, Gallagher placed a call to *Crain's*. In October, the business publication reported, under the headline *"Regulator Reviewing Near North,"* that Near North was under scrutiny by the Department of Insurance.

There was no hint or suggestion of any criminal activity at Near North and the report was careful to note that Near North had already taken corrective measures.

Segal explained to *Crain's* that whatever issues had arisen were due to the rapid growth of the company—revenues in Chicago alone had jumped by fifty percent in the previous five years to about $113 million (representing three-quarters of a billion dollars in premiums and hundreds of thousands of individual transactions)—combined with a computer upgrade. He said that the company often faced fairly minor and technical regulatory issues and that this was the first time Near North had reported anything directly to the Department of Insurance—an assertion that the Department of Insurance confirmed.[6]

Nathaniel Shapo, director of the Department of Insurance, told *Crain's* that voluntary disclosures by insurance companies were not at all unusual. He did concede that the Department had suggested that Near North appoint a board of directors—an unusual step for a privately held company. (By the time of his indictment, Segal had embraced the idea of creating a board and immediately afterward set about bringing in a blue-ribbon group of executives.)

Segal told *Crain's* that the issues reported to the Department—to the extent they actually existed—were in the process of being corrected.

---

6   Brett Gerger, Illinois Department of Insurance affidavit

He also noted that the Department had not imposed any fine or any other financial penalty on Near North and had acknowledged that there was absolutely no evidence of any harm to Near North clients or any insurance companies.

Segal also suggested that Near North was the target of a whispering campaign by competitors in the insurance industry who were exaggerating the scope of the problem for their own benefit. "There's a lot of misunderstanding going on," Segal declared. "We're very good and very successful. That creates anxieties."

The author of the *Crain's* article repeated the political connection theory advanced by Kass in his columns. These references to politicians—in *Crain's* and other media articles—likely cemented the prosecution's belief that getting Segal to wear a wire would enable them to prosecute high-ranking political figures.

Perhaps as a result of the media reports, the Department of Insurance was virtually invaded by prosecutors and FBI agents, who essentially took control of the audit of Near North. They demanded that officials subpoena documents from Near North and ultimately bullied the Insurance Department into rejecting the invocation of the self-help provision.

During this time, the government influence was so pervasive that when Stamp approached a senior management official at the insurance department whom he had known for many years, she said that she didn't know whether she was even allowed to talk to him. This, Segal concluded, was part of the government's playbook—scaring and intimidating potential sources of exculpatory information.

During the audit, one of the examiners told Segal that he was very sorry about how it was going, but that there was a tremendous amount of pressure being placed on the auditors. Another examiner, who spent many weeks in Near North offices as part of her duties, tearfully told Segal she knew, based on her review of his company's records, that he was being treated unfairly in the media.

Segal's defense would discover that the prosecution disclosed confidential information received from the Insurance Department to members of the Takeover Group after they had left Near North and joined competitors. That information was then passed to the media.

The Takeover members also obtained confidential information from the prosecution that they tried to use to their advantage with specific Near North customers.

Near North complained to the Department of Insurance about the attempts to undermine Near North by the Takeover Group, but nothing was done. Segal also believed that the Takeover Group tried to feed privileged information to Republican politicians in the hope they would try to exert pressure on the Department of Insurance. Stamp later told him that after the filing, Shapo received a call from a political operative who was trying to pressure him to take adverse action against Near North.

In a brazen move, the FBI went to Stamp's Springfield office without a subpoena or search warrant and demanded that he turn over his files relating to Near North. A standoff ensued. Stamp, understanding attorney-client privilege, called in his own attorney and ultimately the FBI was unsuccessful in obtaining his files.

Evidence of how the playing field was tilted against Near North emerged in reports to Near North from individuals regarding regulatory violations at Aon that were equally or more serious than the allegations made against Near North.[7, 8] The Department of Insurance invited Near North to file a complaint of regulatory violations, which it did, arising from the following:

- Aon's PFTA had a significant and ongoing shortfall from 1999 through 2001. Much of the shortfall was related to the fact that a large Aon client, a worldwide airline, was not timely in paying

---

7   Aon is in joint settlement talks with Attorneys General in 3 states, WSJ, 022205

8   Aon settles allegations that it bribed foreign officials to get business, Business Insurance, 122011.

its insurance premiums, forcing Aon to make premiums on the airline's behalf.

- Segal was told Aon's president, Michael O'Halleran, who was personally active in insurance sales, was never investigated for not having a valid Illinois insurance license. Matt Walsh, the Take-over Group member who was working at Aon, had also let his license lapse. This was never investigated. (Meanwhile, the Take-over Group made allegations of license lapses at Near North that were vigorously pursued and resulted in fines.)

- An ex-Aon employee called Segal and stated that Aon engaged in a fraudulent scheme with respect to facultative insurance place-ments that involved using false premium billings to maximize rev-enues. In other words, they were charging companies more than they were paying for reinsurance and pocketing the difference.

- In 1998, Aon underbid Near North by fifty percent to do busi-ness with the Chicago Board of Education on a fee-based con-tract. Aon placed a substantial portion of the insurance with a subsidiary wholesaler without disclosing the nature of the con-tract and collected in addition to its fee. (This was no different from what Near North was accused of doing in a contract with the Chicago Transit Authority—except Near North had disclosed its relationship with the subsidiary wholesaler.)

But despite being invited to make the filing, the complaint went nowhere—most likely, Segal believed, due to pressure from the pros-ecution on the Department of Insurance to do nothing.

Years later, in 2005, Aon agreed to pay $90 million to end an in-vestigation by New York Attorney General Eliot Spitzer into conflicts of interest and alleged fraud. No one at Aon was prosecuted criminally, though Aon had to announce publicly that it was required to return a $25,000 contribution to Spitzer at the time of the settlement.

During the summer and fall months of 2001, despite their best efforts, the Takeover Group's original "grand scheme" had failed. But they still saw an opportunity to make money—which, after all, was the whole point. As their goal shifted from ostensibly "saving" the company to all-out destruction, they began negotiating for new jobs elsewhere. As Segal's lead defense attorney Reidy later told the jury: "They weren't getting their millions, and so now they were going to wreak vengeance. They executed a plan for vengeance. They still had a personal profit motive." Berry resigned a second time in August of 2001 and was immediately rehired by Aon. Telephone records later showed that he had repeatedly contacted Ryan directly. Five days after Berry left, Gallagher resigned and also went to Aon. Shortly after that, Walsh resigned and headed for Aon. Lori Shaw, another Near North employee, was next.

Gerber, who had left Near North three months earlier, would soon be hired by Aon, as would Near North employee Michael Blaum.

Segal eventually learned that before Walsh left for Aon, he asked Daniel Watkins, a Near North accountant for nearly thirty years, for Segal's personal tax information from June 2001, using some excuse involving the budget. This, Segal believed, was part of the effort to incorporate phony tax information into their plan to take down Segal. Segal's legal team later obtained emails between Walsh and Berry that suggested that Walsh and Berry were falsely emailing each other about the idea of contacting incoming U.S. Attorney Patrick Fitzgerald. Segal came to view these emails as planted breadcrumbs designed to divert attention from the real plan, which was to enlist the support of Pat Ryan to see if he could exert his influence to get Patrick Fitzgerald to go after Segal.

Though Berry, Walsh, and Gallagher were not considered high-end producers in the industry, Segal learned that they walked into Aon with stock options ranging up to as much as $1 million—far above industry standards. Did Ryan believe that they were going to bring in lots of new business? If so, where would that new business be coming from? Segal concluded they planned to steal it from Near North and destroy the company in the process.

They were made part of the "One Aon Team," a special short-lived section that reported directly to Ryan and O'Halleran. This designation was used to make it appear that Walsh and Berry would not be competing directly with Near North's insurance business. When Segal emailed his attorneys about this development a short time later, One Aon Team abruptly disappeared.

According to reports that later circulated back to Segal, Ryan and O'Halleran, prior to the Takeover Group's arrival, had begun disparaging Near North to prospective Near North clients, suggesting that Near North was having financial difficulties and problems with its PFTA.

In the end, however, Ryan and Aon ultimately received little business in this way. The majority of Near North's high-profile clients were perceptive enough to see what the Takeover Group was trying to do.

Trying to harpoon Near North from the confines of the Aon offices apparently wasn't enough for the likes of Berry, Walsh, and the others. As one of the Takeover members told Jim Meyer before departing for Aon, "Mike doesn't understand that he is sitting on a bomb and we have the detonator to blow it up."

They went to the FBI. And the FBI, and later the U.S. Attorney's Office, were only too happy to oblige.

Chapter 6

The Embezzler Is Caught

"WHY DID YOU PUT IT there?"

It was Tuesday, October 23, 2001, several months before his arrest and Michael Segal was on his cell phone, angrily confronting Near North accountant Daniel Watkins.

Segal was holding the phone sideways. Sitting calmly by his side was Ernest Wish, an accountant with a stellar list of achievements including a term as president of the Illinois CPA Society. Wish's head was cocked to the side so that he could hear both sides of the conversation. "Who told you to put any money into the postage account?" Segal demanded.

The scene would have been almost comical were the implications not so serious. Segal had hired Wish to clean up Near North's accounting department and fix the company's computer problems. By any measure, Wish was a perfect candidate for this formidable task. A decade earlier, Wish had been appointed city clerk for the city of Chicago by Mayor Richard M. Daley, who believed in Wish's integrity and ability to clean up after a series of scandals rocked that office. In fact, Wish had not only restored respectability to the position, but had gone on to become director of the city's Revenue Department.

About a half hour before the phone call, Wish had arrived in Segal's office and gently, almost timidly, informed him that McNichols, Near North's chief financial officer, had reported problems in the petty cash fund—an account that Watkins solely controlled. McNichols threatened to quit, expose the petty cash problem, and infer that Segal was involved. This was a threat Segal believed was designed to get Wish to walk away from Near North before Wish discovered McNichol's alliance with the Takeover Group.

But Wish wasn't leaving. He told Segal that an analysis suggested that as much as $200,000 in petty cash expenditures had been booked to the postage account. This seemed extremely odd, if not downright impossible, because the company's postage expenses were paid by check to Pitney Bowes. Segal and Wish agreed that this had the aroma of embezzlement.

McNichols didn't tell Segal about it himself because a day earlier, on October 22, Matt Walsh had introduced McNichols to the FBI in the hope that he might help them implicate Segal. McNichols agreed to begin wearing a wire to record conversations with Watkins, Segal, and essentially anyone McNichols talked to—even Segal's lawyer—even though U.S. Justice Department guidelines prohibit eavesdropping on conversations involving legal matters.

When Segal eventually saw the FBI report relating to McNichols agreeing to wear the wire, it was single-spaced, unlike most other FBI reports and appeared to Segal to be a laughably amateurish effort to make it look as if McNichols wasn't part of the Takeover Group. Walsh had acted as if he needed to convince McNichols to become a government agent as the two talked back and forth.

So, the government had installed a new player on its team—McNichols—and now the playbook had some new plays. In effect, the FBI was co-opting the Takeover Group to get Segal.

Segal did, of course, obtain cash from the petty cash fund—for cabs and other legitimate expenses. In fact, for some thirty years, he had received $125 each week from petty cash for these purposes. These disbursements should have been posted to the applicable business account, and Segal presumed that was being done. To make sure that all his taxable income was reported accurately, Segal had added at least $50,000 to his own taxable income annually for two decades to cover any personal expenses that the company would have paid if they were misclassified during the record-keeping process. The government ignored this fact—which should have put to rest any accusation of tax law violations.

Now, Wish was suggesting that Watkins at some point had begun charging the cash withdrawals to the postage account and destroying Segal's documented receipts to cover up Watkins's embezzlement.

"That's crazy," Segal declared. "I'll find out what the hell's going on here." That is when he had picked up his mobile phone and punched in Watkins's number, gesturing at Wish to lean closer so he could listen.

They both heard Watkins explain that he had been posting cash to the postage account. "You told me to do it," Watkins insisted.

"I remember nothing of the kind," Segal said.

"You told me to do it twenty years ago," Watkins said, "when our offices were still on Chestnut Street."

"I don't remember that. That's bullshit!" Segal retorted and ended the call.

"Something is very wrong here," Segal told Wish, "and I need you to get involved. You should immediately do a review and analysis and get to the bottom of this. I believe someone is trying to set me up."

Wish said he would investigate and then suggested, "What about calling Harvey Silets? If anyone can figure this out, Harvey can."

For several decades, Silets, a long-time close friend of Segal, had been one of the shrewdest and most powerful criminal defense attorneys in Chicago. A diminutive man with an encyclopedic knowledge of criminal tax law, Silets was already representing Near North on loan transactions, so an expansion of his responsibilities made sense.

Silets was already aware that the Takeover Group had attempted to wrest control of the company from Segal. What he, Segal, and Wish didn't know was that McNichols now was part of the Group, and was secretly recording their conversations for the FBI.

Segal dictated an email to Wish, dated October 23, 2001, recapping their meeting. It made clear that Segal was not involved in any conspiracy. Indeed, it was outrageous that, having discovered an embezzler who had been stealing from Near North for years, McNichols and the government would try to tie Segal to Watkins's petty cash scheme. As sole owner of Near North, Segal had legal access to millions of dollars in retained earnings that he could have chosen to keep as income instead of using it to expand his company.

In the email, Segal expressed his surprise at Watkins's activities and made clear that his long-term policy had been to attribute any cash payments he received for personal expenses to his draw account or the applicable business account. "I was surprised and uninformed as to the characterization of certain miscellaneous expenses that were being referred to as Watkins' classifications," Segal wrote.

McNichols and Wish met a week later, on October 30, and Wish told McNichols of the email and of Segal's surprise at Watkins's activities. The FBI would report that McNichols's tape recorder was not working on that day. Segal suspected that the tape recorder actually was working on October 30, but because the conversation would have been favorable to Segal, the report was falsified.

But whether it was falsified or not, it was clear from the October 31 conversation between Watkins and McNichols that the prosecution knew then of the October 23 email, and Segal's position—surprise and a statement of his practice, which was evidence that there was no conspiracy with Watkins.

Segal understood the gravity of the situation. A trusted employee was engaging in what appeared to be classic embezzlement. This wasn't a matter of ten- or twenty-dollar cab fares; Watkins was in fact undermining Segal's own tax liability by crediting money to postage instead of Segal's draw account. Segal removed all bookkeeping responsibilities from Watkins, in effect ending his ability to create false evidence.

What Segal didn't know at the time—what no one except Watkins knew—was that Watkins had been embezzling money for more than twenty years and was trying to cover it up through the falsification and destruction of records, including the audit trail, relating to Segal's receipt of petty cash. To the extent that he succeeded, he made it possible for the prosecution to allege that Segal was receiving petty cash and to charge him with a criminal tax conspiracy.

Two days after the call from Segal and Wish, Watkins had told McNichols about it, mocking Segal by mimicking him: "Why did you put that there?" Watkins clearly had no idea that his conversation with McNichols was being recorded for the FBI. He admitted that his actions were his own and not directed by Segal. "I always thought postage was a good place to hide it," he said. This recording was further proof of a repudiation of any tax conspiracy, if one existed, prior to November 1.

On October 31, Wish had told McNichols that Segal was asking Silets to investigate the Watkins matter. This was a clear message to McNichols—and now, the FBI—that Segal was trying to halt any wrongdoing by Watkins, not cover it up.

In a November 1 recorded conversation between McNichols and Watkins, McNichols warned Watkins that he would become the scapegoat since he helped prepare Near North's income tax returns. Watkins complained that he had worked hard and now would probably be fired. He suggested that if someone would pay to find him another job, "I'll forget everything I know."

In that same conversation, McNichols asked Watkins if he had any document or record to protect himself. Watkins said there was no written proof that anyone told him to do any of these things—everything had been oral. He said that he hadn't told Segal about a lot of what he was doing.

On November 16, Silets and Wish interviewed Watkins in his office at Near North and subsequently prepared an affidavit in which Watkins said that he had executed the postage scheme all on his own. Watkins was extremely concerned that he'd be fired or worse—who wouldn't be, after being caught with his hand in the till to the tune of perhaps as much as $200,000? The very next day, McNichols taped a phone conversation between Wish and Silets about the affidavit—trampling on attorney-client privilege. During the call, Wish said, "I think this document describes accurately our meeting with Watkins." Significantly, the FBI was now on notice that the affidavit was exculpatory for Segal.

On November 20, Silets and Wish met in Watkins's office to review the draft affidavit. Several handwritten corrections were made and they all agreed that when it was retyped and ready for Watkins' signature, they would meet again.

The following day, November 21, in another recorded conversation, McNichols told Watkins that although there would be great pressure on him to sign the affidavit, he shouldn't sign it. When Watkins said he didn't believe he was being pressured and began to add that Segal had no knowledge, McNichols cut him off before he could say anything further.

On November 23, when it appeared that Watkins was going to sign the affidavit—McNichols made the big reveal: He was working with the FBI on an investigation of Segal and Near North and he was wearing a wire and recording conversations with Segal and others. He quickly arranged for Watkins to meet with FBI agent Patrick Murphy, the agent that McNichols was working with. Watkins was worried that Segal was going to fire him, a fear that likely provided strong motivation to cooperate with the FBI and even to fabricate evidence.

After meeting with Murphy, Watkins agreed to change the account of his actions that he had given to Silets and Wish. With Murphy's help (later disclosed in an FBI recording), Watkins created a new affidavit, which significantly removed the fact that Segal had no knowledge that Watkins was illegally posting cash payments to the postage account.[9, 10]

On November 29, Watkins called Silets to report that he was backing out of his affidavit, that he did not agree with what it said, and that he would not sign it. (This conversation was recorded by Watkins.)

"You were going to get back to me with that statement that we met about ten days ago and I haven't heard from you," Silets said.

"Well, because, I think, uh, I don't agree with the stuff that's on it, so I haven't done anything with it," Watkins said.

"What do you mean you don't agree with it? What I wrote there is what you told us," Silets retorted.

Several seconds passed in silence before Silets prodded Watkins. "Hello?"

"Hi. Yes," Watkins said.

"Did you hear me? Didn't you tell me all those things?" Silets demanded.

"Well, we went over some of the procedures and that, but some of the things in there, um, are not, you know—I'm not comfortable with," Watkins said.

"Such as what?"

"Well, just a minute, let me get the statement," Watkins said. The only sound for several minutes was the sound of rustling pages. What happened during those minutes remains a mystery, but Segal and his defense team came to believe that Watkins, who didn't do anything without approval from Murphy, had reached out to Murphy for advice.

Finally, Watkins spoke again. "Well, like I said, I'm just not comfortable with this statement."

Silets was baffled. "What is it in there that you don't agree with?"

"Let me read over this and get back to you," Watkins said, and hung up.

---

9   Government ID92 - Example of Murphy controlling Watkins while taping Silets.

10   Government ID31 - Watkins taping his conversation with Segal's attorney Silets.

At the time, the sudden reversal was puzzling. But Segal later deduced that because Watkins had begun cooperating with the FBI, Murphy wanted to eliminate Watkins's admissions that Segal had no knowledge of any accounting irregularities—even though Watkins had already confirmed that fact in a recorded conversation with McNichols.

Agents and prosecutors who are willing to violate the law in order to secure a conviction can and do resort to suborning perjury, creating false facts, and hiding exculpatory evidence—but this process is normally hidden from view. Murphy's apparent collaboration with Watkins became an example of this sort of violation being exposed via audiotape, and showed what the government was willing to do to convict Segal.

A transcript of a conversation between Murphy and Watkins revealed the particulars of how Murphy advised Watkins to alter the affidavit.[11]

"Another thought I had was on the petty cash part," Murphy said. "Assuming this is accurate, I saw him put in there when Mike first started asking for petty cash, if you recall the first amounts of denominations he was asking for, it was too much for stamps."

"Sure," Watkins replied. "Because it was two hundred-fifty or five hundred bucks."

"In the context of when Mike started asking that money be put to postage, I will assume it's accurate that the amount he was asking for—(that) it was abundantly clear that he wasn't using it for postage. I'm just trying to make it clear that—shoot down this idea that the thing that Harvey's trying to do to you, I thought putting a phrase in to that effect…."

Murphy then asked Watkins how much he paid for postage. "I would buy two or three rolls at a time," Watkins said.

"How much were stamps back then?" Murphy asked. "Fifteen cents? So, fifty bucks probably. He's trying to box you in there. Add in a 'furthermore, the amounts he typically withdrew at that time'—ah, what did you say the amounts were?"

---

11   Government ID34 - Murphy instructing Watkins how to change affidavit.

"Two-fifty, five-hundred," Watkins replied.

"I don't want to pin you down on those," Murphy said. "Write down something like, 'All of this made it clear to me that these withdrawals were not for postage.' The point I'm trying to make is that even though he never said, 'This isn't really for postage, Dan, this is so I can go do whatever I want to do,' you're a logical human being, you're looking at the circumstances, and it's obvious to you that this was not for postage, contrary to what Silets is trying to say."

Watkins asked, "How does Harvey get around the fact that [Segal] keeps asking me for cash?"

"His point is that Mike was, at that time, asking for small amounts to pay for postage," Murphy said. "And you just kept charging any petty cash for Mike to postage. Rather than asking him what the money is for, you're assuming that he wants it to go to postage, and he's assuming that you are taking care of it properly."

Baffled, Watkins asked, "How do I take care of it properly though? What do I do?"

Of course, that conversation ignored the fact that money was posted to Segal's draw account and that every year Segal added $50,000 to his income to cover any such personal expenses. At Segal's trial, Angela Amaro, a Near North accounting employee would testify that Segal had instructed her to post cash advances to his draw account.

Despite the evidence that Segal made an immediate attempt to investigate Watkins and to cut off Watkins's access to the accounts, Segal ultimately was charged with a Klein Tax Conspiracy, which alleges that two or more people conspired to impede the Internal Revenue Service of its ability to review books and records. It was critical to the prosecution that they be able to show that Segal conspired with someone—and they made that happen by co-opting Watkins.

When the real events of late October and November 2001 came to light, however, they didn't show a conspiracy at all. Rather, the emails and transcripts of that period showed Segal working feverishly to find out what Watkins was doing and trying to stop it.

On November 1, exactly eight days after Segal learned of the embezzlement and acted to stop it, new federal sentencing guidelines took effect across the United States. Under the guidelines, the Klein Tax Conspiracy charge, as it was applied to Segal, was what is known as a "straddle crime," which allowed conduct committed prior to that date to be punished under the new and increased punishment factors.

Courts have usually ruled straddle crimes exempt from ex post facto problems if the crime, though it began prior to the enactment of the law, was completed or was continuing after enactment of the law. These new sentencing guidelines would be invoked at Segal's sentencing to add more than four additional years to his sentence.

Chapter 7

Near North
Is Cyberhacked

In late February 2002, less than a month after Segal's arrest, he ramped up his offensive against the Takeover Group and archrival Aon. His lawyer, Richard Prendergast, past president of the Chicago Bar Association, filed documents in Cook County Circuit Court to amend the civil suit that had been filed prior to any knowledge of the federal investigation. These papers asserted that Near North was a victim of a "crude extortion effort" engineered by Walsh, Berry, Ludwig, Gerber, and Gallagher, with the support and encouragement of Aon. (Mackey was not yet named because his actions on behalf of the Takeover Group were still undiscovered.)

For the first time, Segal went public with the details of how the Takeover Group had engaged in a "campaign of extortion based on false claims," to try to force him to sell Near North. He asserted that the group had "spread tales of improper conduct on the part of Near North and its CEO," and leaked negative information to state regulators, the media, and "apparently" U.S. Attorney Patrick Fitzgerald.

It was becoming clear to Segal that someone had used influence with U.S. Senator Peter Fitzgerald to induce the incoming U.S. Attorney to prosecute him and Near North. Segal's case was unusual because there were no victims named and none would emerge in the ensuing years. What would emerge was a wealth of evidence to show that Segal and the firm he'd built over forty years had been victimized by the Takeover Group.

The lawsuit originally was filed just days before Segal was arrested and accused the Takeover Group of illegally interfering with existing Near North contracts when its members went to work for Aon and other tortious misconduct. Just a few weeks later, in April 2002, as Segal's lawyers were filing motions in U.S. District Court to dismiss the criminal case against him and to suppress his statements during the hotel confrontation, one of his employees made a startling discovery.

A Near North accounting department employee went to Karen Gruca, director of Human Resources, to report she had learned she was going to be fired and was not satisfied with her severance package. Since the employee had not yet been officially notified of the impending firing or its terms, Gruca suspected that someone had hacked into Gruca's emails and passed the information to the employee. Gruca discovered that someone had, in fact, logged into her email the previous night.

The discovery triggered an internal investigation. A computer program was set up to collect data about any intrusions. Sure enough, it was soon confirmed that Near North's email security had been compromised. This was the first clue that the company—and Segal himself—were the targets of a complex, intrusive, and focused computer hacking scheme.

It turned out that David Cheley, a former Near North employee, had been stealing emails during an eight-month period that began four months prior to Segal's arrest.

Almost immediately, Cheley figured out he had been discovered. On April 12, he emailed a former Near North employee who had worked in the computer department to report that he had just read Gruca's email in which she told Tony Swiantek, head of Near North's Information Technology Department, that she noticed someone logged into her email the previous night.

Using the initials TS to refer to Swiantek, Cheley wrote: "So my guess is they will lock down [email] by Monday so I am going in to write [*Chicago Tribune* columnist John Kass an] email this weekend and send it through dial-up via TS's email account. Once that gets sent out and NN gets wind of the person who sent it, all hell should break loose and access to mail will be cut...I think it's time to get this done before the door closes. What I will do is write the email from TS's account and then send it to Kass. To make it fair, I'll also send the same email to the *Sun-Times*. Then I'll delete the email from TS's sent mail before the backups run so it will never show up in the logs."

This was proof of criminal conduct. Surely, with these emails in the possession of the government, there could be no investigation or prosecution, thought Segal. Protecting a criminal, enabling him to continue breaking the law, is itself a crime, he reasoned.[12]

Cheley also seemed to be targeting Swiantek as retribution for being fired. "I think to make it extra fun," he wrote, "I'll put all KG's files from her personal network drive into TS's network drive. That way, if they look at TS's computer, he will have all her HR stuff there. Finally, to make it really interesting, I might want to copy all the NN salary information to every NN network drive. Do you think that's too much? The only conclusion they will make is that it was done by someone in house (T) as this info is not accessible by someone outside. I can pretty much do anything on the network. Perhaps I can print something on a couple of network printers. On Monday morning, there will be [lots] of interesting things for T to explain to management. Buh-Bye, T. :)"

The discovery of this email explained why Near North's employee benefits payroll roster had mysteriously appeared on the desks of several Near North employees who, it turned out, were being solicited by members of the Takeover Group to leave Near North. Some of Segal's best employees, in fact, did leave. Some went to Aon, some to other

---

12   Cheley Non-email related hacking.

companies, draining Near North of talent and strengthening its competition. Cheley had begun stealing emails almost immediately after he left Near North in August 2001. The investigation showed that he left on a Friday—the same day that Takeover Group member Matt Walsh left for Aon—and spent more than six hours over the next two days using his home computer to hack into Near North's computer systems[13], including its email and accounting systems.[14] He immediately began obtaining sensitive financial data and attorney-client privileged documents.

If that wasn't bad enough, a private investigation by the Pinkerton detective service and some ex-Secret Service agents hired by Segal soon uncovered evidence that many of the thousands of stolen emails were passed on to Walsh and Dana Berry at Aon. More ominously, the Takeover Group had shared emails with the FBI, suggesting that the prosecution knew about the hacking, which could be viewed as a crime itself.

From that moment on, Segal was at war with a U.S. Attorney's Office that seemed committed to bringing him and Near North down any way it could, even if no crime had occurred. As far as Segal was concerned, he was up against a government "Conviction-at-Any-Cost" playbook. Segal was about to experience what criminal defense lawyer Harvey Silverglate described in his 2009 book, *Three Felonies a Day: How the Feds Target the Innocent*. In Silverglate's terms, the federal criminal justice system has become, "a crude conviction machine instead of an engine of truth and justice."

But first, just who was David Cheley?

Cheley had been hired by Near North in 1999 as a computer consultant working with the Employee Benefit Department. In April 2001, he was about to be terminated when Takeover Group members Ludwig and Gerber intervened on his behalf and he was moved to a full-time job in another department. Years later, Ludwig admitted spending

---

13   Timeline – August 15, 2001 David Cheley terminated from Near North.
14   Cheley's hacking activities into Near North's computer systems.

hours with Cheley at Near North, and, after Ludwig left Near North, he met several times with Cheley, once for nearly three hours. For the next four months—until Cheley left Near North—Cheley worked on a wide variety of projects, including the administration of the company's computer operating systems—Microsoft NT and Unix—and SQL, a powerful relational database system. Cheley was responsible for changing passwords, setting up network shares, server administration, and remote-access administration. During these four months, Cheley became familiar with the security protocols for all Near North computer operating systems.

Near North's internal investigation would ascertain that prior to his departure, Cheley worked to obtain a wealth of Near North's proprietary information, including high-value technology and intellectual properties that positioned Near North uniquely in the market place as a leading technology innovator. It became clear that Cheley intended to profit by his theft and use Near North's proprietary Surety Bond system as an enticement to be hired at Kemper Insurance. His cyberhacking thefts included a confidential Near North employee database of names, addresses, telephone numbers, Social Security numbers, salary information, and a complete list of user IDs and passwords.

On August 15, 2001, Cheley was terminated. By then, he had figured out numerous unauthorized methods of access to Near North computer systems, servers, and data. As he was leaving Near North, Cheley emailed his wife, saying he would soon be coming into some money. Shortly after that, he was hired by a computer-consulting firm, DHS & Associates, which assigned him to provide computer consulting to Kemper Insurance Services in Long Grove, Illinois. Cheley had barely settled into his chair at Kemper when he began breaking into Near North's computers. For the next eight months, Cheley accessed Near North's computer system almost daily from Kemper computers.

Near North's sleuths, working virtually around the clock for several days, unraveled the cyberhacking scheme by first determining that the company's email system was being accessed from a computer IP address at Kemper's Long Grove facility. Segal called the president of Kemper, who was a friend, and suggested that he meet with Near North's legal counsel and technology people to go over what they had learned.

At the meeting on April 23, 2002, Kemper officials initially denied there was any hacking. But when a Kemper computer expert ran a program that tracked activity for the previous forty-five days, the hacking was evident. Kemper admitted that Cheley had brought personal computers and CD burners into the office in violation of Kemper policy. The activity logs showed Cheley accessing massive segments of Near North's computer records for many hours and burning them onto CD-rom discs. He would then pull out full copies of select documents.

Kemper's activity logs, created with Internet-activity-tracking software, showed that Cheley had been using three Kemper computer workstations and a non-Kemper laptop known as IROAMER to access Near North's email servers from Kemper's computer network.[15] Kemper's head of security, a former FBI agent, excused himself and left the meeting. Segal's investigators would conclude that the former agent specifically left to inform the FBI that the hacking issue was looming.

Everyone at the meeting agreed that the following day, Kemper and Near North would file a complaint against Cheley with the Lake County States Attorney. But Kemper was non-responsive the next day, and Near North determined that Kemper had not filed a complaint but instead hired an outside consultant, Kroll & Associates. In the view of Near North, the consultant was hired to cover up and control the electronic hacking footprints. Soon after, Kemper officials notified the Lake County State's Attorney that the matter would not be pursued. Segal subsequently would learn that federal prosecutor Virgina Kendall had called the Lake County States Attorney and later the Cook County

---

15   Near North sites accessed by IROAMER.

States Attorney to say that the hacking was related to the Segal prosecution and suggested that local law enforcement should back off.

For its part, the media—with the exception of *Chicago Tribune* reporter Ray Gibson—whose reputation for accuracy and fairness was unmatched—ignored the hacking evidence completely.[16] Segal had hoped that if the government was worried about the exposure of their involvement with Cheley and the Takeover Group, prosecutors might negotiate with Segal's attorneys. He also believed that exposing possession of stolen emails by a Fortune 500 company would surely generate media attention. But the matter went ignored by the media and the prosecution proceeded unchecked.

Near North would learn from phone records that very late on the night before Kemper was to have Cheley fired, his unauthorized laptop copied, and his case walked over to the Lake County State's Attorney's Office, telephone calls were made between Takeover Group member Gallagher and FBI Agent Murphy. Segal and others were suspicious there was a leak inside Near North—that Pat Muldowney, an attorney at Near North who was close to Takeover Group member Mike Mackey, who had possibly alerted the other Takeover Group members about the hacking investigation.

The internal investigation discovered that for the 45-day period prior to April 23, Cheley had hit Near North's computer system *more than 20,000 times*. The activity-tracking software was unable to go back any further than forty-five days. But if that was an average period for Cheley, he likely accessed Near North's computer system *100,000 times*. And, Segal learned, there likely was a fourth hard drive, but it was never examined.

Kemper did fire Cheley as promised and Kroll took a statement from him. But Kroll concluded, despite extensive contrary evidence, that Cheley was merely a "curious voyeur" who wanted to know what

---

16   Hacking alleged at Near North, Chicago Tribune, 062402

was going on at his former employer and neither Kroll nor Kemper recommended criminal prosecution. Perhaps most galling was that Kemper allowed Cheley to leave without confiscating the IROAMER laptop. Essentially, Cheley walked away with the evidence of his crimes under his arm.

Later, Segal asked Kemper's president, William Smith, why Kemper did not seek to have Cheley arrested. Wordlessly, Smith pointed toward the executive offices. Segal nodded, realizing that the son of Kemper's chairman worked for Aon.

Even so, the hard drives that were examined ultimately revealed that Cheley had illegally accessed a wide range of email files from Near North, including Segal's personal emails. In total, Near North generated more than 600 pages of specific emails that Cheley had hacked,[17] as well as:

- Segal's complete email files, including attorney-client-privileged documents sent to lawyers working inside Near North and outside counsel

- Current Near North clients

- Near North employees and strategies about retaining employees and business units within Near North

- Strategic Near North business issues

- Near North litigation relating to the lawsuit Near North had filed in Cook County Circuit Court

- Near North litigation matters, specifically Segal's attorney-client-privileged communications with the inside and outside counsel

- Near North litigation matters pending in California

- Near North litigation matters relating to a separate lawsuit against the Takeover Group involving Aon that was pending in

---

17   Attorney-Client privileged Hacked documents log

Cook County Circuit Court, which was used to interfere with a settlement just prior to Segal's arrest

- Near North customer and financial databases

Through the civil lawsuit, Near North demanded that Aon examine the computers used by Walsh and Berry. As a result, Aon turned over 129 pages of emails between Cheley and Walsh and Berry, but declined to turn over electronic records from Walsh and Berry's computer server. The emails that were disclosed showed that, months before Segal was arrested:

- Walsh and Berry were in frequent contact with Cheley and provided him with their direct lines and fax numbers at Aon.

- Walsh and Berry, after being sent copies of privileged Near North emails, solicited Cheley to send them even larger files.

- Cheley gave passwords to Walsh and Berry so they could open encrypted files that Cheley sent them.

- Walsh and Berry received a large amount of highly confidential and proprietary Near North business information, including information about employees and clients.

- Walsh and Berry received many attorney-client communications from Near North, including privileged communications relating to the Takeover Group lawsuit.

Cheley's activities, what motivated him, and the individuals with whom he was aligned, became clear in emails that he sent to Walsh and Berry—using email accounts he created under the names of Lisa Chen, Lisa Fisher, and Lisa Rasmussen. He met and worked with Ludwig, Walsh, and Berry, effectively becoming a member of the Takeover Group. At times, the internal investigation showed, Cheley was pulling documents specifically requested by members of that group.

On September 21, 2001, for example, he emailed Walsh and reported that he had called Ludwig, "a couple of weeks ago and passed some info to him and he was appreciative…I am personally disgusted with what NN has done not only to me, but to the former management group. Anyway, I don't want to go into details here as to what I have or can get and how I do it, but if you're interested in knowing what Segal's plans are, let me know a number to call."

Barely twenty minutes after Cheley pushed the button on that email, Walsh wrote him back providing his and Berry's direct telephone lines at Aon. Shortly thereafter, Walsh and Cheley spoke for thirteen minutes.

Ten days later, on October 1, Cheley sent the first installment of hacked emails to Walsh, who promptly forwarded them to Berry. When Walsh had trouble opening the file, Berry helped him get it open. This first installment included a privileged email between Segal and Sherri Stanton, Near North's general counsel, discussing Walsh's extensive efforts over days to recruit a Near North employee to leave and join Walsh at Aon.

This first installment whetted Walsh's appetite: He asked Cheley to send him a larger file later that day and Cheley was only too happy to oblige. This larger file proved a treasure trove to Walsh. It contained emails concerning several of Near North's significant customers—customers that Walsh and Berry had promised to bring to Aon—including Sony Music, Grupo Modelo (Corona Beer), Key3 Media, and SMG, the industry gold standard for public facility management. These emails also included potential litigation strategy concerning Walsh and Berry. Walsh dutifully passed all of it to Berry.

Cheley continued sending files, including two more packages in October 2001, another in December 2001 and another in February 2002. These concerned Near North's business strategies relating to key clients, including Jupiter Realty and Standard Parking, as well as privileged communications on legal issues to and from Segal, Stanton, and Near North's outside legal counsel. One email passed along was between Segal and attorney Harvey Silets, discussing potential legal strategies against Walsh and Berry regarding specific facts that proved their unlawful conduct.

On March 20, at 3:31 p.m., Cheley sent an email saying, "I still have access to the local network through dial-up and VPN, but I no longer have administrator access…. I am going to have to see if I have Neil's password at home, but if I don't it will be much harder to gain administrative access."

At 11:38 p.m., he emailed, "I have a large file of [Near North] stuff, including information that would surely cause major problems for the company."

And then, less than an hour later, at 12:24 a.m. on March 21, Cheley emailed again. "Great news. I have full administrative access to the entire network. Boy, are those guys dumb over there. I also have access to Tony [Swiantek]'s email again."

The exposure of the systematic hacking made clear that Walsh and Berry were using the stolen emails to advance their own litigation strategy in the lawsuit filed by Near North, as well as to threaten and harass certain Near North employees and solicit others to leave the company. Moreover, the Takeover Group was using the information to pursue customers of Near North. For example, on December 28, Cheley hacked an email from Segal to Near North's lawyers that discussed how Walsh and Gallagher had solicited Jupiter Realty, a long-time Near North customer, during a meeting with Jupiter's vice president. Ten days later, Walsh sent a letter to Jupiter's president and CEO attempting to explain away the meeting with the vice president and counter certain facts in Segal's email.

Cheley passed along a privileged email communication between Segal and Stanton relating to Near North employee Marisa Thielen, who worked in the company's bond department in Washington, D.C. Five days later, Walsh called Thielen three times, spending about an hour in total in conversation. Ultimately, Thielen left Near North and was hired by Aon. Segal believed that Walsh had other motivations in bringing her to Aon.

On August 21, 2001—just days after Cheley left Near North—Segal emailed Stanton and others that he was going to contact attorney Zack Stamp to represent Near North in the self-reporting procedure before the Illinois Department of Insurance relating to the PFTA.[18] The email laid out in detail the facts supporting Near North's plans for making the company's presentation on the PFTA issue.

On August 29, Walsh—who was committed to taking down Near North—called McNichols to report he had "heard" that Near North had matters covered with the State of Illinois, but that the "feds" would not be so easy.

On December 28, Segal sent an email to Stanton and two of Near North's outside lawyers, Thomas Rakowski and David Novoselsky, discussing litigation strategies to respond to the efforts by Walsh and Berry and others to solicit Near North clients. Segal discussed the possibility of filing a complaint against some of the Takeover Group members. That didn't remain confidential for long. Cheley hacked that email the same day and passed it along.

On January 3, 2002, just six days later, Eric Brandfonbrener, an attorney hired by Aon to work on behalf of Walsh, Berry, and Gallagher, sent a letter to Rakowski and Novoselsky saying, "I would like to discuss an ominous report we have just received." Brandfonbrener went on to say that he had information that Segal was considering "filing unfounded complaints with the Illinois Department of Insurance on behalf of Near North and against Dana Berry, Tim Gallagher, and Matt Walsh." He didn't disclose the source of this information, but the only possible source was the hacked email Cheley had sent to Walsh.

In September 2001, Segal sent an email discussing the possibility of

---

18   Zack Stamp, Ex-Illinois Director of Insurance affidavit.

filing a lawsuit against Gallagher and Near North employee Lori Shaw as a way of persuading Berry and Walsh to back off in their takeover efforts. This email was stolen on October 2 and emailed to Walsh, who forwarded it to Berry. It kicked off a series of emails to Brandfonbrener who, on October 3, met with Aon's chief corporate counsel and also had a phone conversation with Berry. On October 4, less than forty-eight hours after Segal's email was stolen, Shaw sent an email to her superior at Aon saying that Segal's "tactic is to come after me and Tim Gallagher in an attempt to pressure Dana [Berry] and Matt [Walsh] to relent in their efforts. He is currently suing me to return my signing bonus and other paid bonuses, which amount to $150,000. I know that Raymond Skilling, Aon's chief general counsel, and the independent attorney Brandfonbrener met yesterday." A month later, when the outside counsel emailed the draft lawsuit against Shaw to Stanton, that email was stolen as well.[19]

It became clear that at about the same time that Cheley was breaking into Near North's computers, Walsh and Berry—and later McNichols—were feeding information to the FBI, specifically to agent Patrick Murphy. In fact, the Takeover Group allegations—fueled by the stolen emails—were the centerpiece of the affidavit used to support the search warrant and arrest warrant against Segal on January 26, 2002.

In June 2002, Near North filed a separate federal lawsuit against Cheley and two other former Near North computer employees seeking damages for the cost of the Pinkerton investigation and other expenses, which, by that time, totaled $645,000.

The Pinkerton investigation was led by David Grossman, a former FBI agent with impeccable credentials whose work in an undercover investigation of corruption in the Cook County Courts had led to numerous convictions. He had gone on to head the FBI computer crimes unit in Chicago before leaving to become a private consultant.

---

19   Attorney-Client privileged hacked documents log, 11/2/01.

Within days of examining the evidence of the hacking of Segal's emails, Grossman paid a visit to the FBI's Chicago office and spoke with two computer crimes agents there—both of whom he had trained before leaving the FBI. Grossman laid out the evidence that Cheley had illegally hacked into the Near North email system. The agents expressed some interest in the information and said it appeared there was a credible case for prosecution. Later, Grossman was told that the computer crimes unit was told to "open a file," but nothing more was done; no investigation was ever conducted. In fact, Grossman learned, the Segal prosecution team took the matter out of the FBI's computer crimes unit and put in the hands of other agents.

The FBI never went to Cheley's home, although they eventually met with him at a rest stop on the Illinois Tollway. The meeting was basically a waste of time. By that time, Cheley's laptop had been purged. Cheley was never charged with a crime. His conduct was essentially condoned and protected by the government. It was but one example of what Segal was up against. It seemed a perversion of justice to ignore a very real crime *against* Segal to prosecute him for something that wasn't a crime. Meanwhile, Aon, a Fortune 500 company, escaped any accountability while benefiting from the theft of Near North documents and clients.[20]

---

20   Overview of Cheley Hacking Activity.

Chapter 8

RICO and
Prosecution Revenge

IN SEPTEMBER 2002, JOSHUA BUCHMAN, an attorney for Near North who had gone into private practice after a distinguished career as a federal prosecutor, requested a meeting with the prosecution team. He did it as a courtesy to inform the prosecution that Near North intended to amend its civil lawsuit against Walsh, Berry and the others to include evidence of Cheley's illegal conduct.

The meeting was held at the office of the U.S. Attorney in the Dirksen Federal Building; in attendance were FBI agents Patrick Murphy and Jane Higgins and prosecutors Virginia Kendall and William Hogan. Of particular concern was the fact that some of the stolen emails had been forwarded to Murphy and the prosecution had not disclosed it.

Hogan was no stranger to accusations of misconduct.[21] In the case against Segal and Near North, Hogan would be accused of engaging in the sort of misconduct that had gotten him fired previously. A decade earlier, Hogan was at the vortex of one of the worst and most embarrassing episodes of prosecutorial misconduct in the history of the U.S. Attorney's Office in Chicago. His conduct was found to be egregious.

Hogan had been the architect of a massive prosecution of the El

---

21   Hogan Boyd case.

Rukn street gang—one of Chicago's most notorious and vicious gangs. A six-year investigation generated multiple indictments and more than fifty convictions. But most of the cases unraveled after disclosures that some of Hogan's witnesses were snorting heroin and having sex while in custody and in government offices. Judges vacated more than a dozen convictions after finding that two key El Rukn members had used drugs while they were government witnesses and in custody. A former prosecutor and other witnesses said that they'd told Hogan that the informants were using drugs but that information was never disclosed to the defense. The sordid affair was the subject of a CBS *60 Minutes* segment and made national news.

In addition, judges found that Hogan had failed to disclose that El Rukn witnesses had contact visits with wives, girlfriends, and others—some in government offices while federal agents or Chicago police officers stood outside. One judge, Suzanne Conlon, ruled that the federal Metropolitan Correctional Center—where the prosecution witnesses were housed—failed to turn over records that would have shown that the witnesses had tested positive for drugs. Conlon ruled that the concealment "was tacitly approved, if not requested," by Hogan, "to conceal evidence that reflected negatively on the El Rukn inmate witnesses." The witnesses had free access to prosecutor telephones—even answering the phones themselves at times—and were provided with clothing, gifts, a camera, headset radios (some of these at taxpayer expense), and even beer. Prosecutors have a duty to disclose evidence favorable to defendants—including evidence of benefits provided to their witnesses. Hogan, the judges ruled, had committed prosecutorial misconduct by failing to disclose this evidence. U.S. District Court Judge Marvin Aspen concluded that Hogan must have known of the drug use. Aspen called Hogan's failure to disclose the information to the defense, "a deliberate and calculated decision."

The U.S. Justice Department's Office of Professional Standards opened an investigation and Hogan was suspended. As reported by the *Chicago Sun-Times* on May 2, 1996, Associate Deputy Attorney General David Margolis formally notified Hogan of his firing, but Hogan refused to go quietly. He filed a lawsuit and following a hearing in 1998, his dismissal was overturned and he was reinstated with back pay. An administrative hearing judge ruled that the Justice Department had failed to prove Hogan had known about the drug use and that, even if the evidence had been passed to the defense, the defendants would still have been convicted. Indeed, the El Rukn members who got new trials because of the rulings were reconvicted.

In another case, Hogan's team was accused of "serial prosecutorial misconduct" by the Illinois Association of Criminal Defense lawyers in the prosecution of Chicago developer Peter Palivos, who was convicted in 2003 of obstruction of justice and sentenced to a year in prison. Palivos contended that the Hogan-led prosecution framed him because he wouldn't testify as a government witness in an unrelated investigation. In what Palivos's attorneys contended was a case of suborning perjury, Hogan's key witness against Palivos, a businessman named Nick Black, stated under oath that the government had not promised him that he would be spared jail time for failing to pay his taxes in exchange for testimony against Palivos. Following the trial, however, Black acknowledged in an affidavit that he was promised a reduced sentence from prosecutors, and at his sentencing, he did in fact receive no time in custody.

The El Rukn case would dog Hogan again years later. In 2014, Earl Hawkins, one of the most infamous of the El Rukn informants—whose lawyer once bribed a judge to fix a double murder case that sent Hawkins to Death Row—was released from prison despite having been sentenced to terms of sixty years for racketeering conspiracy and seventy-eight years for armed violence. Hawkins was released earlier than anticipated after Hogan and another federal prosecutor, as well as two former Chicago police officers, wrote letters of support to the Illinois

Prisoner Review Board. Hawkins was released after he testified in the retrial of Nathson Fields for murder. Fields was acquitted in 2009 by a judge who said Hawkins was not a credible witness. Fields, who spent eighteen years in prison for a crime he didn't commit, then filed a civil suit accusing the detectives who had handled his case of framing him.

After Hawkins was released, one of Fields's lawyers, Candace Gorman, faxed a letter to U.S. Attorney Zachary Fardon in Chicago and Inspector General Michael Horowitz of the U.S. Department of Justice, accusing Hogan of interfering with Fields's lawsuit. Gorman said Hogan wasn't an attorney on the case, but even so he waited outside the courtroom during the proceedings of the case and conversed with the detectives and their attorneys. Gorman said Hogan acted as Hawkins's "personal representative" at his parole hearing. "I ask that you conduct your investigation into AUSA Hogan's role in the Fields civil rights case—or at the very least that you rein him in and keep him away from this case and the courtroom when the case is up," Gorman requested.

Hogan disputed Gorman's allegations, but his efforts to protect government witnesses put him under cross-examination in the 2016 trial of Fields's civil lawsuit. Hogan was questioned for arranging an early release for yet another El Rukn government witness, Derrick Kees, who admitted to taking part in twenty slayings. As the *Chicago Tribune* reported: "Kees tried to get out of a plea deal calling for a 99-year sentence after he said Assistant U.S. Attorney William Hogan, the lead prosecutor in the case, had cut a side deal promising him he'd serve less time."

Hogan denied under oath that he'd made such a promise, yet Kees did, in fact, obtain early release with the support of the U.S. Attorney's Office after seventeen years were cut off his sentence. In December 2016, the jury ordered the City of Chicago to pay Fields $22 million for his wrongful incarceration.[22] Hogan was not disciplined for failing to disclose benefits conferred on his government witnesses. When

---

22 Federal prosecutor takes stand in wrongful conviction case, Sun-Times, 12/9/16.

Fields's lawyers accused Hogan of lying, he claimed, to their disbelief, that he'd simply "made a mistake."

Segal's lawyers realized that while they were on solid ground, Near North's plan to file an amended lawsuit citing the criminal activities of the Takeover Group was not the sort of news that someone with Hogan's background would want to hear. That's why Buchman set up the meeting to present the prosecutors with a draft of an amended complaint explicitly outlining the evidence of the cyberhacking and connecting the dots between Cheley, the Takeover Group, and Aon.

Buchman later stated in an affidavit: "Hogan asked me how Near North felt it could include Cheley and the other individual defendants in the same lawsuit. I replied that the draft complaint alleged a conspiracy among Cheley and the other individuals to unlawfully obtain Near North's confidential information and to use it to engage in unfair competition against Near North." Hogan and Kendall "voiced objections to this allegation regarding a conspiracy among Cheley and other individuals and expressed the government's view that such an allegation was unfounded," Buchman went on. "Hogan characterized the allegation regarding a conspiracy between Cheley and others in pejorative terms."

Segal considered Buchman's affidavit a testament to his courage and his willingness to do the right thing and fulfill his professional responsibilities, even though Buchman was a close friend of Kendall. In fact, they had dined together on the evening of the day Segal was arrested.

Despite the evidence, Hogan and Kendall denied that any members of the Takeover Group had anything to do with the cyberhacking and denied that any of the hacked emails had been communicated to the FBI or any member of the prosecution.

The prosecutors claimed that they had conducted their own internal investigation and concluded that there was no connection between Cheley and the Takeover Group. Hogan and Kendall apparently paid no attention to Eric Brandfonbrener, attorney for the Takeover Group, who acknowledged in the civil litigation that his clients *had* received stolen emails, but claimed they did not use them for competitive trade purposes and instead gave them to the FBI.

Then, spontaneously, Murphy recalled an occasion in the fall of 2001 when a cooperating witness, whom he believed was Matt Walsh, had told Murphy that he had received an unsolicited email from an unidentified sender that may have originated from Near North's email database.

Murphy's comment contradicted Kendall's denial moments earlier and suggested that either Murphy had been hiding the information from the prosecution team up to that point or that Kendall knew about it and had falsely denied any connection.

Kendall asserted that during the government's investigation of itself, the prosecution had not been inclined to interfere with Near North's civil litigation against the Takeover Group. She claimed the government didn't know what kind of business conduct Walsh, Berry, Gallagher, and the others had engaged in after departing Near North. However, an email between attorney for the Takeover Group and prosecutor Kendall was later discovered in which they discussed the review of the civil discovery of phone records from the Takeover Group.

Kendall and Hogan then informed Buchman that if Near North filed the amended civil complaint, the government would have no choice but to take that into consideration when determining whether to charge Segal in a superseding indictment under the Racketeer-Influenced Corrupt Organizations Act, commonly known as RICO. They implied that it might even mean an indictment of Near North itself.

This was an extraordinarily powerful threat. A RICO conviction, with its forfeiture provision, would destroy Near North, eliminate 1,000 jobs, and essentially wipe out Segal's source of revenue to pay legal fees. Three days after Buchman's meeting, Kendall called to advise that Murphy wanted to talk about some emails received by the Takeover Group. Buchman met with Hogan and Kendall, along with agents Murphy and

Higgins. The subject of the meeting was whether Walsh, Berry, and others who were key operators in the investigation and prosecution of Segal had received confidential or privileged emails from "a third party."

At the meeting, Murphy described a series of emails received by Walsh and Berry in the fall of 2001 and in March 2002. These emails appeared to contain confidential information regarding Near North, Murphy said. The March 2002 emails came from Berry and were addressed to someone named Lisa Fisher. Segal's lawyers were aware that this was one of Cheley's pseudonyms. Murphy admitted that one of the emails was a privileged and confidential communication between Segal and attorney Harvey Silets, although Murphy claimed that the privileged material had been deleted or redacted from the copy provided to him. Conspicuously, there was no communication as to who did the redaction. Segal was highly skeptical that anything had been redacted before Murphy received the material. (The defense later learned that at least one more email was sent by Walsh to Murphy's personal address—in February 2002—but this was not disclosed at this meeting.)

The prosecution was now reversing its earlier statement and admitting that hacked emails in fact were sent to their witnesses and shared with the FBI. Moreover, Kendall and Murphy now claimed that they had learned of these email interceptions in the fall of 2001 and spring of 2002, but that it hadn't occurred to them that the emails sent to Walsh and Berry were obtained through illegal activity. This defied logic and common sense. And finally, it was quite clear that there would be no criminal investigation of the hacking.

Buchman later recalled that Agent Higgins did not "actively" participate in the discussions at the meetings on September 17 and September 23, and "made no substantive verbal contributions to the issues being discussed in these meetings." She did not contradict or take issue with anything Kendall, Hogan and Murphy said, nor did she make any statement that indicated that the government possessed information that emails sent to Walsh and Berry may have been obtained through Cheley's hacking.

If there had been any doubt concerning the prosecution's agenda, it should have been dispelled when Hogan called Buchman and demanded that Near North withdraw a press release relating to the hacking and that Near North stop communicating with the media (Never mind Near North's First Amendment right to free speech.)[23]

Five weeks later, Hogan made good on his threat. The grand jury returned a superseding indictment against Segal, charging him with fraud and racketeering. The indictment charged Segal with using millions of dollars in insurance premiums to pay his own personal and business expenses. The indictment contained seven counts of insurance fraud, seven counts of mail fraud, and one count of wire fraud and a RICO charge. The case was assigned to U.S. District Judge Ruben Castillo.

In response, Near North spokeswoman Kitty Kurth said that a five-member independent board, headed by former U.S. Attorney Fred Foreman, now managed the company. Its members included Walter Stowe, who had worked at the FBI for twenty-six years and ended his career as Associate Special Agent in Charge of the Chicago FBI office. "This indictment will not impact the ability of Near North to continue operating our business," said COO John Harney. "We are having a record year under our independent board."

Near North issued a statement saying that if there were any problems with the Premium Fund Trust Account, they were identified by the company's own management and brought to the attention of the Illinois Department of Insurance in August 2001. "With input from the Department, changes were made to the accounting systems and regulatory accounting," the statement said. "This was accomplished by September 2001—well before the recent allegations were made."

---

23   Near North corporate counsel's notes on 3/20 communication.

Kurth said that the charges were not the result of any fraud complaints by customers or clients and that revenue for the first nine months of 2002 had increased by seventeen percent. "Our clients have been very supportive," Kurth said. "We've attracted new business and our revenue has been up in each of the last three quarters."

Where that revenue would wind up was now a matter of serious concern. The RICO charge in the new indictment sought to have Segal forfeit Near North and forfeit $30 million.

The stakes had been raised. Not only was Segal's liberty at stake, but the future of his company and the fate of his 1,000 employees hung in the balance as well.

Chapter 9

Riding Roughshod on Privilege

ATTORNEY-CLIENT PRIVILEGE, THE RIGHT TO keep communications with an attorney confidential, dates to Roman law and is a right guaranteed under the Sixth Amendment to the U.S. Constitution. According to the American Bar Association, "The confidentiality rule...applies not only to matters communicated in confidence by the client but also to all information relating to the representation, whatever its source."

When FBI agents armed with search warrants swarmed his Chicago condominium, his home in Highland Park, the offices of Near North, and a Near North storage facility, they seized a virtual warehouse of documents, mirror images of computer servers, and desktop hard drives. The agents inventoried 6,000 boxes. There was no doubt that these boxes contained an enormous number of attorney-client-privileged documents, and that the FBI had not followed Department of Justice guidelines to protect the privacy of these documents. There was no taint team or privilege team in place when several boxes of files were removed from the office of Sherri Stanton, the in-house general counsel and corporate secretary of Near North. Taken from her office were a desktop computer, her emails and scores of documents. Similarly, there was no taint team at the other search sites, where agents seized desktop computers belonging to Segal and his wife, boxes of documents and Segal's laptop computer.

The lack of a taint team on U.S. Attorney Patrick Fitzgerald's first major case was, Segal's lawyers declared, a violation of Segal's right to counsel and attorney-client privilege under the Sixth Amendment. This violation was part of a larger picture that included the covert taping of defense attorney Harvey Silets, the illegal cyberhacking of Segal's communications with counsel, and the involvement of the Takeover Group. At the time of the search of Stanton's office, FBI agents demanded she speak with them, a particularly aggressive action considering she was the lawyer for Near North and Segal and could invoke attorney-client privilege. When she refused, a subpoena was issued to try to force her to cooperate. Stanton was forced to hire her own attorney to deal with this intimidation attempt. When Stanton said she would speak with investigators if she were given a letter saying she was not a subject of the investigation, the FBI refused. Stanton then announced she was resigning because of "medical problems." Essentially, this hamstrung Segal from exercising a defense strategy that he relied upon corporate legal advice regarding the PFTA regulations.

In late November 2002, Segal's defense team filed a motion asking Judge Ruben Castillo to order the prosecution to return all privileged information and to bar the prosecution from using any of that information to prepare for trial or at the trial itself.[24] The defense knew that the prosecution had more than 11,000 emails to and from Segal. Approximately 9,400 emails and faxes were seized from Stanton's office—half of which were directed to Segal, his internal legal staff, and outside counsel.

In the motion, the defense explained that it had asked the prosecution to return all privileged communications involving Segal, but that

---

24   Doc 80-2 Defendant's response to government's motion to reconsider an order requiring government to return privileged material seized during execution of search warrants, Filed 3/14/03.

the government had refused and told the defense that it was taking the position that attorney-client privilege was an evidentiary privilege that would be decided at trial on a piece by piece basis. In fact, Polales had said that while he did not know whether the government had yet read or used any of Segal's privileged communications, he and co-prosecutors Kendall and Hogan believed they were free to do so. Polales and Kendall did say they would abstain from reading or using any communications until Castillo ruled on the motion, although everyone in the courtroom knew that their promise had to be taken at face value.

On February 2, 2003, Segal's lawyers and the prosecutors appeared before Castillo to discuss a number of issues, including the pending motion to return the privileged material.

Castillo expressed misgivings about the government's conduct. "I will tell you that I am concerned with the manner in which documents were recovered from Mr. Segal in the course of this search and I'm very much aware of the U.S. Attorney's guideline and the fact that with regard to certain searches, I'm aware that even privilege teams are put together to make sure that a defendant's privileges are, in fact, adhered to. I'm concerned that that doesn't seem to have happened in this case. So, with regard to that motion, at this point, the part that the Court is going to grant is to order the government to return all privileged information." This ruling clearly alarmed the prosecutors, who surely did not want to seem to have violated the Citizens Protection Act of 1998, informally known as the McDade Amendment. That Act, which went into effect in the spring of 1999, requires federal prosecutors and other government lawyers to follow state and federal rules of professional responsibility—ethics codes—in other words, the same state laws and ethics rules that all other lawyers are required to follow. Violations can be—though rarely are—punishable by disbarment. Ultimately, Segal's defense team would produce evidence of multiple violations of the Act. Now, Polales was scrambling. Not citing any case law or facts, he began rambling. Referring to the search of Stanton's office, he noted, "I am aware that with respect to the search of a corporate entity, there was an individual's office searched who happened to be a corporate officer in a dual capacity. Now, Your Honor hasn't reviewed the search warrant."

This was an argument that the defense saw as nonsensical and frivolous. "No, I haven't," Castillo replied. "Let me ask you this—I'm sorry to interrupt you, Mr. Polales. There was no privilege team put together when this search occurred, right?"

"Your Honor," Polales replied. "There was no privilege team—there was a direction to set aside material that could arguably be claimed as attorney-client material, and we will get to that in due course during the corporation's investigation. Now, when you have someone who acts in the capacity as a general counsel for a corporation, there are business judgments being made...."

Polales was avoiding the issue and so Castillo said he wanted to hear what Dan Reidy, one of Segal's lawyers, had to say. In a few short sentences, Reidy undercut Polales' arguments as misleading and wrong.

"Judge, a couple of things," he began. "One is that Mr. Segal, at the time of the search, was the president of the company basically, and we believe, and we've cited cases to you, that with respect to certain of the communications between him and the general counsel of the company or outside lawyers for the company, he would have a personal right to assert that privilege. It's not just the company's privilege in our view and we've asserted that.

"In addition, among the things that were seized, we believe—and we don't have complete understanding of it either—were personally privileged documents of his; that is, documents that had to do with his own relationships with his own attorneys. And, as I understand the government's position here, Judge, it is that because they took admittedly—at least I think—privileged-on-their-face documents in the search, they're free to do anything they want with them other than walk in and produce them in court. I don't believe that's the case. I believe that the way the U.S. Attorney's manual—the Department of Justice—in other cases of which I'm familiar—the way they proceed is with one of their taint teams. And what the taint team does is get enough information so that they can make some sort of assessment as to whether or not they wish to assert a crime fraud exception or wish to assert some other means of piercing the privilege.

"But the notion that the government can walk in, go into the general counsel's office at the company, take away all those documents, seize the privileged materials off my client's computer, walk out, look at them, show them to witnesses, do whatever they want with them except introduce them in court, I think, is wrongly conceived in the law; against, as far as I know, the Department of Justice policy and that Your Honor's initial pronouncement of the order would be the correct order.

"They had a chance to do this on a taint basis and make the arguments they make," Reidy continued. "As far as we know, they say they're free to roam through these records as long as they want. That's not the law, Judge."

Polales countered, although he again cited no case law and misrepresented Department of Justice and professional ethics standards, "Mr. Reidy's position is wrong. It's just wrong as a matter of law, wrong as a matter of fact. As a matter of fact, DOJ policies don't give him any substantive rights. They're prudential considerations with respect to a criminal investigation because we know with respect to law offices searches that there are issues. But this is the office of a business."

Abruptly, Castillo abruptly cut him off.

"I think there are easy ways to cut through this," the judge said. "This is what I'm going to do. I'm ordering, in no uncertain terms, the government to return the privileged information. If your position is these are not privileged, I can see that being the subject of another dispute that I'm going to have to resolve. Either return the privileged information—number one—or two: supply the defense with a privilege log of the documents that you are withholding and either have me review them in camera or if you're going to assert something else and you don't want me to review them *in camera*, then at least let me see your privilege log so I can review that. But that's what I'm ordering and I want you to do that within fourteen days. I'm not going to head any defendant into a trial unless I can be assured that it is a fair trial. And right now, I will tell you, it's my conclusion I have some questions, serious questions, about that, as the objective presider of this trial."

Castillo looked at Polales. "Now, you're free, Mr. Polales, if you think I just got out of bed today and got this absolutely wrong—you're free to file a motion to reconsider that educates me further. But I can tell you in no uncertain terms, I have read the materials and I'm troubled by what occurred in terms of the respect that was shown privileged materials in this case."

And with that, court was adjourned.

Two weeks later, the prosecution filed a motion asking Castillo to reconsider his ruling. For the first time, the prosecution contended it had treated potentially privileged material with "extreme caution" despite the lack of a taint team, stating that it "has not permitted the prosecution team or the case agents to be exposed to any materials seized that appear to give rise to potential attorney-client privilege issues."

Further, the motion said that the special agent reviewing Stanton's office "segregated six boxes of documents from his search...and labeled those boxes potential attorney/client privilege. To date, the government agents assigned to this case and the prosecutors working the case have not reviewed the documents contained in those boxes." Polales offered no proof of his claims.

The government's filing was contradicted by a review of the "Draft Report of Inventory" of the search that indicated that the agents did in fact look at attorney-client-privileged documents. The first two lines of the contents list of one box read, "File folders labeled: 'New York Office lease and Gary McHammon (emails, correspondence) *loose-papers litigation, memorandums…'" If the government did not view the contents of McHammon's attorney-client privilege folder, then how was it possible to list its contents? But the contents *were* listed on the inventory sheet, implying that government agents had viewed them.

The inventory said that another box had come from Tim Gallagher's office, even though Gallagher had left Near North in August 2001—several months before the search—and his name had been removed from the door. How could they have known it was his office? Moreover, many of the documents listed as coming from Gallagher's office had nothing to do with anything that Gallagher did for Near North.

The prosecution argued that the Department of Justice policies "are just that, policies, and do not create any enforceable right, claim, or benefit on an accused," suggesting that the policies were something that could be ignored or jettisoned as the prosecution saw fit.

The prosecution then said for the very first time that, prior to the searches, the team of agents was instructed to segregate any materials falling within the scope of the warrant and "deemed by the searching agent to be potential attorney-client information, and to mark the materials as such."

Doug Seccomb, the FBI agent who searched Stanton's office, filled six boxes with documents. Seccomb did not fulfill the definition of a taint team, but none of the documents had been reviewed, the prosecution asserted. The motion did not address a curious question—in the draft of the inventory of the searches prepared by the FBI, the materials listed as being removed from Stanton's office totaled three boxes, not six. It was unclear where the additional three boxes came from.

The prosecution claimed Seccomb segregated privileged documents at the condominium as well, a total of seven boxes in all. "No documents seized during the search of the residence were marked by agents as potentially attorney-client materials," the motion said. There was no explanation as to how Seccomb could have been in two places—Near North and the condominium—at the same time.

"As to the six thousand boxes currently maintained at [Near North's storage facility], no attempt at reviewing potential attorney-client material has been made to date.... As to the computer correspondence, the government team assigned to this case has not reviewed correspondence that may have occurred between the defendant and his personal attorneys relating to this or other matters. As such, the government has properly maintained control of the documents, has exercised extreme caution in its handling of the documents and records."

Segal's attorneys asked for discovery of evidence that a separate taint team was employed in viewing Segal's computer. Segal's forensic team determined that there had been substantial penetration of privileged documents. Castillo, in what seemed to Segal to be a slap on the wrist, responded by imploring the government not to use any of the privileged information obtained and to stop the non-taint-team process.

Rather than address the issue, the prosecution tried to skirt its responsibility by accusing the defense of shifting the burden to the government to catalog the privileged documents—a job that the defense "has had every opportunity to review...for privilege and preserve its right to assert the privilege to this court but has failed to do so." This was ridiculous—the defense really had no idea what documents were in the files.

The defense countered, "The government's newly raised arguments and evidentiary submissions do not merit reversal of this court's previous order. Taken as a whole, the government's submissions demonstrate that there is abundant room for an abuse of Mr. Segal's attorney-client privilege with the government's search and post-search procedures employed here, as evidenced by the government's failure to comply with

Justice Department guidelines regarding searching of privileged materials, particularly the substantial amounts of privileged electronic information contained on laptops, personal computers, and servers seized by the government."

These important possessions never were returned to Segal. The computers would have provided a forensic trail of how the prosecution had violated the attorney-client privilege—which the prosecution did not want the defense to see. This also greatly hampered Segal at trial. As Reidy's response noted, "Indeed, the government's failure to apprise the issuing court in its search warrant affidavit about the likelihood of seizing privileged material, and its failure to have an independent third-party review the seized electronic information for privilege before allowing the prosecution team to access it, both run afoul of DOJ policies."

The response was critical of the prosecution for demonstrating "an insensitivity to safeguarding potentially privileged material from the outset of its planning and execution of searches in this case." The government knew that it would be searching Stanton's office (the defense later found a government document with a map depicting it) and that the agents would be seizing voluminous privileged materials from Near North's computer servers as well as Segal's desktop and laptop computers. Segal's attorneys pointed out that Polales's disjointed argument was not only filled with double talk, but cited regulations that didn't exist and made a mockery of Sixth Amendment protections of attorney-client privilege.

When the defense lawyers and prosecutors returned to court on May 13, Castillo—to the surprise and chagrin of the defense—reversed his prior decision. The order he issued was terse: "Government's motion to reconsider court's discovery order requiring the government to return alleged 'privileged' documents is granted."

The judge offered no reason for this surprising and deeply disappointing reversal, which completely contradicted his earlier statements about the lack of a taint team and the disregard for Segal's rights. The ruling was particularly surprising because Castillo had a reputation as a liberal jurist. Segal now worried that Castillo felt a greater loyalty to his former colleagues on the prosecution team than to the principles of justice and rules of law.

Chapter 10

Fighting Back at the Hacker

"Anyway, I don't want to go into details here as to what I have or can get and how I do it but if you're interested in knowing what Segal's plans are, let me know a number to call."

— Email from David Cheley to Matt Walsh, September 21, 2001

ON JUNE 10, 2003, FOLLOWING Judge Castillo's abrupt reversal on the motion for the return of the attorney-client-privileged documents, the defense team filed another motion requesting that Castillo hold an evidentiary hearing to consider evidence that the prosecution witnesses—Cheley and the Takeover Group—were acting as government agents and thereby violating Segal's Fourth Amendment right to freedom from illegal searches.[25 26 27]

---

25   Doc 97 Defendant's Motion for an Evidentiary Hearing, Filed 6/10/03.

26   Doc 122-2 Defendant Michael Segal's Reply in support of his motion for an Evidentiary Hearing, Filed 8/1/03.

27   Doc 167-2 Defendant's Memorandum in support of their renewed Motion for an Evidentiary Hearing and to Suppress Illegally Seized Evidence, Filed 10/31/03.

Coincidental or not, three days later, a third superseding indictment was returned against Segal and Near North. This indictment was the hatchet that would put Near North out of business. The Takeover Group, which was well informed about the prosecution's plans, had been promising Near North clients that a RICO indictment against the company, not just Segal personally, was about to be filed. Many of those companies now stopped doing business with Near North.

According to the motion for an evidentiary hearing, "For more than eight months, defendant Michael Segal and his insurance brokerage firm, Near North Insurance Brokerage, Inc., were the targets of a complex, intrusive, and focused computer hacking scheme by one of Near North's ex-employees. The hacker pilfered proprietary, confidential, and attorney-client privileged information from Near North's system on a routine basis, beginning at least four months before Mr. Segal's arrest in January 2002, and continuing until as late as April 2002, well after Mr. Segal's arrest.[28] [29] [30] [31]

"At about the same time as the hacker began perusing and stealing copious amounts of this information from Mr. Segal and Near North, a number of other former Near North employees, who were now working for a rival insurance brokerage firm, began volunteering information to the federal government with the intention of destroying Mr. Segal and Near North. These former Near North employees sought to gain a competitive advantage over Mr. Segal and Near North for themselves and their new employer. As the discovery in this case has shown, these former employees became the government's key 'confidential sources' and private agents of the government. The allegations made by Walsh, Berry, Gallagher, Ludwig, and McNichols were in fact the centerpiece

---

28   March 13 2002 email from Cheley to Jongsma re NNIB salaries.

29   Lisa Fisher email to Alabama Worley March 21 2002 re entire access.

30   Lisa Fisher email to Jongsma April 12 2002 re email access being shut down.

31   May 13 2002 email from Jongsma to Cheley.

of the affidavit used to support the search warrant and arrest warrant against Mr. Segal on January 26, 2002.

"[I]t is now clear beyond any doubt that the hacker repeatedly provided the government's principal cooperating witnesses with the most sensitive and critical of stolen and privileged information hacked from Near North's system."

Eric Brandfonbrener, the attorney defending Walsh, Berry, and Gallagher in the Aon civil suit brought by Near North, had admitted as much on April 18, 2003, during a hearing in the civil case. Brandfonbrener confirmed that three emails his clients received from Cheley had been passed on to the government, saying that his clients were "not using these emails except in connection with their cooperation with the government…these emails are only going to the FBI."

Segal's lawyers said that according to their analysis, they did not have to prove that the prosecution explicitly directed its witnesses to obtain stolen information in order to invoke the protections guaranteed Segal under the Fourth Amendment. However, the evidence strongly suggested there was direction. An analysis of the hacked emails showed there were occasions when Cheley downloaded many documents and emails and later went back and obtained specific documents. That suggested that someone was advising Cheley on what to look for.

"Throughout the investigation and prosecution of Mr. Segal, the government repeatedly insisted, in conversations with counsel for Mr. Segal and with counsel for Near North, that its witnesses had no connection to the hacking activity," the defense motion declared. "The government even took the position that, should Near North allege in related civil litigation that there was a conspiracy between the hacker and its witnesses, the government would view that allegation negatively and take it into account in deciding whether to identify Near North as a RICO enterprise in superseding charges against Mr. Segal, or whether to name Near North as a defendant.

"Mr. Segal has gathered irrefutable proof that the government's insistence that there was no connection between the hacker and its witnesses was flat-out wrong."

The motion detailed how the defense investigation of email communications from Cheley showed him referring to "what I've read" in Segal's emails, and stating that if Walsh were "interested in knowing what Segal's plans are, let me know a number to call."

Multiple, transparent, amateurish "cover-up" emails were exchanged between Walsh and Cheley, including one in which Walsh pretended that the hacked information was "sent in error" and "deleted without any review," even though, a mere two hours earlier, Walsh had explicitly asked Cheley to "please resend" a large amount of stolen information. Cheley sent Walsh an additional cache of stolen information less than twenty-four hours later. The defense believed these cover-up emails were worded to make it appear that there was no conspiracy between Cheley and the Takeover Group.

The prosecution knew the Takeover Group was receiving hundreds of selected emails "months before Mr. Segal's arrest" from a purportedly "unknown source," because FBI Agent Pat Murphy finally acknowledged that "several" emails had been sent to the Takeover Group.

"It is clear," the motion said, "that there were frequent communications between the witnesses and the FBI or other government personnel." It was equally clear that, despite the government's agreement to "open-file" discovery in the case, this was being ignored. The defense was not provided with contemporaneous memoranda of key communications between the FBI (or other government personnel) and the witnesses who were receiving the stolen information. "Either there are no contemporaneous records by the government documenting what were clearly critical and highly confidential communications being sent to its witnesses, or those materials have been withheld," the motion noted.

The defense had learned that Ludwig gave a cell phone to Cheley for their private communication and as a result, was able to document more than 300 phone calls (and believed there were many, many more) between Cheley and Takeover Group members. They concluded that when Cheley found something at Near North that he thought was significant, he frequently notified Ludwig, who in turn would inform other Takeover Group members or Agent Murphy. Many such calls were placed on the same day or the day after Cheley hacked into Near North. The motion said that the prosecution had recently disclosed a memorandum of interview that had occurred ten months earlier which suggested there was a cover up of prior knowledge of hacking.

An FBI memorandum of interview is called a "302," because that is the government number assigned to those forms. These are said to be a record of what an agent was able to write down during the interview and the agent's recollection. The FBI does not electronically record interviews. The 302 may list the questions and the answers or simply be a narrative of what the agent thinks the witness said. A witness does not see the 302 or get a chance to correct any mistakes before it is finalized. For these and other reasons, these are problematic documents. For example, taking handwritten notes cannot capture an entire conversation. People talk too fast. And if the subject is complicated, it is nearly impossible to be completely accurate because the agent is simultaneously listening to the witness, trying to understand what the witness is saying and summarizing it by hand. Even more troubling is if the 302 is written up later, because memory is not infallible and often wrong. Things can get left out. Sometimes, it appears things are left out on purpose or false facts are inserted for the purpose of obscuring facts that hurt the prosecution case.

And there is no requirement that the FBI agent write down everything a witness says or that the agent take any notes at all. There's nothing to prevent the agent from stopping the note-taking if the witness says something helpful to the target of the investigation. Because it's nearly impossible to obtain handwritten notes underlying a 302, the FBI has little concern that anyone can prove a conflict between the notes and the final 302.

Segal found numerous 302s that contained false information that inflated his political connections as well as mischaracterizations that were not relevant to the case, including multiple statements that were not attributed by name, but appeared to come from members of the Takeover Group. In addition, there were 302s that attempted to water down the attempts of the Takeover Group to interfere with Near North.

This motion said that the 302 purported to be about a conversation between Agent Murphy and Walsh about supposed non-involvement with hacked materials. Former FBI agent Walter Stowe, a Near North board of director, would later tell Segal this was, on its face, a violation of FBI protocol by Agent Murphy.

According to the motion, the defense "now has obtained evidence of communications between the government's witnesses and the FBI at times coinciding with the hacker's intrusions into files of Mr. Segal and Near North. In still another instance, the defense gathered evidence from a third party reflecting the forwarding of hacked information from a government witness to the FBI via the agent's home email, but the government has not yet produced any 302 or other contemporaneous memorialization of this communication."

In fact, the defense documented 393 calls to the FBI from the Takeover Group dating from August 2001. None of those calls were reported in any 302 and the failure to document each one was a breach of FBI protocol.

"Consequently," the motion stated, "Mr. Segal seeks the aid of this court in holding an evidentiary hearing to get at the truth regarding the nature and extent of the government's receipt and awareness of the stolen materials provided to it by its cooperating witnesses."

In laying out the series of events that led to the unmasking of Cheley, the motion noted that after Kemper officials confronted Cheley about his hacking and fired him, Cheley offered up a four-page handwritten confession on the spot, admitting that for eight months he had hacked into Near North's network and that he had done so while at Kemper and from his laptop at his home. He confessed he had the ability to create, delete, and modify files. After Cheley's hacking was revealed, his personal website was, for a brief period, reprogrammed in such a way that if anyone visited it from a Near North network computer, the person was automatically transferred to the FBI website!

Through the civil lawsuit, Segal's lawyers had obtained access to records from Aon and discovered that, beginning as early as October 2001 and continuing for at least eight months, Cheley had repeatedly hacked and immediately forwarded emails that were "confidential and privileged communications stolen from Near North's network to various individuals, including government witnesses Matt Walsh and Dana Berry." Emails obtained from Aon's servers revealed that Cheley had admitted to Walsh he was also sending information to Ludwig, who was then working for USI, another Near North competitor. Cheley advised Walsh in an email that Ludwig "seemed to appreciate" the information that Cheley had provided. The defense believed the note was intentionally worded to make Cheley's conduct seem more benign that it really was.

Telephone records and emails showed that on that September day, Walsh emailed his phone number to Cheley, saying, "I neglected to give you my phone number in the event you want to reach me." Less than half an hour later, Cheley called Walsh and they spoke for thirteen minutes. Five days after that, on September 26, 2001, Walsh emailed Cheley the work phone numbers for Berry and Gallagher.

On October 1, Cheley emailed Walsh a zip file that included a privileged communication from Segal to his in-house counsel at Near North regarding litigation strategy for Near North's plans to pursue

Walsh, Berry, and Gallagher for breach of fiduciary duty and other claims. He also sent an email from Segal to his wife, Joy, which contained confidential details about trust accounting issues, and the roles that various Near North consultants played in addressing those issues. This multi-page, single-spaced email—drafted before Segal knew there was any federal investigation—memorialized his description of the illegal conduct of the Takeover Group and specifically laid out the false allegations about the PFTA regulatory issues. It listed what steps needed to be taken. The defense believed that this note gave the prosecution an inside look at the defense strategy in the civil lawsuit, a roadmap which allowed the prosecution to control and obscure evidence that would have helped Near North.

Six minutes after receiving the large file, Walsh forwarded it to Dana Berry. Over the next few weeks, Cheley sent Walsh three additional zip files, including one consisting entirely of privileged emails between Segal and his lawyers.

At the same time, Cheley and Walsh engaged in what the defense asserted was a conscious attempt to cover up what was going on. In October, after receiving two zip files from Cheley and asking him to resend one of them, Walsh disingenuously wrote the following to Cheley:

> "I did receive the instructions to delete the information sent, and will utilize it immediately. Thank you. I recognize that these were sent in error and contain information that you did not intend to send. Hence, it has been deleted without any review."

Less than a day later, Cheley sent Walsh another zip file of privileged communications between Segal and his lawyers.

Although the defense was continuing its investigation, it was "virtually impossible without an evidentiary hearing to determine how much stolen information Mr. Cheley transmitted to the government's witnesses, including that transmitted by non-electronic means, such as calls, in-person meetings or the mail."

The motion stated, "Although the emails produced by Aon demonstrate that the government witnesses solicited and received information that Cheley stole from Near North, those materials do not represent the entire universe of communication between Mr. Cheley and any government witnesses, or even the government witnesses employed at Aon. In fact, analysis of the Aon emails reveals that whatever source Aon searched to produce the emails did not retain every email communication between Mr. Cheley and Mr. Walsh's Aon email account."

Hacked Near North emails found on Aon servers also contained Near North's litigation strategy relating to other civil litigation between Aon and Near North over other business matters. At the time, Near North was engaged in intellectual property litigation against Aon for its Surety Bond Master program. At one point, Aon said it was willing to pay a substantial settlement, but then, in a major turnaround, Aon halted settlement talks. Segal speculated that Aon and its general counsel were motivated by learning of the investigation of Near North. On February 8, 2002, shortly after Segal was arrested, Walsh forwarded a hacked email to Agent Murphy's personal address, saying, "As noted in the past, from time to time I received these anonymously."[32] That phrase "as noted in the past" indicated that this wasn't the first time Walsh had passed along such emails.

It was not until September 19, 2002—just days after Joshua Buchman met with the prosecution team and was threatened with the superseding indictment—that Murphy finally prepared a 302 documenting a conversation with Berry on March 4, 2002, six months earlier and five weeks after Segal was arrested. The 302 said that Berry had admitted he received an unsolicited email from "Lisa Fisher" (a Cheley alias) that contained a privileged communication between Segal and

---

32   Walsh email to FBI Murphy home email Pass it on, 020802.

Silets, Segal's criminal defense lawyer. Murphy reported in the 302 that Berry had faxed the email to Murphy after redacting the privileged aspects. The unredacted portion said, "Here is another FYI on some of the plans…I have access to lots of interesting information and I want to make sure it gets to the right person." The defense believed this was part of a cover-up.

The defense motion requesting the hearing noted that it was not clear "what protections the government put in place to prevent further intrusion into Mr. Segal's privileged communications with his criminal defense attorney." It was clear that Berry had provided the email to Murphy the same day he had received it.

Why was this not documented until six months later? Would this ever have been documented at all, if the defense lawyers had not discovered evidence of it? It was difficult to view this as anything but an attempt by the prosecution to hide evidence.

The defense noted that Murphy had prepared a 302 that was dated January 6, 2003 and described a conversation with a "source" who was believed to be Walsh. In the report, Murphy said that the source "had previously related that he received unsolicited emails that contained what appeared to be emails of Michael Segal."

Previously related?

There were no 302s of these previous contacts. The defense believed that this showed that the FBI knew that its witnesses were receiving stolen confidential information, knew that illegal hacking was going on and that nothing was being done about it.

The defense motion also noted that Walsh and Berry had attempted to use their knowledge of the investigation to persuade Near North employees or personnel to abandon the company to work for Aon. Allen Kaercher, the owner of an insurance agency in Nevada that had merged with Near North in 1999, said that Walsh and Berry came to meet with him in November 2002 and told him that he should switch his business to Aon. If he didn't, they indicated Kaercher would suffer legal problems, would hear from the FBI, and that "Things are going to get rough around here." The *following day,* an FBI agent did call Kaercher. No FBI report of that call was ever provided to the defense.

Stowe later told Segal that this was improper and that, had he known of such conduct when he was in charge, he would have fired the agent.

In another instance, Walsh called an underwriter at AIG and suggested that she could be in trouble and the FBI would be calling as part of the government's investigation of Near North. She was in fact contacted, at which point she offered a truthful account of AIG's proper relationship with Near North.

"The government appears to have facilitated their witnesses' receipt of certain court filings that the witnesses have in turn used to their competitive advantage," the defense motion stated. For example, on November 1, 2002 at 11:40 a.m.—the same day that the superseding indictment was entered on the federal court docket—an unsigned copy was faxed from the U.S. Attorney's Office to an unknown destination. At 2:26 p.m. that day, the same document (complete with the original fax line from the U.S. Attorney's Office) was faxed again from the office of Eric Brandfonbrener, the lawyer for Berry, Walsh, and Gallagher. And at 3:23 p.m., the same document—now bearing the fax lines of the U.S. Attorney's Office and Brandfonbrener's office—was faxed from Berry's private line at Aon.

"Although the superseding indictment is... a public filing and would have been available to the witnesses had they sought a copy from the clerk's office, the fact that the government appears to have faxed an unsigned copy of it to counsel for its key witnesses...demonstrates the government's likely awareness that its witnesses expected to and did obtain a commercial advantage from supplying information to the government which the government in turn used in the indictment and prosecution of Mr. Segal," the motion said.

"After assuming control of the hacking investigation, to the exclusion of state law enforcement agencies that Near North had originally contacted, the federal government is believed to have waited several weeks before seizing the hacker's laptop, through which approximately 80 percent of the hacking activity occurred," the motion said. "The government still has not charged the hacker with a single crime, more than thirteen months after he confessed to hacking into Near North 'at least twice a day' over an eight-month period."

An evidentiary hearing would have required that government witnesses testify under oath. Could there be a better way to determine if there was misconduct?

What happened next would provide ample fuel to the contention that the prosecution had been hiding evidence for nearly two years.

Chapter 11

Critical Hearing Denied

THE PROSECUTION OBJECTED TO AN evidentiary hearing primarily on the ground that the defense was trying to get information that might bolster the pending civil case against the Takeover Group and impeach their testimony if they testified at Segal's trial.

The prosecution could have asked Judge Castillo to order the Near North civil litigation put on hold while the federal case was proceeding. But that would have opened them to the risk that Castillo might order a hearing, which could require testimony, which could expose its witnesses to cross-examination and the potential for revealing the depth of the relationship between the Takeover Group and the FBI.

In its response, the prosecution told Judge Castillo that "none of the actions alleged by the defendant indicate any basis to believe that any action by Cheley or the witnesses was undertaken at either the express or implied request of any government actor."

Significantly, the prosecution said the defense had no proof that any of the hacked information was contained in any of the evidence that they had turned over to the defense and that any suggestion that Takeover Group members had provided "stolen" information to the prosecution was "a stretching of potential inferences."

"Indeed, all of the 302s are sourced," the prosecution declared. This was another misrepresentation, as Segal's lawyers had discovered evidence of hundreds of phone calls for which there were no corresponding FBI 302 reports.

The prosecution claimed there was no legal basis for suggesting that Segal's constitutional rights were at stake—although the theft of significant documents from a company and passing them to hostile entities who were, in fact, government witnesses had to be wrong. Turning logic on its head, the prosecution insisted that Segal had no expectation of privacy precisely because these were Near North documents that were typed by secretaries and could be accessed by computer. They further stated that, because Near North failed to deactivate Cheley's passwords after he left, the company itself was to blame for the hacking!

"Cheley was completely unknown to the government, and nothing caused the agents to believe that any information being provided was a result of stolen or improper access to this corporation's computer network.... The fact is that Cheley was completely independent of the government and unknown to the government. There is not the slightest indication that any government agent knew of unauthorized intrusions into the Near North system let alone an illegal hacking of the system by Cheley or anyone else."

Exactly ten days later, the prosecutors ate their words.

"[A]s a result of ongoing discovery discussion with the defense last week," Polales reported to Judge Castillo, the prosecution learned "for the first time" that FBI Agent Jane Higgins had suddenly remembered that she had a set of notes from a January 14, 2002, conversation with members of the Takeover Group.

What wasn't reported to Castillo was that after the prosecution filed its original response, stating that it was unaware of the Cheley hacking until "well after" Near North learned of it, an enraged Segal sent a copy of the response to David Grossman, the former FBI agent who had investigated the hacking on behalf of Near North.[33] Grossman, appalled

---

33 David Grossman affidavit.

by what he saw as a violation of the law and misrepresentation of the facts, on his own initiative paid a personal visit to the special agent in charge of the Chicago FBI office to complain about the misrepresentations. Grossman was told that the matter would be looked into, but he never heard back and it appeared nothing was ever done.

But not long after Grossman's visit, a member of the defense team was summoned to a meeting with the prosecution. The purpose was not specified. There, prosecutors and FBI agents turned over Higgins's notes and said there were some tapes that would be turned over in the future. They offered no excuse—beyond the assertion that Higgins had suddenly remembered them—for why these notes had remained undisclosed for eighteen months.

To Segal, this was ample proof that the government was hiding evidence and attempting to cover up improper conduct.

Buried in these notes were two entries on separate pages. The first page referenced "David 'Chiele' or David 'Shiele'" and said that he "might" be sending anonymous emails to the Takeover Group. Cheley's name was misspelled and his address incorrectly noted.

The second page noted that one email was sent by "hacker."[34]

What?

In its filing, the prosecution reported; "According to Special Agent Higgins, prior to her recent review of these notes, she had no recollection of this information and at the present time she has stated that she recalled that the conversation that led to the notes indicated that one or more of the [Takeover Group] expressed suspicion that Cheley might have been sending anonymous emails to them. She has no present recollection of the second page of notes."

The defense believed that the government was attempting to backdate and cover up events by using a misspelled name and address separated on two pages. This was hardly a *disclosure*.

---

34   1A Notes.

So, after months of denials of any knowledge of Cheley or the hacking, suddenly Higgins and the prosecution *discovered* the existence of these notes? And in a case that was dominating the media, a case in which the prosecution claimed they had provided every document in their file pursuant to the "open-file" discovery process?

The "disclosure" only deepened the suspicion that the prosecution was hiding evidence favorable to Segal. In fact, the full set of notes from this conversation (twenty pages in all) was not turned over until September 2003—two months later. The notes referenced thirty-eight different matters that had been discussed, but not a single 302 was ever offered that memorialized that meeting. The defense later determined that twenty-four of the thirty-eight topics actually were investigated, and that 302s had in fact been prepared regarding each of them—*before* the notes were ultimately disclosed to the defense. It's unclear why the FBI followed up on those twenty-four topics, but never on the Cheley hacking.

Grossman told Segal that it was virtually impossible for all those notes to have been included under one date. Those notes, it appeared, contained multiple subjects backdated to cover up the fact that information was being passed to the government through hacked emails.

Higgins's notes reflected that Cheley lived at DeWitt Place and Pearson Street, which was revealing, since the prosecution had been contending that they didn't know of his existence at that time. In fact, the address noted was within a block of where he actually lived. The fact that Cheley's name was misspelled and his address was not *exactly* correct was used as an excuse for why the notes had been ignored for eighteen months. The information just wasn't specific, contended the prosecution. But that made no sense. It was also curious to the defense that this information came from Higgins, considering that there were no calls to her from the Takeover Group.

Nor did the claim of Higgins that she had "forgotten" and misplaced these notes for eighteen months resonate as genuine. Sensing this, the prosecution immediately requested to amend their filed motion to retract their false statements in the first filing. The following day, the prosecution filed an amended response that said, "Although Special Agent Higgins's notes indicated that the identity of Cheley as a potential sender of anonymous emails was mentioned shortly before the search warrants were executed, that fact does nothing to suggest that any of defendant Segal's Constitutional rights were violated by the government."

Even in their amended response, the government presented further false facts by calling Cheley's emails anonymous and by calling Cheley the "potential" sender, though the government had proof of his role in the attachments to Segal's lawyers' filings before the court. The facts uncovered by the defense belied the prosecution's claim that Cheley's identity was mentioned "shortly" before the warrants were executed. In fact, he was identified well before that time.

Incredibly, the prosecution contended that there was "not a hint of a suggestion" that Cheley was controlled by the Takeover Group or that the Takeover Group was the motivating force behind Cheley's hacking. The prosecution was trying to squeeze an elephant through a keyhole—arguing that Cheley was acting on his own, for his own motives, and therefore, that his illegal activity "may not be laid at the government's doorstep."

Moreover, the prosecution's amended response said the FBI agents had not received "material" information that they knew or should have known was stolen. This, essentially, was a watered-down concession that the agents had indeed received stolen information—which should have been a matter of deep concern standing alone—but that it wasn't important or valuable to the case.

But who was making that judgment? The prosecution, of course.

Who would be the best judge of it? The defense, of course.

But would the defense get to see all the information? No, the prosecution said.

On August 1, the defense fired back.

"Before its amended filing, the government unequivocally stated that it knew nothing about the hacking activity and that it never received any hacked information from its witnesses. The court and the defense now know that both of these statements were one-hundred percent false."

The disclosure of the notes made it clear that before Segal's arrest—indeed, prior to the submission of the affidavit for the search warrant—the prosecution knew the hacker by name, where he lived, that he was sending hacked information to Takeover Group members, that those individuals were cooperating with the government, and they had received hacked information relating to Near North's Premium Fund Trust Account—"the centerpiece of the government's case" against Segal. The defense said it was time to put government agents under oath regarding evidence of misconduct.

The defense noted that on July 17, 2003, after the government was allowed to file a corrected response, the prosecutors "assured the defense that it would promptly produce that afternoon what it described as approximately an "inch worth" of additional documents from the government's confidential source files. Although the defense deadline to respond to the prosecution's amended response was August 1, the prosecution didn't deliver the materials—even though the defense made several phone calls and sent a letter dated July 29. The prosecution arrogantly ignored the defense and Judge Castillo did nothing about it.

"The government's progressive pattern of overstated and increasingly hedged assurances, attempting to distance its investigation from the hacker and its key witnesses, have proven to be consistently and disappointingly wrong," the defense motion concluded.

"The government then retreated even further, but still gave unwavering assurances that its agents were never aware of any improper conduct by Cheley until well after Mr. Segal's arrest, and there was nothing that could have even remotely caused its agents to believe that any information being provided by its witnesses was the result of stolen information hacked by Cheley. Now, the recently disclosed FBI notes lay waste to that assurance as well.

"Mr. Segal is entitled to an evidentiary hearing to get at the truth, and neither Mr. Segal nor the court can be bound to rely on assurances by the government that have repeatedly fallen short of reality."

The defense noted that the prosecution "does not dispute that Mr. Segal and Near North were thoroughly searched in an invasive and blatantly illegal fashion; that substantial amounts of confidential and privileged material were taken, including a post-arrest email from Mr. Segal to his criminal defense lawyer; that certain government witnesses procured an unknown but provably substantial amount of the stolen material; that the government witnesses [the Takeover Group] had been working very closely with the government at the time they received the hacked material; that a government witness [Walsh] forwarded a hacked email to the lead case agent's [Murphy] personal email address just a week after Mr. Segal's arrest [a violation of FBI protocol]; that the witnesses were highly motivated by personal and pecuniary self-interest to cooperate in the investigation of Mr. Segal; that the witnesses were a source of key elements of the search warrant affidavit for Mr. Segal's residences and business; and that the government was aware in the fall of 2001, several months before Mr. Segal's arrest, that its witnesses were receiving emails involving Mr. Segal and Near North from a purportedly 'anonymous' source."

The defense also said that during the time the Takeover Group had access to Segal's and Near North's "most confidential documents," there were numerous FBI contacts with the witnesses which were not recorded in any way. "Only a hearing can hope to establish whether any additional confidential and privileged material illegally stolen by the hacker and repeatedly given to the government's key witnesses, both before and after the government prepared and executed three search warrants, and before and after Mr. Segal was arrested and engaged initial trial counsel, was directly or indirectly provided to the government."

The prosecution argued that even if evidence was illegally obtained, they hadn't intended to use it, so there was no harm to the defense. But the issue was not whether the prosecution intended to offer any evidence stolen by Cheley and passed to the witnesses and then to the FBI, but rather whether the prosecution made any use of the illegally obtained information during *any* part of its investigation of Segal and Near North.

The defense said Segal should not be forced to accept any government assurances as to when it knew of Cheley, whether it received hacked information or whether Cheley was acting on his own or at the behest of the Takeover Group, especially after the prosecution's prior statements were shown to be "flat-out wrong."

"Now, backed into a corner and unable to dispute that it knowingly received hacked information from its witnesses, the government has resorted to 'plan C' and asserts that it did not 'induce' Cheley to steal information, and that its agents did not receive any 'material' information which they 'knew or should have known was stolen.' Yet the government's latest fallback position ignores the applicable law."

The reference to the case as "open file" was misleading as well, the defense said. "While the defense is glad to have been promised an 'open file,' 'open file' has not meant a 'complete file,' and has not meant access to all clearly relevant cooperating witness and source files that we now know contain information showing the government's knowing receipt of hacked information."

Not only had the agents failed to make a record of a substantial number of conversations with the Takeover Group at the same time they were receiving "copious amounts of stolen information," the prosecution had "failed to explain...the yawning gaps in its case file with respect to contacts with its cooperating witnesses and the conflicting statements that its cooperating witnesses and their counsel have been making to another court about their receipt of stolen materials and their provision of those materials to the government."

The prosecution's contacts with the Takeover Group were numerous and frequent, yet remained largely undocumented by the FBI. For example, the defense pointed out that Gallagher, who left Near North in the summer of 2001 to join Aon and was used to set up the meeting that resulted in Segal's arrest, called the FBI main number or a mobile number of an FBI agent more than sixty times. A total of twenty-one of those calls were placed prior to Segal's arrest and the execution of the search warrant. That tally doesn't include any FBI return calls or any that Gallagher may have made from his home or office phones. Yet, the first 302 of an interview with Gallagher was dated July 12, 2002—ten months after his first cell phone call to the FBI.

"It defies belief," the defense declared, "that between September 2001 and July 2002, Mr. Gallagher never said anything substantive that should have been put in a 302 or otherwise memorialized. The absence of any contemporaneously memorialized contacts with Gallagher during this period is compounded by the fact that the hacker's activity was at its most intrusive and frequent during this precise period."

The FBI similarly failed to contemporaneously memorialize its extensive initial interviews of Dana Berry and Matt Walsh. In the civil litigation, Walsh said under oath that by the time he started getting hacked emails, he had "already been extensively interviewed by the U.S. Department of Justice." Berry admitted to the same thing.

According to the defense investigation, McNichols placed or received two hundred and twenty-five phone calls to or from an FBI number between October 24, 2001 and June 18, 2002. About one hundred and fifty of these occurred prior to Segal's arrest. Yet, only a fraction of McNichols's contacts with the FBI was ever recorded. McNichols, the defense noted, had supplied the government with a document titled

"NNIB Petty Cash Reimbursement – 2001," which he had obtained from Dan Watkins, the embezzler. And from October 2001 through April 24, 2002, when Cheley's hacking stopped, McNichols's cell phone records showed he either placed or received fifty-six calls to or from numbers belonging to Berry, Walsh, or Aon. There were another twelve calls to and from Jeff Ludwig or his employer—and, again, this did not include any calls McNichols made or received from his home phone or any other landline.

The evidence, the defense noted, raised several significant questions:

- Why was there no contemporaneous FBI record of Matt Walsh telling the government, in the fall of 2001, that he had received a number of confidential emails involving Segal and Near North from a purportedly unknown source?

- Why was there no record in the prosecution's files of Walsh forwarding hacked emails to Agent Murphy in February 2002, or any of the other occasions "as noted in the past" where Walsh received purportedly anonymous emails involving Segal or Near North?

- How could the prosecution reconcile the statement in open court in the civil litigation by the lawyer for Walsh, Berry, and Gallagher that his clients did not use the hacked emails "except in connection with our cooperation with the government" and that the emails were "only going to the FBI"?

- Why was the first FBI report of contact with Gallagher dated July 12, 2002, when more than sixty calls were placed from Gallagher's cell phone to an FBI number prior to that date?

- Why had the government contacted Berry on September 19, 2002—two days after Near North's lawyer met with the prosecution to discuss the company's filing of a civil suit based on the Takeover Group's involvement in the hacking activity, and then wrote up a report saying that, more than six months earlier, Berry had received a privileged post-arrest email between Segal and his criminal lawyer Harvey Silets?

- How could the government's contention that it was not aware of earlier email until September 2002 square up with Berry's claim that he sent the email to the FBI "upon its receipt" in March 2002?

- Why was it not until January 2003 that a 302 was prepared saying that Walsh "had previously related" that he received emails containing documents hacked from Near North containing emails of Segal?

Segal's lawyers ripped the prosecution's claim that Near North had confronted Cheley "over a month" before the prosecution learned of the hacking allegations. In fact, the defense noted, Kemper had been specifically asked not to confront Cheley after Near North uncovered the hacking, but did so anyway on April 24, 2002. The defense motion noted that given former FBI agent David Grossman's direct contacts with the FBI's Cybercrime Squad and the other extensive activity by the FBI, the prosecution's claim that it did not learn of the hacking allegations until over a month after Cheley was confronted on April 24, 2002 is "flatly incorrect."

Nonetheless, on August 7, 2003, Judge Castillo denied the defense motion for an evidentiary hearing. Although he left the door open ever so slightly for reconsideration of his ruling, this turned out to be a mere tease. He did not relent. No such a hearing ever was held.

The judge declared: "Segal's theory that the government witnesses [the Takeover Group] were acting as agents of the government, which is the basis of his request for an evidentiary hearing, is supported by many detailed and specific facts. Unfortunately, we find that his theory, and the facts supporting them, are at this time too conjectural, speculative, and attenuated to warrant what is presently framed as an extensive, invasive, and far-reaching inquiry."

Castillo determined that at least one of the prosecution's witnesses "took affirmative steps" to obtain information that had been illegally hacked from Near North's computer network and that the prosecution was aware of the illegal hacking. He also concluded that the prosecution had failed to properly document communications with the witnesses that could have shed light on the relationship between the FBI agents, the cooperating witnesses, and Cheley.

But then, for reasons hard to fathom, Castillo said evidence of knowledge by the prosecution was "flimsy" as was evidence that Cheley and the Takeover Group were working in concert to obtain information and pass it to the prosecution.

There are times in the prosecution of a case when judges must essentially try to read the tea leaves to determine the intent of agents and witnesses. Here, however, despite powerful evidence, Castillo rebuffed the defense.

"In short," the judge wrote, "Segal fails to offer any specific, detailed facts that support the premise that the witnesses were acting as government agents and thus we conclude that the facts presented are simply too conjectural and speculative to support an evidentiary hearing at this time."

No specific, detailed facts?

Segal wondered if Castillo had read the defense briefs at all.

Segal and his legal team were disappointed. There was much conjecture that Castillo was either protecting the government or the reputation of the office.

Underlying all of this was the distinct possibility that the prosecution was resisting an evidentiary hearing because it might reveal that attorney-client-privileged documents were in the hands of the prosecution in violation of the McDade Amendment. It couldn't have been lost on prosecutors that Sal Cognetti, Jr., the defense attorney for Near North, had been one of the framers of the McDade Amendment.

Cognetti had joined the case after the indictment of Near North. Segal had asked Dan Reidy, his lead defense attorney, to represent Near North as well. But Reidy said that would likely be a conflict of interest and that even if a waiver was granted, defending the company would take a great deal of time and money.

The McDade Amendment was named after U.S. Representative Joseph McDade, a Pennsylvania Republican. Segal reached out to former Democratic Congressman Dan Rostenkowski, a personal friend, who arranged for Segal to meet with McDade.

During that meeting, McDade recalled how aggressive prosecutors were and how little oversight there was in his case, which resonated with Segal. McDade said he was initially defended by a high-profile and expensive Washington, D.C. law firm, but later switched to a smaller firm in Scranton, Pennsylvania. A lawyer from that firm—Sal Cognetti—had won McDade's acquittal by putting on a vigorous defense and rigorously challenging the prosecution's misconduct. After the acquittal, McDade went back to Congress and teamed with Cognetti to draft the McDade Amendment legislation that overrode a prior presidential executive order that federal prosecutors would be exempt from a congressional mandate requiring compliance with federal and state canons of ethics. That exemption, combined with immunity from civil liability for their conduct in pursuing a conviction, had left prosecutors virtually bulletproof.

After the meeting with McDade, Cognetti, as a courtesy to McDade, called Segal and offered to answer any questions and to be of assistance. When Near North was indicted, Segal retained Cognetti. In part, Segal wanted him on the team because he was not from Chicago. He would have no allegiances and would not be subject to the pressures that sometimes affect local attorneys who know they will be practicing in the same courtrooms year after year. Every lawyer knows that they aggravate or anger a judge at their own future peril.

Subsequently, Cognetti filed a motion asking Castillo to reconsider his denial of the motion for an evidentiary hearing[35], noting that Near

---

35   Motion for Reconsideration of Their Renewed Motion for Evidentiary Hearing and to Suppress Illegally Seized Evidence, 2/4/04.

North and Segal were the victims of thousands of unlawful hacking in-trusions; that the hacker specifically targeted and accessed confidential attorney-client-privileged communications, many of which related to the criminal charges; that at least one of the cooperating witnesses af-firmatively solicited information from the hacker; that the government was aware of the unlawful computer access; and that there were frequent (approximately four hundred) undocumented contacts between the co-operating witnesses and the government during the relevant period.

Cognetti noted that the prosecution's poor documentation of con-tacts among the FBI agents, the witnesses, and Cheley "leaves the re-cord purposefully and permanently incomplete. Further fact-finding at an evidentiary hearing is necessary and warranted."

After the defense filed its original motion for a hearing, it discov-ered that the prosecution had performed numerous search queries on Near North computer data. Cognetti showed how the prosecution ran searches on Near North and then minutes later, Cheley hacked into the Near North computer system, apparently to obtain whatever the government could not get in its own search. Cognetti presented a chart showing that during these searches, there were frequent phone calls be-tween witnesses and FBI agents. None of these phone calls during this period of "start-and-stop searches" were memorialized in 302 reports. A hearing, Cognetti declared, was the only way to get to the truth.

"Nothing more is required to warrant an evidentiary hearing," his motion said. "Nor can the defense offer additional facts without an evidentiary hearing, given the incomplete record of the government's investigation and voluminous undocumented contacts with its cooper-ating witnesses."

Powerful and persuasive as the motion was, Castillo was not moved. He denied it.

Chapter 12

Covering Up Misconduct

In her book *LICENSE TO Lie,* about prosecutorial misconduct in the case that brought down the late Republican Senator Ted Stevens from Alaska, as well as other high-profile cases such as the conviction of accounting firm Arthur Andersen LLP, author Sidney Powell observed, "When anyone other than a prosecutor hides evidence or makes false statements in court or to a federal agent, it is a federal crime or crimes: subornation of perjury, witness tampering, and so on."

While acknowledging that there are many honest and fair-minded prosecutors, she noted that "a disturbing number fail to disclose exculpatory evidence to the defense."

In a prosecution, the presiding judge is the primary check on government misconduct, presuming that he or she is willing to fulfill that responsibility. Senator Stevens, who lost his reelection campaign because of his conviction, ultimately saw his conviction vacated because U.S. District Court Judge Emmet Sullivan, who presided over the case, ordered an investigation and concluded that "again and again...the government was caught making false representations."

However, as Powell noted, what happened in the Stevens case is "vanishingly rare." The failure of the government to turn over evidence favorable to the defense is "extremely difficult to discover because the prosecution has complete control over the evidence gathered by its investigators.... Even when the evidence is fortuitously disclosed, after the defendant is convicted, judges are reluctant to order a new trial, so they sweep the evidence under the rug."

In the Segal case, however, evidence of misconduct, including multiple misrepresentations by prosecutors and the suppression of exculpatory evidence, was not only discovered, but was exposed *before* the trial.

Through the efforts of management information system staff members at Near North and forensic experts, more than 400 pages of documents were prepared, bearing dates and times, detailing the eight months David Cheley spent hacking into the Near North computer system. When these documents were overlaid with the emails that he had hacked and then overlaid once again with the email communications among the members of the Takeover Group, Cheley, and FBI agent Murphy as well as the limited number of records of the telephone calls among them all, it became very clear that Cheley's activities were not those of some independent party, nor were they independent from the actions of the government witnesses or the FBI. This was tantamount to a violation of Segal's Fourth Amendment protection against unreasonable search and seizure.

When the prosecution became aware of the documents, which were filed in Near North's civil lawsuit against the Takeover Group and Cheley, a federal subpoena was promptly issued for the entire case record. Near North redacted the contents of the attorney-client-privileged documents, but the prosecution was informed that a number of these had been hacked.

At the point when the defense confronted the government with all of this evidence, the prosecution essentially had a choice. It could begin a criminal prosecution of Cheley and the members of the Takeover Group, who used the hacked information to interfere with Near North's business and to promote the business of Aon, Near North's competitor. It could even consider prosecuting Aon, since the Takeover Group members under its roof were stealing business from Near North.

Or, it could, by doing nothing, essentially protect Cheley, the Takeover Group, and Aon, and protect itself from accusations that they violated FBI and Department of Justice regulations and policies, including canons of ethics and the 1999 McDade Amendment.

The prosecution chose to protect the first high-profile case by U.S. Attorney Patrick Fitzgerald. And the result? Cheley got a complete pass, as did Aon and the Takeover Group. Aon and the members of the Takeover Group were never threatened with any prosecution for conspiring to breach a secure computing system or, in Aon's case, for maintaining hundreds of hacked Near North emails on its computer servers. The prosecution essentially reaped the benefit of the Takeover Group's game plan to wrest control of Near North from Segal, crippling Segal's ability to pay for legal and accounting work needed for his defense. The prosecution also had access to confidential and privileged documents belonging to Segal and Near North. Perhaps just as significant, the prosecution had the benefit of what was essentially a "managed leak" of information, via the Takeover Group, that portrayed the prosecution favorably and cast Segal in a disparaging light.

For example, immediately after Segal was arrested, Matt Walsh solicited APCOA Standard Parking, a valued Near North client for two decades, about moving its business to Aon. Although APCOA did not go with Aon, the company did bail on Near North, moving to another major insurance brokerage. Targeting Near North through the media was a Takeover Group tactic, and who would know better than Walsh what to tell a reporter to dirty up the company? Because he didn't get the APCOA business, he apparently tried to dirty up APCOA, too. After APCOA rejected Aon, Near North spokeswoman Kitty Kurth received a telephone call from a reporter at the *Detroit News*. The reporter said that he had received a call from a former Near North employee who suggested that he should investigate Segal and Near North and their connection to APCOA. He was told that the FBI had been investigating Segal and Near North in Detroit, before Segal was arrested in Chicago, and that the FBI in Detroit had butted heads with the bureau in Chicago because neither division knew the other was investigating Segal and Near North.

Of course, all of this "information" passed on to the reporter was false—there had been no investigation in Detroit at all. At least in this instance, the Takeover Group's efforts to use the media in its attempt to destroy Near North had failed. But not for lack of trying.

Agent Murphy, in an action that looked very much like someone doing the bidding of the Takeover Group, contacted an insurance risk manager at the Los Angeles International Airport several days before a multi-million-dollar contract was to be awarded to Near North. After Murphy contacted the risk manager, the business—which represented more than a year of effort on the part of Near North employee Penny Campbell—was awarded to Aon. Murphy later called Campbell in what Segal saw as an attempt to cover up his interference and complimented her for her reputation as an insurance professional. She described the interaction as intimidating. Other Near North clients contacted by the FBI included Major League Baseball, Starwood Hotels, and H2O Plus. Segal believed H2O was selected because the owner was a friend of Aon's Pat Ryan who had not favored Aon with his business.

Perhaps one of the strongest pieces of evidence that hacked emails—or the information derived from them—wound up in the prosecution's hands was revealed by examining the timeline of Cheley's hacking, the notes taken (and not disclosed for eighteen months) by FBI Agent Higgins, and the grand jury testimony of former Near North employee Steven Coleman. The hacking report prepared by former FBI Agent David Grossman showed that at 11:41 a.m. on December 11, 2001, Cheley hacked into the Near North computer system and accessed emails between Sherri Stanton, Near North's in-house counsel, and Karen Gruca, director of Near North's human relations, relating to a letter sent by William Snow, a former Near North employee who had left the company more than twelve years earlier. Snow had been a participant in the company's former profit-sharing plan and was requesting a distribution of $162,000. One of the emails outlined how Snow said that his prior requests in past years to receive a distribution had been denied under Near North's "bad boy" provision.

This provision, which had not been used at Near North for more than a decade, applied to employees who left Near North to work for a competitor—thus "bad boys." Under the provision—as permitted by the federal Employee Retirement Income Security Act—Near North could withhold profit-sharing distributions to these employees until they turned sixty-five. Snow would not turn sixty-five until 2009—another eight years.

After Segal was arrested and the prosecution continued to present witnesses to a federal grand jury, a curious thing happened. Three months after that email was sent, on March 28, 2002, Coleman, who had worked at Near North from 1985 until late in 2000, appeared before the grand jury. Prosecutor Virginia Kendall appeared to be trying to develop evidence of pension-related crimes by Segal or, if no crimes could be discovered, to establish evidence of unscrupulous or vindictive behavior by Segal. Kendall asked Coleman if he was familiar with the manner in which the profit-sharing and pension plans were handled at Near North.

"Generally," Coleman said.

"What is your understanding of what they were and how they operated?" Kendall asked.

"Well, there was a pension plan that I think was frozen and I was never part of that pension plan," Coleman testified. "So that was a prior—probably people that were there prior to my being in the company."

Prior to the establishment of the 401(K), Segal's company had provided company-sponsored profit sharing and made generous contributions of 15 percent to the profit-sharing plan and 10 percent to the pension plan.

"Are you familiar with something called a bad boy list?" Kendall asked.

"Yes," Coleman said.

"What's a bad boy list in connection with the pension plan?" Kendall asked.

"Bad boy list—my recollection was—is people that left on bad terms from the company and their pension or profit-sharing plan, regardless of whether it was vested or not, until they reached retirement at age sixty-five, something like that."

"How did you get on the bad boy list?" Kendall asked.

"Most of the people that were on the bad boy list were there before I was—before I was really very involved with the company," Coleman said. "I think, basically, you left to compete—if you left to compete. That's my general understanding."

"So," Kendall continued. "Mr. Segal froze their pension accounts?"

"I wouldn't say froze it," Coleman replied. "But deferred them taking it until age sixty-five or whatever was normal retirement."

The only information ever turned over to the defense that mentioned the name of Snow—the man protesting his "bad boy" status in December 2001—was the report of Agent Higgins dated April 3, 2002. Those notes were prepared six days *after* Kendall asked Coleman to explain the meaning of the term "bad boy" to the grand jury. No FBI report of any interview in which Snow's name came up prior to Coleman's grand jury appearance was ever disclosed. How, the defense wondered, did Kendall have knowledge of the specific term "bad boy list"—unless the prosecution was privy to emails about Bill Snow, the only person for whom the term had been used in years?

The defense concluded that the source of the prosecution's knowledge was certainly not any interview that was—according to the FBI's own notes—conducted six days after the grand jury testimony. The information had to have come from the Takeover Group, which had to have gotten it from Cheley's hacked emails.

With such clear and powerful evidence on the table, Castillo's refusal to grant an evidentiary hearing was the most painful pretrial loss for the defense team in the case.

Chapter 13

Castillo Turns Away

*"There is no greater tyranny than that which
is perpetrated under the shield of the law
and in the name of justice."*

—Baron de Montesquieu, *The Spirit of the Laws*

AN ASTUTE AND CYNICAL CRIMINAL defense attorney once offered this bit of analysis, based on years of experience: "Everyone wants the justice system to be fair and the judges to be unbiased, except when they are on trial. Then, they want the judge on *their* side."

It is a rare defendant who does not attempt to plumb the inner workings and feelings of the judge presiding over the case. Each time the case is called to order, a defendant studies the judge's words and tone and body language in an attempt to divine some clue as to whether the judge is leaning toward the prosecution or toward the defense.

Michael Segal was no exception.

As the shock of his abrupt arrest and interrogation waned and the case moved into the courtroom for pretrial proceedings, Segal was cautiously encouraged by Judge Castillo's attitude and demeanor on the bench.

Ruben Castillo was nominated to a federal judgeship by President Bill Clinton in 1994 and was confirmed in 1995. A native of Chicago,

Castillo's father was Mexican and his mother was Puerto Rican. He worked nights as a Cook County Circuit Court clerk while earning a law degree from Northwestern University School of Law. He worked for five years as an associate at the prestigious law firm of Jenner & Block, and then became an Assistant U.S. Attorney. After four years of prosecuting cases, Castillo became the regional counsel for the Mexican American Legal Defense and Educational Fund (MALDEF), a national organization dedicated to protecting the rights of Latinos. After three years at MALDEF, Castillo returned to Jenner & Block as a partner, where he remained until his judicial appointment.

At the time of his nomination, Castillo told the U.S. Senate Judiciary Committee that after graduating law school, "I have had the privilege of serving various clients from all walks of life, from some of the Corporate 100 organizations to individuals who had literally no assets, and I have always enjoyed the role of being the advocate for those clients, but I really came to a conclusion that I would like to have only one client from now on, and that client being justice, per se, and that is why I want to be a federal district court judge."

In 2004, as Segal's trial approached, he took comfort in Castillo's reputation as a liberal judge and hoped that those words spoken a decade earlier still rang true. And he was buoyed when a well-regarded criminal defense lawyer told him that years before, he had had a case before Castillo and when the government couldn't produce a dubious forensic arson report, the judge dismissed the prosecution.

At the outset of the pretrial hearings, Castillo nodded warmly and made friendly eye contact. And when the judge brought the prosecution up short and granted a hearing on the defense motion for a hearing on the improper seizure of attorney-client-privileged documents during the post-arrest searches, there was tangible cause for optimism. Castillo clearly had an independent streak and was not about to be intimated by the prosecution.

After the ruling, one newspaper headline declared, "Judge Blasts Segal Prosecutors." That was a mixed blessing. While Segal welcomed favorable publicity, he also feared that Castillo might react negatively. That fear was confirmed when the judge, without explanation, granted the prosecution's motion and reversed his decision.

That marked a turning point in Castillo's outward demeanor. From then on, he no longer looked Segal in the eye or nodded to him in greeting. In fact, Castillo avoided making any physical gesture that could have been interpreted as an act of cordiality.

Perhaps Castillo felt he was under heightened scrutiny because he was being mentioned as a possible nominee for the 7th Circuit U.S. Court of Appeals. His Hispanic background and unblemished record made him a sterling choice, and some members of the media even suggested that he might ultimately be the first Hispanic on the U.S. Supreme Court. Castillo's judicial resume also included his service on the U.S. Sentencing Commission, where he had served since 1999 when President Bill Clinton appointed him vice-chair of the commission, a position that effectively doubled his salary. The sentencing commission was extremely powerful because it had the responsibility for setting the sentencing guidelines for all federal crimes. In effect, Castillo was among those who decided the formula for determining how long people such as Segal would spend in prison if convicted. During Segal's trial, Castillo mentioned to the jury, arguably inappropriately, that he was the recipient of two appointments by President Clinton—information that underscored his prestige and undoubtedly conferred some extra authority on his rulings and comments from the bench.

Castillo was approaching the end of his first six-year term on the commission and despite his reputation as a liberal judge, some members of the legal community were speculating that he was becoming more conservative—that is, more pro-prosecution—to encourage the Republican administration to reappoint him.

Segal had hoped that the strength of Reidy's motion, heavily supported by documentation and case law, would make it difficult for Castillo to deny a pretrial evidentiary hearing. The judge's earlier criticisms of Polales had offered some hope of a decision favorable to the defense. But at the same time, Castillo once had worked in the same office as Polales, Hogan, and Kendall. Protecting the U.S. Attorney's Office certainly wouldn't hurt Castillo's ambitions, Segal believed.

After Castillo's ruling, Reidy told Segal he would not be raising or challenging prosecutorial misconduct issues going forward because he believed that Castillo would rule in favor of the government and take offense at such motions. Reidy said Castillo would not want to be in a position of appearing to protect the government. Segal thought the opposite was true—that the defense had to challenge the prosecution at every turn and that challenges were a necessary part of the system of checks and balances. Now, he felt the system was eroding and he silently began to question Reidy's reasoning.

Still, in the run-up to the trial, the defense filed motions to reconsider the denials of all of its previous motions for evidentiary hearings. The answer from Castillo was the same: "Motions denied."

The defense also moved to dismiss the RICO charge as a vindictive act by the prosecution. Near North attorney Joshua Buchman's affidavit was clear: When the defense told the prosecution that they intended to amend the Near North civil suit against the Takeover Group to include the allegations of Cheley's cyberhacking, prosecutor Hogan—the man with a past history of being accused of prosecutorial misconduct—said in no uncertain terms that if that happened, Near North would likely be facing a RICO charge. Undeterred by the threat, Segal's lawyers filed the amended complaint and in short order came the RICO charge.[36]

Two and two make four, the defense told Castillo. "The facts here create a presumption of vindictiveness under existing law, and are es-

---

36   Josh Buchman affidavit.

pecially troubling given that the allegations in the civil suit that the government so strongly objected to have been substantiated with clear and irrefutable evidence of its witnesses' connection to the hacker and illegally seized evidence."

Additionally, the defense contended the RICO indictment was a First Amendment due process violation because it interfered with Near North's independent Board of Directors' right to pursue a civil lawsuit to protect the company.

It boiled down to this—the defense had forensic proof that Cheley funneled stolen information to Walsh, Gallagher, Ludwig and Berry, and that these prosecution witnesses and Cheley conspired to acquire confidential, proprietary, and privileged Near North information by illegal means to harm Near North and Segal. All Segal wanted to do was what any citizen in that situation would do: Get the bastards who did it.

Again, Castillo ruled for the prosecution. There never was another favorable ruling for the defense. Segal would not get a full vetting of the facts and issues prior to trial.

The downhill cascade had begun.

Emboldened, the prosecution filed a sweeping motion that could only be characterized as an attempt to fatally hobble the defense at trial. The motion asked that Castillo bar the defense from presenting evidence of "outrageous governmental misconduct" and from attacking the conduct of the FBI agents or the prosecution.

The motion was so broad that if granted, it would preclude the defense from bringing up the issue of the doctored evidence used to manufacture a crime. The motion asked that the defense be forbidden from trying to connect the financial devastation of Near North—a $250 million company of 1,000 employees that was the product of Segal's life's work—to the investigation and prosecution of the case. It would even bar evidence of Segal's family needs.

Castillo ruled that motion, like the others, was "absolutely granted."

The motion left Segal facing trial with his hands essentially tied behind his back. The jury would not only be prevented from learning the details of how Segal's case was built, but would also be kept in the dark about the human consequences.

Chapter 14

The Accounting
Battle Begins

By the time jury selection began in April 2004, prosecutors had piled on a fourth superseding RICO indictment against Segal and Near North. Consistent with the prosecution playbook, the charges in these superseding indictments were only slightly different, yet each one created a new round of unfavorable publicity.

Segal stood accused of thirteen counts of mail fraud, one count of wire fraud, seven counts of making false statements to the Illinois Department of Insurance, three counts of embezzlement, one count of making a false statement to the federal government, one count of conspiring to defraud the IRS, and one count of violating the Racketeer-Influenced Corrupt Organizations Act—the RICO charge.

The Illinois insurance regulations relating to the financial responsibilities of an insurance broker set out in very specific language that any money received for procuring insurance shall be held in a "fiduciary capacity" and not be misappropriated or withheld.[37] The broker is responsible for ensuring that the entity that provides the insurance is paid. Any broker who "knowingly misappropriates" $150 or less is

---

37 Illinois statute re PFTA.

guilty of a misdemeanor. Subsequent violations of $150 or less are a Class 4 felony. Misappropriation of more than $150 is a Class 3 felony.

Significantly, nowhere in the statute do the words "trust" or "trust accounting" appear—despite what the prosecution would claim over and over again. In addition, the statute provides that once a premium payment has been received by a broker from an insured, it is considered "paid" to the carrier. Hence no loss, or risk of loss, can occur after a premium is paid. A valid RICO prosecution predicated on two or more dishonest services, mail fraud charges required evidence of either a loss or risk of loss of money or property to clients of Near North. Nevertheless, Castillo allowed the case to proceed.

The charges against Segal were layered like an onion. On the outside was the RICO charge, which although it was originally conceived as a weapon against organized crime, over time had been brought against public officials and private corporations. There is substantial literature on how RICO has been misused by vindictive prosecutors. In Segal's case, there was never any allegation of involvement with organized crime. The first RICO charge against Segal was filed as a retaliatory act and additional superseding RICO indictments against both Near North and Segal came after the defense sought a pretrial evidentiary hearing on prosecutorial misconduct. One of the most onerous of all criminal laws, the RICO statute allows the government to seize all manner of property and essentially financially wipe out a defendant.

The prosecution of Segal and Near North also was in direct conflict with the provisions of the McCarran-Ferguson Act, which excludes the insurance industry from most federal regulation. The Act gives primary responsibility to states—not the federal government—to oversee the insurance business. As a result, each state has its own department of insurance with its own rules and regulations.

But when Segal refused to wear a wire, the government ignored the statute and used the federal mail fraud statute to accuse him of defrauding customers of their right to his honest services. The mail and wire fraud charges accused Segal and Near North of willfully defrauding insurance customers. The prosecution claimed that Near North customers were at risk of loss because the company wasn't forwarding their payments to the carrier. But, in reality, there were no victims. The government would provide no evidence that any customer failed to get their insurance. Likewise, there would be no evidence that any insurance company failed to get the premiums paid to Near North for the insurance. In fact, many major insurance companies wrote letters of support for Near North and Segal.[38]

To get around this, the prosecution would present testimony from a leveraged witness who stated that checks were held as to the payment of premiums, but left out that normal practice was to wait until the last day to collect premiums due to insurance companies to avoid cancellation. In fact, the government's own evidence showed that Near North at times advanced three million dollars to insurance companies so that their clients would not experience cancellations.

The trial would be a battle over accounting. The prosecution's sleight of hand was clearly designed to suggest that Near North and Segal had somehow embezzled more than $20 million.

The defense intended to prove that there was no evidence that even a single disbursement from the Premium Fund Trust Account was made in violation of state insurance regulations. The defense planned to show that the prosecution, by ignoring selected provisions of the Illinois Insurance Code sought to create the false impression that Illinois insurance brokers were required to segregate customer payments into a trust account. The defense would show that Illinois provides that the PFTA is a commingled, fungible account that is in no way subject to the accounting procedures and requirements of a true trust account.

The prosecution estimated that it would take at least two months to

---

38   AIG & Chubb letters of support.

present its case and evidence. It spoke volumes that there would be *no victims to testify against Segal*. Undaunted, the prosecution was going to depend on witnesses who were under pressure to testify or face possible prosecution themselves as members of a "conspiracy."

There had been an expectation that government witnesses would include dozens of current and former Near North employees, most significantly the members of the Takeover Group, as well as Daniel Watkins, but that would not be the case. The only member of that group that would be called to testify would be McNichols.

Watkins pleaded guilty earlier in the year to stealing more than $70,000 from Near North, although Near North records indicated the amount was closer to $250,000. As part of his deal with the prosecution, he had agreed to testify against Segal at trial. Segal's lawyers intended to attack Watkins as a witness who could not be believed after cutting a deal. After all, the defense could show that Watkins was recorded by McNichols saying that he had no written record that he could rely on to prove that he was only doing what Segal told him to do. But all the preparation regarding Watkins would be for naught—he was never called to testify.

The prosecution intended to try to show that Near North wrote off customer credits. The prosecution contended that when a credit owed to a customer had been on the books without a demand for payment by the customer, the credit was written off. The prosecution intended to argue that nearly $500,000 had been written off, although its sole evidence was predicated on a document, which would come to be known as Exhibit No. 119, which had been created by McNichols.

The charge of making a false statement to the government stemmed from the ambush interview of Segal on the day he was arrested. Segal was accused of lying when he told the FBI agents he knew nothing about Watkins posting cash expenditures to the postage account. In fact, the jury would never have to decide that count because the prosecution—after highlighting it during its opening statement—quietly dismissed the charge mid-trial. The defense believed that the charge was dismissed because the prosecution no longer wanted Agent Murphy to testify. They left it to the defense to actually tell the jury that the charge was no longer in the case.

The defense intended to attack the prosecution's case by showing that the government's "accounting" evidence was unsupported by any working papers, that exculpatory working papers were withheld, and that the documentation submitted had not been prepared according to Generally Accepted Accounting Principles (GAAP), the gold standard of accounting used to create financial statements.

Although there are areas of accountancy about which competent professionals may have differing opinions (such as depreciable assets, intellectual property, and the value of business "good will"), none of these concepts were relevant to an insurance brokerage's use of a PFTA. One would expect that given that the basic core of accounting is arithmetic—2 plus 2 equals four—forensic accounting evidence would be similar to DNA testing in its accuracy. The prosecution had all of Near North's accounting records for more than two years prior to the trial, and had also subpoenaed records from third parties. Yet, no team of government accountants was ever assigned to analyze these records.

The defense planned to show that the base numbers used by the government for its "accounting" conclusions were flawed and the results were only as good as the methodology employed. In fact, not a single government witness had analyzed the PFTA deposit requirements using methodology prescribed by the Illinois statute and regulations. Instead, each government witness used his own "estimate" methodology. This alone accounted for the tens of millions of dollars in differences. Instead of assembling a team of auditors to pore over the records, the government had simply accepted dubious documents from the Takeover Group as the foundation for the prosecution. The defense intended to show that the prosecution must have known that this was wrong and that the Takeover Group members were most decidedly not "whistleblowers." Instead, they were determined to destroy Near North. Their "accounting records" should have been viewed with extreme skepticism or dismissed outright instead of being embraced and relied upon by government.

By the time a jury had been selected and the prosecution and defense were preparing to give their opening statements, Segal's forensic accountant, Andrew Lotts, and his team had invested thousands of hours looking into Near North's books. Segal had spent nearly $4 million to pay for the reconstruction of Near North's books and records, as well as an analysis of the PFTA by certified forensic accountants. They were ready to answer the accounting charges, defend Segal, and undermine the prosecution witnesses.

Chapter 15

A False Picture

AT TRIAL, THE PROSECUTION'S PARADE of confusion, misstatements, misdirection, and false evidence began with the testimony of Norm Pater, the former chief financial officer for Near North, who said that Near North had a reconciliation use deficit in the Premium Fund Trust Account, and that he had prepared a series of ratio charts to show it. Pater said he passed these charts to another employee, Steve Coleman, and *assumed*—he had no proof—the charts were passed to Segal. Of course, Pater could have sent the charts directly to Segal, but since he had not, the government's script called for him to imply that Segal had knowledge of the Takeover Group's contrived PFTA deficit reconciliation.

Pater went so far as to say he had left the documents with Segal's secretary, but that conflicted with other trial evidence, which showed that he emailed the documents only to Coleman. Had Segal seen these numbers back then, he certainly would have challenged them.

One by one—Pater was just the first—the prosecution trotted out witnesses it claimed had knowledge of a PFTA-use reconciliation deficit. Estimates were magically transformed into exactitude.

Virtually all the prosecution's witnesses were leveraged—meaning they testified after being told by the prosecution that they risked facing criminal charges or some other liability as a result of their employment at Near North. The exception was Tom McNichols, who engineered the Takeover Group's false accounting evidence and began cooperating with the FBI and wearing a recording device well before Segal was arrested.

Some witnesses had been approached by the FBI at their homes—a well-established and intimidating FBI tactic. There were usually implications that their names would end up in the newspaper along with Segal's unless they cooperated. This was no idle threat. There was intense media scrutiny of Segal and Near North after his arrest and the press was ready to pounce on even the slightest hint of wrongdoing. Some witnesses were threatened with conspiracy charges, another tactic to hush up witnesses who might provide favorable evidence for Segal. Most witnesses had to hire lawyers, particularly those who were called before the federal grand jury.

This became particularly clear when nearly a dozen prosecution witnesses, torn between what they knew to be true and the pressure to comply, changed portions of their testimony during cross-examination. The list included the lead-off witness, Pater, and as well as David O'Gara, Steve Coleman, Charles Caufield, Roger Torneden, Thomas Jackson, Christian Perez, Angela Amaro, and Cindy Niehaus. All had given initial statements—under oath to the grand jury or in FBI interviews—that Segal's lawyers considered beneficial to the defense, but all eventually became witnesses for the prosecution. Segal subsequently analyzed the trial record and concluded that these government witnesses perjured themselves or, at least, denied statements they'd made during the investigation or in their grand jury testimony. When cross-examined by the defense, virtually all of them testified that every insurance client had received their insurance, every insurer had received full payment on time, and that there had been no misrepresentation by Near North.

Pater admitted that he became a prosecution witness after a surprise visit to his home by the FBI in January 2002 was followed by subsequent meetings with agents and prosecutors. He said a written statement was finalized after it was modified and changed numerous times.

Then he testified before the grand jury. Pater's family came to court to support him—an indication, Segal believed, that they were worried about his exposure to repercussions, including criminal charges, if he didn't help the prosecution.

Pater's testimony flipped and flopped. He initially claimed during prosecution questioning that the Near North books were in good condition. During cross-examination, he said they were not.

During his direct testimony, Pater said that he was the Chief Financial Officer (CFO) in name only. Segal, he said, was really the CFO. This was the prosecution's way of telling the jury that Segal had knowledge of and control over accounting decisions.

However, during cross-examination, Reidy pressed him on the issue. "Yesterday, you testified that he was the CFO."

"I considered him the CFO," Pater said.

"But you didn't say 'considered,' said Reidy. "You said *he was the CFO.*"

"Then he was the CFO," Pater said.

"In fact, when…you were first interviewed by the government… you told them *you* were the CFO, didn't you?"

"I had the title of CFO," Pater said, stubbornly.

Reidy went on to point out that on numerous occasions—including in his statements to the FBI and grand jury, Pater always referred to himself as the CFO.

"Was the first time you ever said that Mr. Segal was the CFO at the time you were there when you testified in court here yesterday?" Reidy asked.

"I believe so," Pater admitted.

"And the other times, when you took an oath and testified to the grand jury, you testified three times that you were the CFO, didn't you?"

"Yes," Pater admitted, bringing the tally of changed testimony to four, just on the topic of who really was the CFO.

This was one of several instances in which the power and influence of the prosecution during Pater's direct testimony was evident.

For example, Pater, under direct examination by prosecutor Hogan, compared Near North to a "Ponzi scheme," which essentially is a financial investment scheme that ultimately collapses when not enough subsequent investors can be found to continue paying returns to the early ones.

Reidy showed that introducing this hot-button concept with no real connection to the evidence was yet another attempt by the prosecution to mislead the jury.

Reidy focused on that testimony during cross-examination. "Do you recall saying that you knew what a Ponzi scheme was?"

"Uh-huh," Pater said.

"A Ponzi scheme is where somebody goes out and gets money from investors and says I'm going to give you a—"

"Twenty percent return," Pater interrupted, finishing Reidy's question.

"And then they take the money from the next investor and pay that—is that right?"

"Right."

"There's nothing in a Ponzi scheme that requires somebody to pay for insurance, is there?"

"I don't—I don't think so," Pater stammered.

"Okay," Reidy said, "So a Ponzi scheme is just about asking for money, telling people you'll give them a return on it, taking that money in and using new money to pay the return on the old money, is that right?"

"Correct."

"But nobody in a Ponzi scheme is having anything to do with actually having to get insurance and deliver it to the person who's paying the money. That's not part of a Ponzi scheme, right?"

"No," Pater admitted.

"In a Ponzi scheme, the person doesn't get anything unless they're one of the early ones, right?"

"Correct."

"And at Near North, *everybody* got their insurance, right?"

"To my knowledge, yes."

Although he was a prosecution witness, Steven Coleman, who had been Near North's chief operating officer, testified that Pater had indicated to him that he did *not* believe that Near North had reliable financials that would have provided accurate accounting components for even the estimated PFTA-use reconciliation. Coleman, who said that Pater was in fact the CFO, testified that he fired Pater because he was doing a poor job. "I don't think he was a very effective [CFO]," Coleman testified.

Another witness who changed his testimony was Christian Perez, who was auditor for the firm of Deloitte & Touche. Perez admitted, on cross-examination by defense attorney Sal Cognetti, that there was no "missing" money.

"Was there an attempt on the part of Near North to book all transactions relating to Mr. Segal's draw account?" Cognetti asked.

"I believe so, yes," Perez said.

"So, all those records were transparent? They were on the books and records of Near North, correct?"

"Yes."

"There's no hidden company someplace that you found for Near North, did you?"

"No."

"No flow of money to some secret company hidden offshore someplace—you didn't find anything of that, did you?" Cognetti asked.

"Don't recall finding anything of that nature, either."

Tom Jackson, also of Deloitte, testified similarly. Cognetti asked him, "Did you ever see any drain of money to an offshore account or any hidden corporations or this money going any nefarious place?"

"No," Jackson said. "I did not."

The cross-examination of former Chief Financial Officer Don Kendeigh by defense lawyer Thomas McNulty directly undermined the prosecution's scenario. McNulty questioned Kendeigh about Near

North's books and records and asked, "So, there was never anything prepared that you're aware of where somebody intentionally tried to mislead anyone?"

"That's correct," Kendeigh said.

The cross-examinations demonstrated that the prosecution was relying upon unsubstantiated testimony from intimidated lay witnesses who were being passed off as "experts," although none had actually performed an audit.

In addition, the prosecution misrepresented the regulations to describe the PFTA as a trust account to imply that it was a traditional trust account that would require non-commingled accounting. The prosecution inserted the word "trust" into their filings in paraphrasing parts of the statute, which was a perversion of the language of the statute. The law actually requires an audit trail of the brokers' use of deposits and disbursements—a deficit use reconciliation—which is not the same as an overdrawn or negative bank account. This misrepresentation was part of a prosecution strategy designed to suggest that money was taken or missing.

Cognetti cross-examined Anthony Senese, who had been in the accounting department at Near North, about the potential for bounced checks, a phenomenon that would have been expected to be common if the PFTA was underfunded. The questioning also gave Cognetti a chance to underscore the defense assertion that if no one lost money, there was no deficit.

"You never bounced a check?" Cognetti asked.

"No," Senese said.

"And all the insurance companies were always paid?" "Correct," Senese said.

"And all the insureds always got their insurance?" "Correct," Senese replied.

Pater was followed on the stand by two accountants—Milton Marcotte and Ron Heitzman from the firm of McGladrey & Pullen—

along with Dennis Poggenburg, from Hales & Company, which was retained by Near North to prepare a marketing analysis of the company.

The prosecution repeatedly told the jury throughout the trial that three separate audits were performed at Near North—by Deloitte & Touche, by McGladrey & Pullen, and by Hales & Company. In fact, although Deloitte & Touche was engaged to perform a balance sheet audit, the company never completed it. Moreover, the firm did not perform an independent analysis of Near North's PFTA reconciliation. Instead, the firm adopted Norm Pater's calculations, which were not supported by any work papers, and were, by Pater's admission, incomplete and inaccurate.

McGladrey & Pullen *did not perform an audit at all,* and actually recommended that Near North consider obtaining one. And the Hales personnel had been working to market Near North to potential investors—they weren't even certified public accountants or auditors. That didn't deter the prosecution from misrepresenting the work performed by all three firms.

None of the prosecution witnesses testified that they conducted or even knew anyone who conducted an accurate accounting of the PFTA. Every single prosecution witness who testified about the PFTA admitted that taking accrued receivables (cash in the bank) and accrued payables—the method the prosecution employed—was not an actual measure of the state of the PFTA. It was an estimate at best. The fact was that if three accounting components were not reconciled with the books and records and subsidiary and aged accounts, it couldn't even be called an estimate. True accounting should generate one definitive answer, just as DNA testing establishes one single identity.

Ultimately, the trial transcript of witness testimony would total about 4,500 pages, and about 1,500 of the pages came from these initial prosecution witnesses. Despite all of these pages, there was not a word of testimony that the PFTA at Near North was measured either by the Illinois Insurance Code regulations or an accounting conducted by the Generally Accepted Accounting Principles.

The prosecution's five primary accounting exhibits, which formed the basis for the time-of-offense conviction, were the results of known incomplete and inaccurate work engineered by McNichols. This was the same accounting strategy the Takeover Group had used in their attempt to extort Segal. The defense believed there really was no indication that anything McNichols touched was reliable. For instance, on the day McNichols left Near North for good—four days before Segal's arrest—he modified a key financial document on his computer related to cash-flow records. There was no doubt that prosecutors were coordinating their efforts with the Takeover Group at that point. Why else would McNichols, in January 2002, be changing a document dated in 1999? McNichols added millions of dollars of old accounts payable, which created false negative PFTA reconciliations. On the same day as the modification, McNichols called Walsh, Berry, Gallagher, and Ludwig of the Takeover Group, as well as the FBI Agent Murphy, cementing this suspicion.

Later, during closing argument, Polales emphasized the importance of McNichols to the prosecution, saying, "I think McNichols was a very important witness in this case. He had a lot to say, put in a lot of documents that were critical."

The accounting system at Near North, by virtually everyone's testimony, was a disaster because of a botched computer Y2K conversion and upgrade that left accounting unable to accurately measure receivables and payables—the core components of even an estimated PFTA reconciliation analysis. To say that it was a mess was an understatement. Segal knew it. His financial officers knew it. The accountants knew it. The task of reconstruction was left to McNichols and his outside consultants. At the time, Segal had no idea that McNichols was part of the Takeover Group, but later, it became obvious that he'd used his control of the accounting components—through omission and commission—to present a bogus picture. This became the core of the Takeover Group's leverage and was adopted by the prosecution.

The prosecution knew about the Y2K computer and conversion problem, but tried to sway the jury through innuendo, conjecture, manipulated evidence, and by characterizing Segal as a wealthy and politically-connected man who only cared about "lining his own pockets."

This strategy produced a steady drumbeat of unsupported testimony that the PFTA-use reconciliation was negative and out of balance because Segal was taking out money—either to prop up his business, expand new businesses, or enrich himself.

Pater, who had no love for Segal and who had demanded that the prosecution provide written assurance that he was not a target before he would agree to cooperate, had gotten the ball rolling, but even he had to dilute his testimony when talking about the PFTA, using words such as "approximation," "indicator," "benchmark," "estimate," and, that old favorite of vagueness, "ballpark." Despite these mushy words, Pater insisted that these estimates were close enough to the statutory method to be good enough.

However, in the end, on cross-examination, Pater had to admit that he could never testify that his PFTA calculation provided a full picture of the balance. He admitted that any calculation without reconciliation of insurance payables and receivables was meaningless. The system in place at the time had been capable of balancing it up, but that would have required extensive time and effort that Pater did not expend.

The bottom line was that the only way to accurately keep track of a PFTA was on a cash commission basis, policy by policy. And Pater, who was near retirement, didn't do it that way because it was too much work. Brokers in states with PFTA requirements *do* keep track that way.

Brokers in many other states—including Iowa and Wisconsin, for example—don't have to keep track because there is no PFTA-use reconciliation regulation at all. Of course, no one could explain why federal prosecutors would pursue an alleged violation of state insurance regulations in Illinois when half the states did not even require PFTA reconciliation.

Moreover, the failure to do it the way it was done wasn't a crime—and had nothing to do with the charges against Segal and Near North. In Illinois, if there is a violation of the accounting regulations, it is not a felony if there is no loss of money—and ultimately, Judge Castillo would so rule. There is no required financial reporting as to PFTA reconciliation in Illinois.

The government's total accounting evidence for the negative PFTA reconciliation use was based on ratio charts prepared by Pater, who said he'd relied on only three accounting components: cash in the bank, insurance premiums receivable, and insurance premiums payable; proper reconciliation requires five components. The prosecution, apparently concerned by exposure on cross-examination that these three component numbers were not reconciled and that Pater had left out critical accounting components, called another witness at the last minute.

Charles Caufield, a former outside auditor for Near North, was presented as a concerned witness who read about the trial in the newspaper and came forward to help the prosecution. Segal felt this statement should have been insulting to the jurors or any third party as a "B" type tactic similar to Prosecutor Polales hauling in a cart full of boxes implying evidence everyday at trial.

Caufield told the jury that he had performed work for Near North during some of the same years that Pater covered in his testimony. He implied that he'd conducted audits using the same method that Pater had used and that they included a full PFTA reconciliation. He stated that there had been a deficit in the PFTA every year. Because his own records did not support his testimony, the prosecution played a shell game of mixing and matching years when he did reconciliations with years he did not perform reconciliations.

Prosecutor Hogan asked Caufield, "Have you got any problem with Norm Pater's calculation of the trust deficit in that fashion?"

"No," Caufield said.

"That's how you'd do one, wouldn't you?"

"Right, correct."

"Any problem with the way Norm Pater calculated the trust deficit?"

"No."

While Segal was in law school, he worked for Caufield at an accounting firm. Segal had a great deal of respect for Caufield, and later hired him to perform auditing services at Near North. Segal believed then—and his belief was never shaken—that Caufield was an honorable man who must have been cajoled or perhaps threatened by the prosecution. During a trial recess, Segal reviewed Caufield's work papers provided by the prosecution to look for Caufield's petty cash analysis documents. Segal believed these would support his defense. But *the petty cash analysis documents were missing.* Segal believed that was no coincidence.

On cross-examination, Caufield was forced to admit that when the FBI first questioned him, he'd said *there wasn't any deficit at all.* He claimed he was interpreting the FBI questions in a technical fashion. He also admitted that his method involved five accounting components—not three, as Pater had used—and that his methods involved a completely different computation.

Despite those admissions, Polales, in his closing argument to the jury, would emphasize only Caufield's direct testimony. "He told you that Norm Pater's calculations were right and that there was no problem with his calculations, that Norm Pater calculated the trust deficit the same way he did. It was a pretty much elementary calculation."

Reidy, in the defense closing argument, also focused on Caufield's testimony, pointing out its weaknesses and unreliability. Reidy noted that Caufield testified that for about seven years, beginning in 1987, he calculated a PFTA deficit. "And on cross-examination, it was clearly established that he had twice before been interviewed—by the IRS one time and the FBI another time...and that he had indicated to them that he had never had any such concern and or raised any red flags or any issues with Mike Segal," Reidy said. "And so, I'm going to tell you that not only should you not credit his testimony whatsoever, but you should just reject it outright and you can do that quite easily, not only based on what he did before you in this courtroom, where he admitted perjuring himself to you, but also just based on the circumstances and the facts and whether they fit what is likely to have happened."

Years later, after Segal was released from prison, he confronted Caufield, who refused to discuss his testimony. He did admit he had not come to court because he had read about the trial in the newspaper.

Caufield was followed by Kendeigh, who, in addition to being chief financial officer at Near North (after Pater left), was a certified public accountant. Kendeigh conceded that he had used the same flawed methodology that Pater had used—an unreconciled accounting procedure that used three components rather than the five required for accuracy.

But notwithstanding the improper methodology, Kendeigh calculated that the company and its subsidiaries were actually $1.5 million to the good as far as the PFTA was concerned. Near North's smaller subsidiaries did not have the accounting problems that Near North had. Those companies had different computer systems and, more significantly, their accounting was not being compromised by McNichols. The Kendeigh era at Near North—which lasted until the fall of 1999—was notable because he supervised the company's disastrous attempt to convert the accounting system. In fact, he conceded that the last good numbers that he ever got were in October of 1998. He said that after the new system was put in place, he had no faith at all in the numbers. "There was a *complete lack of accuracy to the numbers*," he testified.

Asked on cross-examination to grade the conversion process he oversaw, Kendeigh gave it a "C" or at best a C+." Two years later, the prosecution, in seeking a lengthy prison term for Segal, would falsely quote Kendeigh as having said that there was no problem with the accounting numbers during the entire time he worked at Near North.

In the spring of 1999, Jeffrey Ludwig hired the management consulting division of McGladrey & Pullen to reorganize workflow and personnel issues in Accounting—*not to do an accounting*. After several months, McGladrey concluded that the computer system was in such bad shape that until that more serious problem was addressed, there was little point in reorganizing the department.

Their recommendation?

Go back and fix the accounting conversion issues. And they tried, spending months and months on the project. But the system was still a disaster.

Nonetheless, the prosecution attempted to portray McGladrey's work as an accounting of the books and records that determined there was a PFTA deficit as of October 19, 1999, *even though the firm had done no audit or accounting analysis*. This was embodied in Government Exhibit No. 81, which purported to show a $23.8 million negative PFTA-use reconciliation.[39] It was, however, an exhibit that McGladrey did *not* prepare. (An extensive forensic analysis by Andrew Lotts subsequently proved this was false and that it in fact had been created a few months after McNichols joined the Takeover Group, so likely was his work.) In addition, the one-page document did not include a date, who prepared it, any reference to supporting documents and had multiple inconsistent terminologies.

Segal could not get over that this document was not directly challenged by his trial attorneys and included in a McNichols' cross-examination.

During questioning by the prosecution about Exhibit No. 81, Ron Heitzman of McGladrey testified that he compiled the numbers of that report between October 13 and October 15, 1999. But, on cross-examination, he admitted that was impossible.

Near North attorney Sal Cognetti asked, "What were you doing then? What were you doing between the 13th and 15th of October?"

---

39   Exhibit 81.

"That was the normal correction phase project [that] would have been ongoing during that time frame," Heitzman said.

"And you were familiar with the activity at Near North during those days, correct?"

"From a supervisory standpoint, yes," Heitzman said. "I wasn't on-site every day."

Segal knew that was false—he had never met or even seen Heitzman at Near North at all.

Cognetti then focused on the much-discussed, ill-fated computer program, known as Sagitta.

"You were familiar with the fact that there was a lot of problems with Sagitta, correct?" Cognetti asked.

"Yes," Heitzman said.

"Were you ever made aware that the Sagitta program was down on the 13th, 14th, and 15th of October?" Cognetti asked.

"No," Heitzman said. "I wasn't."

So, Heitzman had been caught in a lie when he claimed he compiled the numbers during those days. And it wasn't the first time, as when he testified that a prosecution exhibit presented by Polales depicted bank reconciliations, but were in fact actually just balances.

Ron Marcotte, who also worked for McGladrey, testified that the reconciliations of accounts receivable and payable were nearly complete by mid-October. However, the records presented in court showed that testimony was false as well. In fact, Marcotte's McGladrey documents showed that the work on the accounts receivable discrepancy was only thirty percent complete and the payables reconciliation was only fifty percent complete.

Other Near North records showed nearly the same tallies—a far cry from nearly one hundred percent. But that didn't stop Polales from telling the jury during his closing argument that the work was, in fact, one hundred percent complete.

Polales asked Heitzman if he had had a final report, which was called the transition report. This also was represented as an accounting, although it was not.

"Yes," Heitzman said.

"And you brought it up to snuff and you gave it to the company, is that right?"

"Yes."

The prosecution presented this report as a "dramatic discovery" by McGladrey of a PFTA violation, even though Heitzman's testimony was clearly inconsistent. Prosecutors suggested that Heitzman terminated the assignment with Near North because of a negative PFTA reconciliation. The defense was troubled that Polales's evidence of meetings where Segal was informed of this "discovery" included emails where the date and subject matter headings were deleted. Polales used Heitzman to misrepresent to the jury that McGladrey prepared Exhibit No. 81, the $23.8 million negative PFTA reconciliation, and to validate the supposed admission by Segal that he didn't care about the consequences. Unfortunately, the defense never seriously challenged the inaccurate testimony that was apparent from the government's own exhibits.

In November 1999, Heitzman prepared the company's final invoices because the firm was ending its engagement. One of the bills was for research on the Illinois insurance regulations relating to premium fund trust accounts. Heitzman testified that the bill was altered following a clandestine meeting with Ludwig, who summoned him to the lower-level lobby of the John Hancock Building. The purpose of the meeting was to perpetrate a fraud—to change the invoice to make it appear that McGladrey had been doing an accounting analysis and to cover up facts that would support the Takeover Group's plan to strongarm Segal into turning over the company to them.

Polales tried to downplay Segal's discovery of the change by eliciting the evidence during his direct examination of Heitzman.

"He asked that I change the wording on the invoice," Heitzman said.

"What did you agree to do?" Polales asked.

"I agreed to do that," Heitzman said.

During cross-examination, Reidy strongly suggested that the altering of the bill demonstrated improper conduct by McGladrey & Pullen.

It was clear to Segal that the change of the bill was a cover-up and further proof that McGladrey was doing the bidding of Ludwig, McNichols, and the Takeover Group. Segal learned through one of his own attorneys, Ed Joyce, who had had a conversation with the in-house legal counsel at McGladrey, that their employee witnesses had been under tremendous government pressure and that the company had incurred substantial legal fees to address their major concerns about how the witnesses would be portrayed in the Segal prosecution. Even so, it appeared that Heitzman was willing to misrepresent the services he'd performed for Near North.

Next came Dennis Poggenburg, who worked for Hales & Company, a Wall Street investment-banking firm with a contract to market Near North. Poggenburg was not an auditor nor was Hales an auditing firm. Poggenburg had produced a marketing report that extolled Near North for its innovations and suggested it had a bright future.

But under pressure from prosecutors, Poggenburg changed his outlook on Near North by 180 degrees. After the prosecution built Poggenburg up as the most knowledgeable of its witnesses about how a PFTA worked, he did testify that the proper way to conduct a PFTA analysis was to examine it on a *consolidated* basis—across the entirety of Near North's companies—not just look at Near North's Chicago PFTA individually.

That was significant because in July 2000, McNichols sent a report to Segal outlining the consolidated company's trust position, showing that there was a $633,000 *surplus*—even though Near North's PFTA was supposedly about $7 million out of balance—again, based on estimates and guesswork. This suggested that there was no cumulative PFTA negative reconciliation—despite the fact that the prosecution kept saying there was. Moreover, the testimony was that if premiums are not paid within forty-five days, the insurance carriers unilaterally cancel them—which meant it was impossible to have a cumulative deficit.

It was striking that none of the prosecution witnesses could agree on the proper way to calculate a PFTA account reconciliation balance. That confusion apparently did not bother prosecutors.

Another prosecution exhibit showed the deficit to be $6.9 million in July 2000, ballooning up to $29 million by April 2001, and then up to $35 million by June 30, 2001.

Poggenburg testified to a $24 million negative reconciliation figure, although he admitted that *he had not conducted an actual review, and that everything he knew was based on information supplied to him by McNichols.*

Poggenburg was asked, "How many times did you ask for the financials [from McNichols] or the balance sheets, rather, as of June 30th of '01?"

"My records show at least six times," Poggenburg said. "Not that we asked for them. We got six different versions."

"You got six different versions?" "Yeah," Poggenburg said.

An affidavit from forensic accounting analyst Andrew Lotts, prepared later, characterized Poggenburg's analysis as "flawed and at the core unreliable." (Poggenburg contradicted his own testimony under cross-examination.) Yet the $35 million figure for the PFTA reconciliation deficit would become the sole source of Segal's forfeiture amount.

Poggenburg also testified:

- That the PFTA account had never had a negative balance.

- His calculations came with highlighted footnote disclaimers because the numbers were suspect, the quality of the staff was poor, and "we could vouch for nothing in terms of the financial statements."

- The calculations used non-statutory methodology.

- The calculations were based on unreconciled accounting components and were unreliable because they were not audited—although prosecutor Hogan claimed the accounting components were reconciled.

- That the complete reconciliations between the subsidiary and the general ledger balances had not been available for review.

- He had no idea how many bank accounts comprised the PFTA—allowing prosecutor Hogan to make a misrepresentation that a $10 million temporary loan obtained by Segal was not on deposit as of June 30, and that it was used to pay owed premiums.

- No reconciliations were performed on Near North's bank accounts.

In his closing argument before the jury, Hogan would claim that $35 million "is not something that we're just making up here. There's plenty of evidence for it."

But in fact, Jeff Cappel, a Poggenburg associate, testified that they *never determined if there was a deficit or whether any money went anywhere*, suggesting that there wasn't a deficit at all. Asked if it was "taken for granted that there was a $20 million hole that needed to be plugged," Cappel said, "Correct."

Segal discovered after the trial that another government exhibit, which was not presented in evidence, showed that the PFTA had a $7.7 million surplus.

In the end, most of the "accounting" evidence came from McNichols, the only member of the Takeover Group to testify. There was no Matt Walsh on the witness stand, no Dana Berry, Devra Gerber, Jeff Ludwig, Mike Mackey, or Tim Gallagher.

The prosecution hauled in speakers and electronic equipment—everything but popcorn—for what appeared to be the playing of selections from the more than 600 hours of conversations taped by McNichols, Walsh, and Watkins. It spoke volumes that in the end, not a single tape was played. Not a single second of any tape and notably none of the tape recordings of Segal's defense lawyer, Harvey Silets. None of the conversations between Agent Murphy and Watkins were aired, including the conversation in which Murphy instructed Watkins how to change his affidavit in a way that would implicate Segal—an example of the creation of false evidence. Nor did the jury hear Watkins's unsuccessful attempts to persuade Segal's wife, Joy, and Segal himself to make damning admissions about his expenditures. And they did not hear conversations between McNichols and Watkins during which McNichols was advising Watkins that he could have a problem and to not make admissions as well as what he should say.

There were references to the tapes, though. During cross-examination by Reidy, McNichols admitted that he had secretly tape-recorded Segal, Walsh, and Watkins.

"Others?" Reidy asked.

"Those were the folks I was trying to tape," McNichols said. "If other people would come into the room or were in conversations, yes."

"And after you would do this taping, you would provide the tapes to the FBI?"

"Yes, sir."

"And was it your intention in having those conversations to try and get inculpating material on the tape recorder?"

"Objection," prosecutor Kendall interjected. "Overruled," Castillo said. "You can answer."

"I was just trying to find out what was going on in these conversations," McNichols said. "I was trying to conduct my business at that time."

"So," Reidy said. "Are you telling me then, that in the course of doing these conversations with people, you only conducted your own business? You didn't try and find out anything a little extra for the FBI?"

"It was my understanding I was to conduct business as normal," McNichols said.

"So, on no occasion did you ask any question of the three men that we've just identified that was meant to elicit something that would be useful for the FBI?" Reidy asked.

"It was meant to be useful in figuring out what was going on," McNichols said.

"But just your desire to know what was going on—not the FBI's desire to know what was going on—is that right?" Reidy asked.

"In conjunction with what I was trying to do was to find out what was going on, yes," McNichols said.

"I just want to make sure I understand," Reidy said. "Did the FBI ask you to go find out what was going on as to certain subject matters?"

"I believe I addressed the subject matters that I was going to try to find out what was going on."

"And so, basically, with respect to your tape recordings, all you were doing was going about your daily business, doing the tape recordings as you went, is that right?"

"Yes, to the best of my knowledge."

"And, did you make a couple of dozen of these tape recordings?"

"I believe so."

McNichols was left to carry the weight for the Takeover Group, though Walsh, Gallagher, Ludwig, and Berry were the primary architects of the attempted takeover of Near North.

Prior to trial, the prosecution subpoenaed accounting records from insurance companies through which Near North brokered, apparently in an effort to identify non-payment or delayed payment by Near North. In the end, the prosecution never introduced any evidence from this fishing expedition. The implication was that they'd found nothing wrong. None of that evidence was ever disclosed to Segal's defense, not even that the insurance companies had been subpoenaed.

Significantly, McNichols was forced to admit that despite the prosecution's depiction of the Takeover Group as a band of noble employees intent on saving Near North, they had no intention of reporting any deficit as Segal had done when he voluntarily reported the situation to the Department of Insurance. Segal's action had essentially put the company under an umbrella of protection and eliminated the Takeover Group's claim of leverage by threatening to report the deficit.

Reidy asked McNichols, "Now, in this plan…there wasn't any part of this plan to go to the Illinois Department of Insurance, was there?"

"No," McNichols replied.

Segal believed that the Takeover Group knew that there was no real deficit reconciliation, but created a phantom crisis to try to pressure Segal into accepting their takeover plan. Once Segal self-reported, they realized their crisis would be exposed as non-existent.

The defense was hampered in its effort to cross-examine McNichols because of what appeared to be the prosecution's failure to disclose a due diligence report prepared by PricewaterhouseCoopers on behalf of Fireman's Fund and AIG prior to their agreement to lend and invest $20 million in Near North. This report was never disclosed to the defense, although it undoubtedly contained information favorable to Segal and Near North. The company refused to turn it over to Segal, even though he had paid for it. AIG told Segal the prosecution told the company not to disclose it to him.

As part of its due diligence investigation, PricewaterhouseCoopers reached out to Kendeigh. Although Kendeigh was by then gone from Near North, PricewaterhouseCoopers wanted to know the status of the PFTA accounting during his tenure as chief financial officer. It is unlikely that he provided any negative information—if he had, it certainly would have become part of the evidence against Segal. What is known is that Berry apparently got wind of the contact. An FBI 302 reported that Berry claimed Kendeigh told him that he had lied to PricewaterhouseCoopers and said that the Near North PFTA deficit was about $5 million, when it was closer to $15 or 20 million. None of this was even close to what Kendeigh testified to at the trial, suggesting that Berry provided false information to the FBI.

The PricewaterhouseCoopers audit of Near North, had it been made public, could well have blown a massive hole in the prosecution's case. But, until the day—if that day ever comes—that the details of the audit are finally disclosed, the truth will remain hidden. One telling tidbit did emerge. At one point, Segal was informed that PricewaterhouseCoopers had said that McNichols would have to be fired as chief financial officer as a condition of any loans and warrants being made. That effectively apparently rendered the due diligence report a negative for the prosecution because of the negative conclusion about McNichols.

Ultimately, forensic accountant Andrew Lotts would determine through his analysis of Near North records that the PricewaterhouseCoopers report had to be exculpatory because by Lotts's analysis, the PFTA deficit was a fiction and the PFTA reconciliation prepared by McNichols was false.

Fireman's Fund and AIG did lend money to, and invest in, Near North. Would they have done so if the report they'd received showed a $35 million PFTA deficit, as the prosecution contended?

The answer to that question can only be a resounding NO.

Chapter 16

Sleight of Hand

THE SAME SLEIGHT OF HAND the prosecution used to present the status of the PFTA was used to try to show that Segal and Near North had pocketed more than $500,000 in insurance premium credits owed to customers. Because the prosecution could not show any losses to customers or insurance providers, it characterized these purported credits as "losses."

McNichols testified that he attended a meeting on December 30, 1999, during which he, Matt Walsh and Dana Berry approved writing off $556,000 in credits. Segal was not at the meeting, but under the questioning of prosecutor Kendall, McNichols read an email that he said he sent to Segal afterward about the write-offs detailing how, of about $11 million receivables outstanding, $1.7 million remained open. Checks for $3.1 million had been received and $6.3 million were "corrected through adjustments." Most of the adjustments were made "in consultation with the appropriate" account executive, the email said.[40]

The last page set out $566,000 in write-offs that McNichols claimed Segal had approved, although no evidence was presented as to when Segal did so.

Kendall repeatedly asked questions of McNichols that made it appear that he sent the email, but that email never was sent—it never left

---

40   Shirley McCurty email 01/21/04.

the "draft" file in his computer. McNichols subsequently claimed that he printed out the email and attached it to the documents and sent them physically to Segal, claiming that the email system would not allow him to attach the documents to the email. This claim was untrue—McNichols had emailed numerous attachments to Segal many times.

The prosecution had to know that the email had never arrived—Segal's computers, seized during the searches in 2002, were in the prosecution's custody.

It took Reidy's cross-examination of McNichols to elicit the truth.

"Isn't it a fact that you [wrote] that email in your machine and that you never pressed the send button?" Reidy asked.

"When you send a package like this," McNichols responded, "you take a copy of the email and put it on top of the package so that it goes to Mr. Segal with the package."

"I'm not talking about a package that went to Mr. Segal," Reidy snapped. "I'm talking about your testimony that you sent that email to Mr. Segal. Did you send it to him by pressing the send button?"

"No," McNichols replied.

Although Reidy had caught McNichols in a lie, inexplicably, it seemed to Segal, Reidy dropped his questioning on the issue rather than try to bury him by pointing out the falsity of his statement. At the defense table, Segal was becoming depressed, fueled by the growing sense that Reidy was not following up when he should. Segal feared the jury wasn't getting the point. Later, following the cross-examination of McNichols, Reidy told Segal that he could "have gone after" McNichols. Segal was stunned.

Polales attempted to suggest to the jury that Near North was able to write off these credits because the clients were never notified that they were owed money, but he too got tripped up.

Addressing David Brower, a former Near North account executive, Polales said, "I take it that with respect to these aged credits, in your experience, much of whether or not the client knew about the credit would depend on the nature of the relationship between the account executive and the customer."

"Correct," Brower replied.

"Because it was not the practice to send out written notification to the clients of the existence of a credit," Polales said.

"The initial credit memo would have been sent to the client when it was created or generated," Brower said.

"You think so?" Polales asked.

"I believe that to be the case, yes," Brower said.

Polales, recognizing his premise had been rejected by his own witness, dropped the subject.

Even McNichols was forced to agree—though his affirmation came during cross-examination by Cognetti.

"And, by the way," Cognetti asked him, "When invoices would come out from Near North, there would be invoices sent to the customers reflecting that they owed Near North money or that Near North owed them money, correct?"

"The invoices, yes," McNichols said.

"The invoice would reflect that?" Cognetti asked. "Right," McNichols said.

Contrary to the assertion of the prosecutors, this meant that clients of Near North had been indeed informed of credits they were owed by the company—which meant there had been no fraud.

McNichols also testified about three documents he said he had prepared in what turned out to be the sole exhibit to support the prosecution claim of improper credit write-offs. These documents were presented as Group Exhibit No. 119 and all were initialed and labeled as "group exhibit" by Agent Murphy in an attempt to present them as related. In fact, the evidence showed they were not related at all. The three documents were:

- The email that McNichols testified under oath that he'd sent, but which never left his computer.[41]

- A "table page" that the prosecution said listed the write-offs of credits that were due certain clients and made up the sole basis of the charges in the indictment relating to the credit write-offs.[42]

- A 50-page spreadsheet that was misrepresented as the work of Marie Salazar, a Near North employee, but was in fact the work of someone else at Near North. The spreadsheet supposedly provided backup analysis for the write-offs on the table page, but in fact contained none of the specific names of clients. Moreover, the accounting scenario in the email did not tie in to the accounting totals on the spreadsheet.[43]

In the prosecution's inventory report of the January 26, 2002 search of Near North's offices, three boxes were said to contain documents from McNichols's office. This was very curious, because McNichols gave his notice and left Near North several days before the search. His assistant reported that the office was cleaned out after he left. Yet the government's inventory of McNichols's empty office included a highlighted section that was part of Exhibit No. 119.

So, how did it come about that the FBI reported it had collected three boxes of documents from an office that had been stripped clean after McNichols walked out the door? Could it be that when McNichols was working as a government informant—prior to the search—he removed documents from his office and gave them to the FBI?

Salazar never testified, probably because she was interviewed prior to the trial by the FBI and a report of that interview—which took up four pages of single-spaced type—said nothing about whether she'd

---

41 Exhibit 119 - McNichols email that was never sent.

42 Exhibit 119 - Table page.

43 Exhibit 119 - 50 page spreadsheet.

prepared the spreadsheet or had any knowledge of it. Moreover, she told the FBI that what the unsent email called "write-offs" were actually "either bad debts that were not going to be collected or credits that could not be found on the payables statement from the carrier."

So, of course, the FBI agents and prosecutors knew that the claim of improper write-offs was a fiction. Unfortunately, Reidy never called Salazar to the witness stand.

Prosecutor Kendall referred to the table page as an integral part of the spreadsheet, but in fact, in the unsent email, McNichols referred only to a single attachment—the spreadsheet. Moreover, the accounts listed in the so-called table page did not appear in the spreadsheet. The table page was presented as evidence that Segal had approved the write-offs of the five premium credits totaling $566,000, even though there was no mark or signature that could be said to be Segal's. Nevertheless, the prosecution would, in its closing argument, refer to the document as having been "initialed" by Segal. The prosecution contended that the spreadsheet backed up what they presented, but the figures didn't correspond—there was a difference of several hundred thousands of dollars. Basically, Exhibit No. 119 was prosecutorial sleight-of-hand designed to prejudice the jury.

Despite having had Near North's records for two years, as well as having asked the Department of Insurance for the information, the prosecution never presented any verification of the amount of credit write-offs based on any basic accounting analysis that showed the origin of the supposed debits or credits or any link to any supporting document. There was no document analysis that explained or proved how much—or if any—of the amounts were owed to customers. McNichols, by his own admission, said there were thousands of transactions moved to suspense accounts for investigation in an attempt to reconcile general ledger numbers. And, throughout the trial, there was ample testimony that the disastrous computer conversion created a system of unbalanced and duplicate accounts receivable, debits, and credits. There were any number of reasons why a credit shown on the Near North books might not represent actual money owed to a client. But, predictably, the prosecution, whenever it found any credit write-off, just *assumed* it was a valid credit—an assumption that could have been verified or disproven had the prosecution simply engaged an accountant to analyze Near North's books.

Most significantly, the prosecution misrepresented the Illinois insurance regulations, which actually impose a specific category and regulatory duty on only one very precise category of "credits"—*return premiums*.[44] A return premium credit is the result of an insurance carrier issuing an endorsement to a policy of insurance to reduce the policy premium. There is a big difference between writing off return premium credits and *improperly* writing off credits. If the credit was applied to the account in error or in duplicate, there was nothing legally wrong with reversing the error.

At no time during the indictments and the trial, did the prosecution ever cite the last paragraph of the state regulation, which states that a credit, instead of being returned, can be applied to a customer's account. In fact, Kendeigh, former chief financial officer, was asked during his testimony, "During your three-year tenure at Near North, did you ever once learn that Near North was improperly writing off credits of customers?"

"No," Kendeigh said.

The testimony of David O'Gara, a former senior vice president at Near North, was particularly illuminating on the issue of prosecutorial pressure on witnesses. Under questioning by Polales, O'Gara testified that he noticed that Maya Saviks, a woman who owned a commercial painting business, was owed a $3,000 credit. O'Gara said that he asked his boss, Bill Hines, about how to handle sending the money to Saviks. According to O'Gara, Hines asked if Saviks was asking for the money.

---

44   Return premiums IL Statute and Higgins affidavit.

When O'Gara told him no, but that the records showed the money was owed to her, Hines allegedly replied, "Why would we send money to someone who's not asking for the money?"

Near North's books and records did not contain a verified transaction relating to Maya Saviks, although her husband may have been a Near North client in the past. After a newspaper reported about credit write-offs and Near North, Saviks called the U.S. Attorney's Office and asserted that a credit was owed to her.

O'Gara reported that Hines told him that if O'Gara was interested in giving the $3,000 to Saviks, he should go directly to Segal and ask for a check. His tone suggested that was a fool's errand because Segal would not give him the money. O'Gara testified that he never knew whether Saviks was paid.

Hines was never called by the prosecution, possibly because what O'Gara quoted him as saying was not true.

Reidy eviscerated O'Gara during cross-examination, forcing O'Gara to admit that when he first was interviewed by the FBI, he said that he was not aware of any policy at Near North about not returning insurance premium credits.

"And then you told them that you weren't aware of any incidents wherein an account in which you were involved had had a credit go unreturned, isn't that right?" Reidy asked.

"I thought I told them about Saviks in that interview," O'Gara said. "Do you remember that as you told the FBI that you didn't recall a single instance when a customer went uncredited, they said to you, 'Oh, we think we know that it's true that they did.' Do you remember that?"

"Yes, I remember that," O'Gara said.

"And do you remember that the FBI agent got up and walked out of the room so that you could talk to your attorney about whether or not you wanted to change your answer that you'd already given them that no credit went unreimbursed?" Reidy asked.

"That's correct," O'Gara said.

"And…when they came back, you changed your story, right?"

"I corrected my story," O'Gara said.

Reidy pounced.

"When you say 'corrected,' are you telling the ladies and gentlemen of the jury that you had forgotten about this credit story of yours at the time that the FBI asked you their first series of credit questions and you told them that there were no problems with credits at Near North to the extent you knew?"

"There were a series of questions that I was answering," O'Gara said. "And as we got into the questions, I realized when they said, is there a single one that sticks out, I remembered about Saviks."

Reidy continued, "And this was when they said to you, not, 'Is there a single one that sticks out?' What they said to you was, 'We have information to the contrary of what you've just told us.' Isn't that what they said? And that was the reason why you and your attorney wanted to talk before you talked any more about credits, because the FBI was telling you, hey, we have some information you might be wrong, that there might be a policy or an instance where credits weren't repaid—correct?"

"That's correct," O'Gara said.

"So," Reidy went on, "it's fair to say that when you were first interviewed by the FBI, prior to having that separate little conversation with your attorney, you told a story about credits that is contrary to the one that you told here today in court, right?"

"I don't know that it's a hundred-percent contrary," O'Gara protested.

"Now, as you sit here today," Reidy said, "your understanding of your arrangement or relationship to the government is that you are not at the present time a target of their investigation—right?"

"That is my understanding," O'Gara replied.

"And you do understand that, in the government's view, you *are* a subject of their investigation—right?" Reidy asked.

"I understand that," O'Gara said.

"And you have been told by the government that one of the things they are investigating is whether or not you engaged in any misconduct in violation of federal law in connection with your employment at Near North—right?" Reidy asked.

Flustered, O'Gara replied, "I don't know. I may have been told that, but the words get kind of confusing that I personally am under investigation."

At that point, Reidy asked his last two questions.

"Mr. O'Gara, who decides if you move from subject to target of the U.S. Attorney's investigation?"

"I assume they do."

"They—the government?"

"Yes."

One of the credit write-offs presented to the jury involved a $91,800 credit to the Texas Rangers Major League baseball team. In fact, there was never a credit due to the team. What had happened was that the Rangers' check was in the mail to Near North just when Near North generated its bills for the next cycle, resulting in a double payment by the Rangers. So, this $91,800 item was never a "return premium" within the meaning of the Illinois Insurance Code; it was the reconciliation of an accidental double payment, and therefore is governed by different legal standards than are "return premium" credits.

Prior to trial, the prosecution had said that Near North had made the same kind of "return premium" payment to the Milwaukee Brewers baseball team, in the amount of $100,000—but dropped this allegation when Near North proved it wrong.

In another example of prosecutorial misrepresentation, Segal and Near North were accused of writing off a credit of $4,793 to St. Chrysostom's Episcopal Church. This allegation was reported widely in the Chicago media, and generated an editorial cartoon in the *Chicago*

Sun-Times that depicted Segal stealing from nuns.[45] That image was particularly hurtful to Segal because he had long nurtured close relationships with local religious leaders and friends of different faiths. Over the years Near North had donated $10,000 to St. Chrysostom's in support of a summer camp at the Cabrini Green public housing development.

In fact, Near North's accounting records showed that it did owe a credit to the church—a mere $44, as a result of the church overpaying its invoice by that amount.[46] And because the overpayment was the church's mistake, it was not a "credit" within the meaning of the Illinois Insurance Code—the government knew all of this, even had the invoice in its possession, demonstrating to Segal once again, the prosecution's willingness to drag in anything that might make him look bad.

Ultimately, accounting work done on behalf of the Segal and Near North defense would establish that more than $24 million in credits were returned and adjusted during the time covered by the indictment. What became clear to Near North was that the federal government did not have any actual analysis or documentation proving that credits were due or stolen. In fact, the Department of Insurance did perform a review of insurance company statements and determined that every credit *had been posted* to the clients' accounts. After that, the Department of Insurance asked Near North to provide an accounting of more than 200 individual customer accounts, including the insureds that the prosecution said Near North had cheated.

The Near North review showed *no credits were taken.*

However, the Department of Insurance never responded to the Near North review of the more than 200 individual customer accounts. There was no way to know why nothing was ever disclosed—whether nothing was done or whether the Near North findings were confirmed

---

45   *Sun-Times* 02/17/02 Nuns article.

46   Credit write off for St. Chryostom's Episcopal Church.

but not disclosed. If it was the latter, Segal's defense was entitled to know about it under the law because it was exculpatory. And if it was because nothing was ever done, Segal had to wonder if that was because the Department was intimidated.

There were insurance experts who were willing to testify that Near North's practice of crediting customer accounts was specifically authorized by Illinois insurance regulations. Such testimony would have rebutted the prosecution's implication that anything other than returning the credits was improper. One expert would have testified that the regulations apply exclusively to customer credits issued by insurance carriers and that customer credits from other sources, such as overpayments to customers, duplicate payments by customers, and accounting and bill errors, were outside the scope. But no such experts were called as witnesses for Segal or Near North.

Chapter 17

The Mystery of Exhibit No. 5

FORMER IRS AGENT MATTHEW ROGOZ spent so little time on the witness stand that his testimony took up less than six pages of double-spaced transcript. But during that brief appearance, he provided some of the most unbelievable testimony of the entire trial—testimony that cost Segal an extra forty months in prison.

Rogoz's claimed discovery of what was known as Exhibit No. 5 was the sole evidence to establish Segal's guilt of a Klein Tax Conspiracy, the "straddle crime" that boosted Segal's prison sentence based on federal sentencing guidelines that had been amended on November 1, 2001.

The document was dated October 18, 1989, and purported to be a memorandum from Dan Watkins to Segal. On its face, the document outlined an arrangement in which Watkins would provide Segal with cash and that the cash would be charged to Near North's postage account. It stated, "I am now preparing separate envelopes from petty cash and charging postage for the following: Every Monday: $125, $370; the last Monday of each month: $150, $250, $500. Is this okay?"

This was followed by the words "yes" and "no." Next to the word "yes" were the initials that purported to be "MS." This became known as the "squiggle" or "scribble" that the prosecution argued—with no proof—was made by Segal and showed that he had approved the arrangement.

The prosecution's theory was that Segal spent these funds on personal expenses, and had conspired with Watkins to hide the income by misrepresenting it as postage expenses, which he then failed to declare on his income tax returns.

The events surrounding Exhibit No. 5 and how it came to be introduced at Segal's trial suggested to Segal that it was manufactured *after* Segal's arrest. By the time Rogoz was called to testify, he had left the IRS and gone to work for the U.S. Department of Veterans Affairs Inspector General's Office. The defense speculated that Rogoz changed jobs because of the pressure as a result of the Segal prosecution. After the trial, Rogoz, a well-respected agent, returned to work for the IRS.

Rogoz appeared nervous as he testified about how, on February 13, 2003—more than a year after the searches of Segal's homes, office and the offices of Near North—he was looking through one of the more than 6,000 boxes seized by the FBI. This box, he said, came from Watkins's office.

Prosecutor Polales asked Rogoz, "Were you looking for that document?" "Not this particular document, no, sir," Rogoz said.

"Did you know that document existed?" "No, sir."

"Did you have an information that that document existed?" "No, sir."

Oddly, Rogoz never explained what he had been looking for more than a year after the seizure of the materials.

To understand exactly why Exhibit No. 5 is of dubious provenance, one must go back in time to October 2001, when Watkins's embezzlement was discovered. Segal took immediate action to stop the embezzlement and fired Watkins.

At the time, Segal's lawyer, Harvey Silets, was preparing an affidavit for Watkins to sign indicating that his embezzlement was something Segal had no idea was going on. But before Watkins could sign it, he became a government witness. Tape recordings of his conversations with McNichols about the embezzlement were very revealing. In one conversation, Watkins said:

- There was no document in existence that would protect him in the embezzlement scheme.

- There was no written proof that anyone told him to do those things.

- Segal did not know that Watkins was using Near North checks for personal use—nor did he know about Watkins posting cash disbursements to Segal in the postage account.

- He knew only about the $125 cash envelopes for Segal, for cab fare.

Not once did Watkins mention the memorandum that would become Exhibit No. 5. In fact, his statements dovetailed with what Segal knew—there were weekly cash envelopes of $125 for cab fare and miscellaneous expenses. It defied common sense to think that somehow Watkins forgot about the memo—a memo that the prosecution contended was the driving force behind more than twenty years of conduct. Segal never denied receiving extra cash beyond the weekly $125 envelope for cab fares. But he had long-standing instructions that the amounts be recorded and posted to his draw account. Ultimately, at tax time, he reduced his net bonus pay by the amount posted to the draw account. In other words, he consistently reimbursed the company for any money he drew out for personal use. The IRS knew this. The gross amount of his bonus pay was reported every year.

While there had been testimony confirming that Segal's cab fare withdrawals and other cash withdrawals were posted properly on the company books, there was no testimony at all that Segal ever directed anyone to post petty cash withdrawals to the postage account. There also had been testimony that when Segal asked for additional petty cash for travel or other purposes, petty cash slips were prepared to properly account for the money.

Why would Segal put his initials of approval on a document that called for petty cash envelopes that Segal did not want?

The answer was he didn't.

Because Watkins was stealing the money. As was pointed out repeatedly during the trial, cash is hard to trace, hard to find. But the defense did fid some uses of cash by Watkins. In April 1990, for example, he used cash to make a deposit on a new home. Ultimately, Dennis Czurylo, a former IRS agent and forensic accountant hired by Near North, documented the use by Watkins of more than $100,000 in cash and estimated that the true amount probably was closer to $250,000. By examining Watkins's bank account, the defense determined that Watkins had been visiting a currency exchange near State Street and Chicago Avenue. Unfortunately, most of the exchange's records had been lost in a flood. So, there was no way to get a full accounting of the theft. Other evidence showed that Watkins went to a local grocery store and bought money orders.

The defense further learned that Watkins, whose duties included replenishing and reconciling the petty cash account, was covering up his embezzling by shredding the petty cash withdrawal slips that were supposed to be credited to Segal's draw account—thereby destroying any audit trail.

Watkins had had plenty of opportunities to give the prosecution and the FBI the memorandum, if such a thing had existed, prior to Segal's arrest. He had been copying Near North documents for the FBI for weeks and that document wasn't among them. And, though he had scanned scores of documents onto his Near North laptop and then turned the entire laptop over the FBI, that document wasn't on the hard drive.

So where did Exhibit No. 5 come from?

On direct examination, Rogoz testified that he found it in Box No. 133, but during cross-examination, he changed his story, stating that he'd found it in a file folder that had been seized during the search of Watkins's office. It was never clear who actually collected the documents from Watkins's office that day.

No matter where or when Rogoz supposedly found Exhibit No. 5—in a box or in a folder—it was clear that there was no listing of the document on the extremely detailed government-prepared inventory of the items taken from Watkins's office. The inventory for Box No. 133 listed no documents with dates even remotely close to the August 18, 1989 date on the memo, nor were there any documents of a similar type. In fact, that inventory did not list any document as coming from or being in a file folder.

As a government witness, Watkins had made recordings of conversations. He also was a source of information for the search warrants. And he clearly was aware that the search was going to take place before it actually happened. On the day of the FBI search of Near North offices, a Near North security camera captured Watkins unlocking the front door to allow the FBI to enter.

What was clear, however, was an FBI tape recording of a conversation on November 1, 2001, between McNichols and Watkins, during which McNichols asked Watkins if he had any document or record to protect himself. Watkins said *that there was no written proof that anyone had told him to do any of these things—everything was verbal. He also said he hadn't told Segal about a lot of what he was doing.*

On another tape, Watkins can be heard talking to himself, expressing dismay that he had been caught embezzling and that he would have to move into a trailer, apparently because, without his source of illicit funds, he would no longer be able to afford his house payment.

"If I hadn't embezzled the money, I'd still be in pretty good shape," he said. "I took it in steps. We can't afford it. We just can't. This way, we can live in the trailer, put this thing inside, we can come back from it." Watkins had left his recorder on and was talking to himself but basically admitted his embezzlement going back to 1990, when he purchased his house.[47]

So, for all of this time, Watkins never mentioned the existence of the memorandum. Why? Because it did not exist.

So, when was it created? There were some clues.

On January 3, 2003—nearly a year after Segal was arrested and the searches were carried out, the IRS interviewed Watkins. A report of the interview was prepared. This hugely critical memorandum was NOT discussed. Not once.

Did Rogoz make note of his discovery of Exhibit No. 5 on February 12, 2003, the day he said he fished it out of a file in a box? If so, no report was made. There was no shouting of "Eureka!" There is no report of Rogoz telling anyone about it—not a fellow IRS agent, not the FBI, and not any members of the prosecution team. This most significant discovery was never noted. Not once.

Moreover, the day after the search, Watkins told a Near North co-worker—in a conversation that was recorded—that prior to the search, he had already cleaned out his office and that there was very little for the FBI to remove.

Exhibit No. 5 is mentioned for the very first time in Rogoz's report of an interview with Watkins conducted on March 4, 2003—exactly twenty days after Rogoz's alleged blockbuster discovery. Watkins told Rogoz he had no recollection of preparing the document.[48] A memory failure, perhaps, or more likely, he never prepared it. In the interview, Watkins identified the squiggle as Segal's initials, specifically calling them "left-handed." Although Segal is, indeed, left-handed—as anyone would know after working for Segal as long as Watkins did—he does not write with the backward slant often associated with left-handers. But Rogoz certainly used the style of the squiggle to strengthen his

---

47   Government ID92 Watkins embezzling.

48   Exhibit 5.

assertion. When he testified before the federal grand jury on May 15, 2003, Rogoz referred to the initials as "left-handed."

Cross-examined by Reidy, Rogoz acknowledged that he really did not know who initialed the document.

"And you are aware that this document was submitted to both the FBI and IRS Questioned Document Examination Laboratory?"

"I'm aware it went to the IRS lab, but I did not know it was at the FBI lab," Rogoz said.

"And, do you know whether or not the IRS lab attempted to make any handwriting recognition of the squiggle?" Reidy asked.

"No, sir, I don't know," Rogoz replied.

That, at least, was a true statement. But it was remarkable that one of the lead agents on an extremely high-profile prosecution discovered what was the prosecution's sole evidence of a conspiracy between Watkins and Segal and didn't bother to submit the document for forensic testing or even ask if anyone else did?

Without any forensic testing, the question of who made the squiggle on the document was unknowable.

Prior to the trial, but many months before Rogoz said he made his discovery, Segal had provided the prosecution with examples of his handwriting. Later, during a session in the grand jury, a juror was examining several documents presented by FBI agent Higgins. The juror remarked that the signatures that Agent Higgins said were made by Segal looked different and questioned whether Segal or someone else had actually signed the documents.

The prosecution never disclosed any report of any analysis of Segal's handwriting, nor did the defense lawyers ask for such a report. Reidy later told Segal that Hogan had intimated that "indentation" analysis showed that the 1989 memorandum was underneath another document that Segal had clearly written on. However, the history of the trial was such that if there was any evidence that pointed to Segal's guilt, the prosecution did not hesitate to introduce it. And no indentation analysis was presented. (The unsupported claim of an indentation was a tactic that Hogan had used in another high-profile trial, which resulted in accusations of misconduct against him.)

The defense inexplicably did not conduct any of its own testing on Exhibit No. 5 to try to determine if it was possible to tell when the document was generated.

However, the defense did call Segal's former executive assistant, Denise Mayo, who had worked directly for Segal for years and who regularly saw him sign and initial documents. She also was familiar with Segal's practice of authorizing her and others to sign and initial documents in his stead.

Prior to her testimony, Mayo had examined scores of documents and was able to determine that Segal made some of the initials or signatures while others were made by her or other staff members at Segal's direction. Regarding Exhibit No. 5, Mayo was adamant that the squiggle or scribble was *not* made by Segal.

After hauling in a gurney loaded with boxes stacked about four feet high—in a move Segal viewed as blatant attempt to suggest the evidence was vast—Polales made two separate, gratuitous references to Box No. 133 during his cross-examination of Mayo.

At one point, he started to show Mayo a copy of Exhibit No. 5 and said, "Let me show you—got so many documents—Box 133. Take a document from the Box 133, which is, I think, is the box Mr. Rogoz testified about."

A few minutes later, during a colloquy with Judge Castillo about exhibits, Polales said, "Kind of hard to keep all of these documents straight, so I apologize. I just want to make the record clear, Your Honor. I've been taking them out of Box 133." This tactic was an obvious attempt to "prove" the document was found in Watkins's office and put in box 133—although there was no record of it.

And, in a bizarre moment during the cross-examination of Mayo, Polales attempted to imply that perhaps Segal had signed his initials upside down because that was the way Exhibit No. 5 was presented to him for his approval.

That led to an almost comical series of questions by Segal's attorney, Thomas McNulty, about Exhibit No. 5.

"You've already testified that when we look at it, that doesn't look like Mr. Segal's signature or his initials to you," McNulty said.

"No," Mayo agreed.

"I'm going to turn it 45 degrees." "No."

"I'm going to turn it upside down. Does that look like Mr. Segal's signature that way?"

"No."

It would be long after Segal's trial and the demise of Near North that the U.S. Tax Court would dismiss a civil tax assessment instigated by prosecutor Hogan based on Exhibit No. 5. But that would be far too late for Segal.

Chapter 18

What the Jury Didn't Hear

ABOUT A MONTH BEFORE THE trial began, Segal and Tony Swiantek, Near North's IT manager, met with the defense team in the office of lead attorney Dan Reidy at Jones Day, one of the largest law firms in the nation. Segal had serious concerns about how the case was being handled. Castillo had shot down the defense pretrial motions and Segal was starting to discern a lack of total commitment on the part of his own team, particularly Reidy. Segal had sought out Reidy because he was one of the top trial lawyers in Chicago. Prior to coming to Jones Day, Reidy had been a top prosecutor in the U.S. Attorney's Office in Chicago. He was one of the architects of the Greylord investigation, an undercover investigation of corruption in the Cook County court system that eventually convicted more than one hundred people, including at least seventeen judges.

From 1984 until 1987, Reidy and Castillo had been fellow prosecutors in the U.S. Attorney's Office in Chicago. During most of that time, Reidy was the First Assistant U.S. Attorney, the number-two position in the office, and, in effect, had been Castillo's boss.

After the first RICO indictment came down, Reidy informed Segal that he would be working less hands-on in the case. Segal interpreted this to mean that other Jones Day lawyers would step in and that he'd

185

be charged a substantially lower hourly rate. In fact, Segal discovered that Reidy was concerned that Segal would not have enough money to pay for Reidy's time as the case grew more complex. And he told Segal that he could not represent Near North because it would require too much time and besides, it might be beneficial to the case to introduce another legal team into the courtroom. Segal believed that Reidy had done an extremely professional job in drafting and filing pretrial motions attacking the case on Constitutional grounds. But it had appeared to Segal—and this suspicion was later confirmed by a close friend of Reidy's—that Castillo's refusal to grant a pretrial evidentiary hearing had surprised and disappointed Reidy.

Segal believed that money was on Reidy's mind when he was asked if he would like to have overnight trial transcripts prepared; Reidy quickly responded that it would cost at least $100,000. The true cost, Segal later was told, was only $25,000 but the overnight option was not ordered.

With the threat of forfeiture of assets because of the RICO charge, the possibility that Near North and Segal might be unable to pay their legal fees was a reality that could not be ignored—and Reidy said as much. While, legally, a lawyer may petition the court to withdraw if his fees are not paid, Segal was up to date on his payments and still fighting to keep his business going. He also was unaware that Reidy would present hardly any defense.

That certainly was not apparent at the pretrial meeting in Reidy's office overlooking the Chicago River. Over four hours, Segal and Swiantek presented six-inch binders of write-ups of accounting issues and other matters they knew would be raised by the prosecution. Reidy took notes and wrote down the names of more than twenty-five potential witnesses and the substance of the testimony they could provide. These included accounting expert Andrew Lotts, who was ready to testify that he and a team of forensic accountants had determined there was no deficit in the PFTA. Reidy was given copies of lawyers' interviews with Richard Rogers and Ron Hartsock, two of Segal's regulatory experts who had worked for Zack Stamp, the attorney representing Near North at the Department of Insurance. Rogers was a former deputy director of the Consumer Division, and Hartsock was also a former deputy director who had co-drafted the PFTA regulations with Richard Seligman, a lawyer who had worked for Near North.

Rogers was prepared to testify that the accounting system in place at Near North in 2001 was based on the accrual method of accounting. The Insurance Department determines an insurance producer's compliance with the PFTA regulations exclusively by using the cash basis method of accounting. Switching between the two methods, Rogers knew, required significant adjustments to the numbers. Rogers also was prepared to say that the Insurance Department would not have shut down Near North, since it was only an administrative body and did not have that authority. The most severe remedy would have been a license revocation, but that would surely have been a last resort. Significantly, the department would not, according to Rogers, have issued a citation based on irregular treatment of the receivables and payables.

For his part, Hartsock would have testified about what an appropriate remedy might have been if there were a misuse of the PFTA. At the very least, an insurance producer would be required to open a separate PFTA, which Segal had actually done. Hartsock would have testified that an agency cannot be cited under the PFTA regulations for "misappropriating a receivable" and the department does not consider payables or receivables in determining whether a PFTA is in balance. As to credits owed to insured—a hotly debated issue at the trial—Hartsock would have confirmed that an insurance agent need not inform the insured that a credit has been applied against past due amounts.

Segal provided Reidy with a list of clients whom the prosecution claimed had been cheated out of insurance credits, but who in fact were prepared to testify to the contrary—that Segal and Near North had stolen nothing. For example, Don Haufe, risk manager of Waste Management, Inc., the company the prosecution claimed had been cheated out of $300,000—eighty-five percent of the stolen insurance premium credits—had offered to travel from Phoenix at his own expense to testify that no such credits were owed or stolen.

As the trial progressed, whenever Segal brought up the question of why these witnesses weren't being called, particularly when the extensive forensic analysis by Lotts showed no credits were owed, Reidy ignored him.

In late May 2004, on the day before the prosecution was scheduled to complete the presentation of its case, Segal joined Near North's defense attorney Sal Cognetti for breakfast at the Union League Club on Jackson Boulevard—just a couple of hundred feet from the Dirksen Federal Building where trial was being held.

"So, Sal," Segal asked, "When will we be putting our witnesses on the stand? What's the strategy? What will we attack initially?"

Cognetti was taking a sip of coffee and at Segal's query, he paused, then slowly lowered his cup.

"I'm the third peg of a three-legged stool," he said. And then stopped. The implication was clear—Reidy was calling the shots and it didn't look as if any defense witnesses would be called at all.

Segal left the table in shock—understandable for a man whose livelihood and—more significantly—his personal liberty were at stake. He hurried outside, jumped into a cab and went immediately to Reidy's office. He found Reidy working with Czurylo, a retired government investigator who had an impeccable reputation, who previously had told Segal that the case against him was the worst he had seen brought by the government in more than twenty years.

"What about our witnesses?" Segal asked Reidy. "What witnesses are we going to put on?"

"Didn't anyone around here tell you that we are putting on a limited defense?" Reidy asked curtly.

"No. No one told me that," Segal said.

Reidy tried to brush him off, saying he had to get back to his trial preparation.

Early on, Reidy had said he thought he could win the case. Gradually, he had backtracked. And now this. Segal flashed back to a moment before the trial when Reidy had asked Segal point-blank if he would like to settle—meaning plead guilty and avoid a trial. Segal had quickly and firmly vetoed that as ever being a possibility.

"I thought you said we could win."

"Not after all the things they've thrown at you," Reidy said.

Segal decided that Reidy must have never taken the time to read and understand the accounting evidence and as a result had completely lost confidence in the defense. Segal also realized that Reidy had never discussed in concrete terms what the defense would be. Now, the full implication of Reidy's comment about being less hands-on after the RICO count came down became clear: He was going to make himself scarce and there wasn't going to be much time spent on defense witnesses. Segal learned that Reidy had disparaged the forensic accounting witnesses proffered by Segal for a lack of precision.

Ultimately, the failure of the defense team to bring in a single accounting witness to attack the prosecution's evidence during the guilt phase of the trial would be understood as a critical error since the analysis would have shown that there was no breach of PFTA reconciliation. This was the defense that Segal had bargained for, but it was not the defense he got.

It was puzzling that Reidy held the meeting, accepted the binders of evidence and Segal's list of witnesses and then decided to use none of it without telling Segal. Segal immediately wished he had paid closer attention. He felt as if his life were slipping through the cracks.

It made no sense to Segal that no one from the team of defense lawyers and investigators ever discussed the interviews with the authors of the statute or incorporated the substance of those interviews into its arguments, Segal was stunned.

"Not sticking with my original attorney, Harvey Silets, was the biggest mistake of my life," Segal later said. "Harvey was a fighter, but early on, Harvey was concerned that he wasn't getting his phone calls returned by prosecutors. I knew that to be one of the many ways the prosecution can obstruct a defense. That is one of the reasons I turned to Reidy. I really didn't know him, but I was influenced by a recommendation from a friend who thought it would be good to have someone who had worked for the U.S. Attorney."

In the end, there would be only two witnesses called by the defense—Denise Mayo, who testified that Segal didn't make the so-called squiggle on Exhibit No. 5, and Thomas Jackson.

Jackson, of Deloitte, was called to specifically rebut the testimony of Don Kendeigh, Near North's former CFO, who had testified about a conversation Kendeigh had with his predecessor, Norm Pater, relating to a supposed meeting Jackson had had with Segal. The testimony had been offered—over the defense objection as hearsay—in prosecutor Hogan's continuing effort to portray Segal in a negative light.

Kendeigh had testified that Pater claimed that Jackson said "that Mr. Segal threw him out of his office when he tried to follow up on this conversation about...the financial statements with the trust out of balance."

"Threw Mr. Jackson out," Hogan had repeated, a prosecutorial tactic designed to make sure the jurors understood what Hogan believed was important.

"Yes," Kendeigh replied.

And so, Jackson took the witness stand and was questioned by defense attorney Thomas McNulty.

"You had occasion while you were doing tax work for Deloitte & Touche to deal with Near North and specifically Mr. Segal, did you not?"

"Yes, I did," Jackson said.

"And you met with Mr. Segal from time to time, did you not?" "Yes, I did."

McNulty asked Jackson if he recalled meeting with Segal in August 1996.

"Yes, I do," Jackson said.

"Sir, has Mr. Segal ever thrown you out of a meeting?"

"No," Jackson said firmly.

"How would you characterize your dealings with Mr. Segal in terms of the level of professionalism?"

"I've always found Mr. Segal to be very professional, very cordial, and very friendly in any meeting I've ever been in with him."

"You don't recall a single time where you ever said to either Mr. Kendeigh or Mr. Pater that Mr. Segal had thrown you out of a meeting?" McNulty asked.

"No," Jackson said. "I do not."

It certainly appeared that Hogan had been caught in yet another instance of introducing false testimony and covering up exculpatory evidence. This, however, carried greater impact than any tedious accounting misrepresentation the jury might have had difficulty following. This false story about Segal throwing Jackson out of his office because Jackson was concerned that the PFTA balance was something a jury could easily grasp and might just influence their understanding of the case.

And then, with little sound or fury, that was that—the defense rested its case. There were no more witnesses. There was no testimony to correct the prosecution's mischaracterization of the PFTA as a traditional "trust account" rather than a commingled account.

After spending millions of dollars, including a $600,000 infusion just before trial, Segal felt as if he had been cast adrift in a dinghy without oars in the middle of Lake Michigan.

191

The thousands of hours and millions of dollars spent to finally reconcile Near North's books had been successful—the prosecution's estimates, ballyhooed throughout the trial by witness after witness, had been undercut as inaccurate and wrong. But the defense team's opportunity to present this powerful counterattack went unexploited. Reidy had already decided, without informing Segal, that the case would be framed and argued *not as an accounting case but as one of intent*. The message to the jury would be essentially that Michael Segal wanted his company to thrive and succeed, and for that reason, he would not siphon money away for his own purposes at the expense of the company. Segal saw this strategy as a betrayal, pure and simple. He concluded that by avoiding mounting a challenge to the government's accounting testimony, Reidy had cut down on the time he would have to spend on the case. He decided that Reidy had not wanted to take a chance that if Segal's assets were tied up by a RICO conviction, he'd never be paid for a full-blown defense.

And so, the defense did not use the best evidence they had—a forensic accounting analysis that refuted the prosecution in every instance.

Segal was devastated.

Chapter 19

The Exploitation
of the Media

*"Few, if any, interests under the Constitution are
more fundamental than the right to a fair trial
by impartial jurors, and an outcome affected
by extrajudicial statements would violate that
fundamental right."*

—Gentile v. State Bar of Nevada

THE TENSION BETWEEN THE MEDIA and the right to a public and
fair trial has long been a matter for debate among prosecutors and defense attorneys—who want their respective sides to be favorably represented—and journalists, who believe that protecting a jury from the
press is the job of the court, not the media. But anyone with any savvy
realizes that the proliferation of the media makes it very difficult to
news-proof a jury, short of locking them down completely.

The media are not subject to the same restraints as officers of the
court. If leaks of information do occur, journalists are only too happy
to take advantage of them and publish what drops in their laps—ide-
ally, before their competitors do. In the case of Segal, the Takeover

Group had no compunction about parceling out tantalizing tidbits to the media. The damage to Segal and Near North was demonstrable.

Long before his trial, Segal had concluded that some members of the Chicago media were determined to print everything that was detrimental to him and Near North and to ignore anything that Segal said in response. There were no "victims" in a classic sense to interview—no insurers lost money and every customer got the insurance they paid for. And so, the media was only too eager to hang on the false claims of the Takeover Group beginning as early as April 2001. And following Segal's arrest, the press corps, seemingly more than ready to ingratiate itself with the new U.S. Attorney, began repeating those falsehoods without attempting to speak to Segal directly. To make things even easier, the U.S. Attorney's media spokesman, Randall Samborn, regularly handed out three-by-five cards pre-packaged with accusations.

Segal watched helplessly as mischaracterizations and ridiculous claims were aired—all of which had the potential to poison the prospective jury pool. Every scrap of information was pounced upon, ranging from the unproven claim that Segal was a "power broker" to a claim that he took his dog to Gene and Georgetti's Restaurant. But even if those things were true, where was the crime? Meanwhile, save one instance, reporters failed to mention the extensive hacking and behavior by the Takeover Group. No reporter noted that the prosecution was unable to produce even one Near North client who claimed to be a victim. In early June 2004, after twenty-three days of trial, the jury was looking forward to a recess of two weeks. With closing arguments in sight, Cognetti filed a motion requesting that Castillo restrict statements to the media by attorneys, parties, and witnesses in the case. Segal had put together an extensive analysis tracking the communications among the Takeover Group, government parties, and the media over a long period of time. Reidy didn't support this idea, but Cognetti, an outsider, was not as accustomed to the relationship between the media and U.S. Attorney's Office in Chicago.

Cognetti noted that "throughout the pendency of this case, the communications of certain trial participants with the media—notably, the communications of certain cooperating government witnesses—have posed and continue to pose a substantial likelihood of prejudicing the right to a fair trial.

"Second, throughout this trial, the government's lawyers and agents have been in close and frequent contact with Steve Warmbir, a reporter for the *Chicago Sun-Times*, who has recently written articles that were published in the *Chicago Sun-Times*, which if read by members of the jury would provide them with the very information that this Court barred from presenting at trial."

The motion was largely the work of Albert Alschuler, a law professor at the University of Chicago and among the nation's most esteemed legal scholars. In addition to holding many prestigious academic positions, he had been a former special assistant to the Assistant Attorney General in charge of the criminal division of the U.S. Justice Department. He was a prolific and highly regarded author on subjects such as plea bargaining, sentencing reform, privacy, search and seizure, civil procedure, legal history and ethics, false confessions, courtroom conduct, jury selection, and other topics in the field of criminal justice.

In other words, Alschuler knew what he was talking about.

Precedent for the motion was an order approved in 2000 by the Fifth Circuit U.S. Court of Appeals in the prosecution of Louisiana Insurance Commissioner Jim Brown. In that case, the appeals court upheld a federal judge's order restricting statements to the media by all trial participants. The motion also quoted the 1966 U.S. Supreme Court ruling in the case of *Sheppard v. Maxwell*, which held that the physician had received an unfair trial on the charges of murdering his wife due to the trial judge's failure to protect the jury from massive, unfavorable press reports.

Nearly thirty years earlier, the Seventh Circuit U.S. Court of Appeals in Chicago had held that lawyers' statements concerning pending litigation could be restricted when those statements posed a "serious and imminent threat" of interference with the fair administration of justice. The proposed order was in complete accord with the Illinois Rules of Professional Conduct and the American Bar Association Model Rules of Professional Conduct, which state that violators may be subject to sanctions by state and federal bar associations. Specifically, the ABA rules state that a prosecutor in a criminal case shall: "except for statements that are necessary to inform the public of the nature and extent of the prosecutor's action and that serve a legitimate law enforcement purpose, *refrain from making extrajudicial comments that have a substantial likelihood of heightening public condemnation of the accused.*"

The media had feasted on Segal's case and the Takeover Group exploited that interest by making every element as salacious as possible. The prosecution likely wasn't unhappy with the torrent of adverse publicity. Although Segal had never worked for a government agency or been elected to public office, he understood what it meant to come up against the political machine in Chicago, and the media continually implied that he was a politically connected and influential person. This reinforced the image the prosecution was trying to convey.

At one point, Segal reached out to *Chicago Tribune* columnist John Kass to have breakfast in an attempt to try to level the playing field. After keeping Segal waiting for two hours, he finally joined him at a Greek restaurant in downtown Chicago. As he sat down, Kass jokingly warned a waitress to be ready to call the police if she saw them wrestling on the floor. Segal asked how he could get his story across and Kass implied that perhaps Segal should cooperate with the government. In fact, Kass suggested that Segal had no chance in court because Daniel

Watkins had secretly taped conversations at Near North for the pros-ecution. That had been a stunner—Segal and his defense lawyers had not yet been informed by the prosecution that Watkins had worn a wire or was cooperating with the prosecution.

Segal suggested that Kass's friends from the Takeover Group were involved in the theft of emails from Near North and perhaps *that* was worth writing about.

"I'm not going to be included in that, am I?" asked Kass. Segal said nothing, although he knew that the defense had found an email written by David Cheley, commenting about sending a stolen email to Kass.

In the end, before they parted, Kass had offered that Segal wasn't "like the rest" nor like some politicians—he had succeeded through hard work. Segal wasn't "a bad guy," he said.

As they walked out, Segal joked, "If I have to go away, will you send me a subscription to your newspaper?"

Wordlessly, Kass patted Segal on the back and walked away. Years later, after Segal was released from prison (there had been no gratis subscription), Kass and Segal crossed paths in another restaurant. Kass approached and said, "You must hate me."

"I should, but I don't," Segal replied with a wry smile and walked away.

Three voluminous lists were attached to support Cognetti's motion. The first was an index of 201 stories and articles about Segal and Near North that had been published since May 2001, "nearly all of them nega-tive and prejudicial." The second was a list of 305 telephone and email exchanges between Takeover Group members Timothy Gallagher, Matt Walsh and Dana Berry and members of the media during that same time. The third itemized 572 telephone exchanges between Takeover Group members and members of the prosecution team during that same time frame—the majority of which were never detailed in any FBI reports.

As substantial as those numbers were, they didn't tell the whole story. They were compiled from records provided to Segal and Near

North in response to subpoenas and discovery requests in the civil law-suit against the Takeover Group and Cheley. "Because these records reveal only calls initiated by the cooperating witnesses and calls from only a portion of the phone lines they used, the records are incomplete," the motion said.

The defense team had analyzed the dates and times on the three lists and concluded: "Cooperating witnesses have given news of forthcoming government actions to the media before this information was available to either the defendants or the public and, for their own personal and economic reasons, have engaged in a systematic campaign to destroy the defendants' public reputations."

The motion recounted the calls FBI agent Murphy made to Matt Walsh and Dana Berry on the day Segal was arrested. It detailed how, beginning at 6:30 a.m., Walsh was a media-calling machine, dialing up the WBEZ (NPR) newsroom, the WBBM (CBS radio) newsroom and the WGN television newsroom. The prosecution's press release announcing the arrest of Segal was not issued until about 3 p.m. that day—more than eight hours later. The following morning, January 29, 2002, Kass published a column titled, "Rest Assured, Political Pals Feel Segal's Pain." Newspapers in Los Angeles, Las Vegas, and Washington, D.C.—all cities where Near North had an office competing head-to-head with Aon—published articles about Segal's arrest.

The analysis showed that on February 22, 2002—the day that Segal was arraigned—Gallagher telephoned the FBI at 7:12 a.m.—two hours before the arraignment occurred. Exactly eleven minutes later, Gallagher called Kass at the *Tribune*. Seven minutes after that, Gallagher called the FBI again and then Gallagher called Kass once more. The following day, the *Tribune* published an article about Segal.

The list went on and on.

Gallagher called Kass and the FBI regularly throughout the spring and summer of 2002, and—not one to play favorites—Gallagher also frequently contacted the *Sun-Times* reporter Steve Warmbir, along with other news outlets as well. In one eight-day stretch in October 2002, Gallagher called Warmbir nine separate times and during the same period was calling the FBI at least five times. Following these calls, Warmbir wrote an article headlined: "Feds Turn Up Heat On Insurance Mogul."

More calls from Gallagher and Walsh to Warmbir and the FBI followed. Two weeks later, on November 15, 2002, Warmbir published another exclusive article: "Segal Gave Heavyweights Sweet Deals on Insurance," based on a document obtained from an unnamed source. The document was described as a "VIP list." (In the later civil litigation, Gallagher would be accused of attempting to obtain it just before he left Near North.) The article suggested that Segal and Near North were providing discounts to curry favor with "powerful politicians" and "business bigwigs."

The analysis of material hacked by Cheley had revealed an email describing ongoing hacking of sensitive information and how some of it was being sent to the *Sun-Times*. In response, Segal set up a meeting with *Sun-Times* publisher John Cruickshank, who asked Segal to give him copies of the analysis of the stolen emails and communications.

In February 2004, *Chicago Tribune* reporter Ray Gibson telephoned Kevin Lampe, Segal's spokesman, and said that the prosecution had notified him that they would be unveiling another superseding indictment. Lampe would learn that whoever had talked to Gibson had specifically pointed him to a particular paragraph alleging that Segal had attempted to apply improper political pressure on regulators at the Illinois Department of Insurance. It seemed a blatant effort by the prosecution to get news media coverage.

These, Cognetti's motion said, were "only a small portion of the communications between the government's cooperating witnesses and the media. As is shown...the government's cooperating witnesses were in frequent telephone contact with certain members of the news media in the days and hours immediately preceding news stories that have been published regarding defendant Segal and defendant Near North.

"The evidence...shows a pattern of frequent communication between the government's cooperating witnesses and the FBI and also a steady flow of information from the witnesses to certain members of the media. This conduct has interfered with the defendants' right to a fair trial.

"Despite the Court's daily efforts to ensure that jurors are not influenced by outside sources, the conduct referenced herein is prejudicial to the defense and jeopardizes the defendants' right to a fair trial," the motion concluded.

It came as no surprise to the defense team when Castillo denied the motion.

Chapter 20

Showtime: Final Arguments

THE PRESENTATION OF THE CASE was finished. There would be no more testimony, no more exhibits and no more cross-examination. It was—as some lawyers call it—showtime.

During closing arguments, prosecutors and defense lawyers walk into the spotlight one last time to sum up all that has come before and leave the jury with the particular impression they have been working so hard to prove. Having been bound by strict rules about what they can and can't say throughout the trial, they are now unleashed to speak directly to the jury about whatever they wish—with the understanding that as long as they stick to the facts they've presented, there can be no objection by the other side. In courtroom dramas on the screen or stage, this is the climax.

In contrast to opening statements, when prosecutors and defense lawyers offer the jury a preview of what the evidence *will* show, closing statements provide an opportunity to tell the jurors what the evidence *has* shown. In spite of the latitude lawyers are given at this point in the proceeding, closing arguments are one of the most abused aspects of criminal trials. After months, perhaps years of preparation, in their zeal to win a conviction, prosecutors will at times play fast and loose with the rule of sticking only to the facts presented. Indeed, some former prosecutors have acknowledged over the years that when it came time to deliver their closing argument, they lost their self-control or, worse, were so concerned about losing that they intentionally crafted their argument to ensure a victory—even if it opened the door for a reversal by a court of appeals. The prosecution of Segal had been fueled by falsehoods, misstatements, and egregious overreach all along, so it was unlikely that the closing would be any different.

In February 2004, just prior to Segal's trial, the Seventh Circuit U.S. Court of Appeals noted in the case of *U.S. v. Mitrione*: "We consider claims that a prosecutor has tainted a trial with improper remarks under a two-step inquiry. We first consider the remarks in isolation. If they are improper in the abstract, we then consider them in the context of the entire record and ask whether they denied the defendant a fair trial. Only if the remarks undermined the fairness of the proceedings will we overturn a conviction."

In Segal's case, misrepresentations of the trial record during the prosecution's closing arguments were rampant. The prosecutors basically said whatever they wanted to say. Segal was baffled by how the system could go so far off track.

Throughout the trial, there had been little pretense about how the prosecution had guided the jury to despise Segal, but the name-calling in the closing arguments was remarkable, the epithets almost endless:

- Thief
- Embezzler
- Liar
- Ruthless
- Crook
- Fraud artist
- Schemer

- Tax cheat

- Political fixer

The prosecution is allowed two closing arguments, intersected by the defense's own. In this case, Hogan opened and was followed by Polales. Both hammered Segal as a man who "cooked the books," stole hundreds of thousands of dollars in cash from Near North, and "spent it like a drunken sailor." This, in spite of the fact that their own witnesses—leveraged and threatened with their own prosecution—had acknowledged during cross-examination that Segal was not like the man the prosecution portrayed him to be.

Under cross-examination, the government's witnesses had described Segal as a major insurance producer who paid himself less than he paid his executives, although he was entitled to much more. They testified that he was simultaneously operating fifteen to twenty companies, had an incredible work ethic, and was clearly passionate about the success of Near North. But that testimony was ignored or glossed over, along with any recantations, explanations, or clarifications that contradicted the government's scenario.

The prosecution's closing refrain focused on cash, cash, and—cash. They insisted that Segal had improperly received $150,000 or more in the form of envelopes containing cash, despite the only evidence testimony being the $125 cab fare Segal regularly received.

Hogan "reminded" the jury that Norm Pater, former Near North chief financial officer, testified that Watkins "routinely" brought an envelope containing $2,000 to $3,000 to Segal, and that he (Pater) had "stayed out of it because it was not an area he wanted to go into because it was an arrangement between two people that had been going on long before he ever got to the company."

There was every kind of wrong in that statement.

Pater had never testified to giving Segal $3,000 in cash. He'd actually said that he gave him an *unspecified* amount of money on *one* occasion and filled out a petty cash slip as to the amount and date so as to properly account for the money. Pater had never testified that there were routine transactions between Watkins and Segal.

Hogan told the jury that Near North employee Angelo Amaro had testified that Segal had gotten $3,000 to $5,000 weekly, in white envelopes. "Say it's $3,000 a week," Hogan declared. "That's $150,000 a year....not a nickel of that is reported on his tax returns."

But Amaro *had never testified to cash in white envelopes* nor had anyone else. (The closest reality to this statement was that, when the FBI had searched Segal's condominium and found several bundles of cash in a safe, they had photographed the money next to white envelopes they'd brought themselves.) Ultimately, even the U.S. Probation Office, during its presentencing investigation, found no support for that argument. In fact, Segal's forensic accountant, Dennis Czurylo, had traced more than $100,000 to Watkins. This was money the prosecution chose not to trace or, if they did, failed to disclose their findings to the defense. It was remarkable that even though Watkins was a cooperating witness—in effect, he was owned by the government—the prosecution at first said Watkins had taken only $7,000 and in the end never acknowledged that it was more than ten times that amount.

"So, Mr. Segal and Mr. Reidy, doing their job, went out to investigate and to try to tear down Mr. Watkins's credibility and to attribute as much of this petty cash as possible to him," argued Hogan. "And I don't know exactly what it was that they did or how long they did it or how much it cost, but what they came up with was about $1,500 that the government didn't find." This was an interesting misrepresentation, since forensic investigators had turned over evidence of Watkins spending tens of thousands of dollars in embezzled cash prior to the trial.

Although there had been no testimony stating that Segal had been aware of Watkins's embezzlement, let alone that he'd tacitly agreed to allow it, Hogan told the jury, "Did [Segal] let Dan Watkins dip into the account himself with a wink and a nod? Why not? There was plenty of cash to go around. He thought it was all his money at the company anyway. Let Dan Watkins take a little bit of it." The implication that Segal would not care that Watkins had stolen more than $100,000 was insulting to the jury, Segal thought.

Hogan then told the jury that Cindy Niehaus, another Near North employee, also was one of the people who identified Segal's squiggle on government exhibit No. 5, "that is, the approval for Dan Watkins to book the cash he was giving to Mike Segal to postage."

Again, just plain false. Niehaus had never testified about Exhibit No. 5 nor authenticated Segal's initials on that document.

The prosecution's closing was a litany of false evidence and mischaracterizations. Hogan claimed that another Near North employee, Mandi Miglets, had testified that she saw Watkins "frequently bringing petty cash in envelopes to Mr. Segal.… It was often. It was a usual practice, several times a week, that the envelopes were a half-an-inch thick and that she would see Mike Segal take cash out of the envelopes."

In fact, the only testimony on that subject from Miglets was that she'd seen Segal get his usual Monday morning $125 for cab fare.

Hogan told the jury that Near North employee Linda Callahan had testified that Segal told her to book cash to postage. Not true. Callahan had testified that cash for cabs and miscellaneous expenses were booked to petty cash expenses.

These prosecutorial misstatements subsequently would take up more than twenty-five pages of Segal's post-conviction brief. The prosecution misstated insurance law, misrepresented the testimony of numerous witnesses about issues of petty cash, and falsely claimed, for example, that Segal funded lavish personal Christmas gifts as Near North business expenses.

In a desperate attempt to persuade the jury that Segal did not properly account for money he received, Hogan argued, "There's not a single receipt in this case, in all of the evidence, that comes from Mike Segal." That statement ignored the American Express bills that had been placed in evidence, listing every transaction Segal had made. It further implied that any receipt of funds by Segal that was not offset by a receipt was unlawful, even though the evidence had shown that when cash was booked to Segal's draw account, the funds were either reimbursed or reported as income on his tax returns.

Hogan suggested that Segal had spent thousands of dollars inappropriately at Tiffany's for gifts and at Hermes for ties. In fact, the prosecution knew that Near North routinely gave five-year and ten-year longevity awards to employees consisting of Tiffany clocks and watches. None of those expenditures was improper or illegal.

Hogan told the jury that Karl Maheia had worked for Near North from 1984 to 2002 and worked for Sentry Fire, a Near North company, "for a while," while at the same time serving as a driver for Segal's wife, Joy on Tuesdays, Wednesdays, and Thursdays.

In fact, since Joy Segal had tutored him and personally paid for his college education, Maheia had volunteered to drive her and did not get paid for it. There was no evidence that his work was done on the clock of any Segal company.

Testimony had established that verifying the accuracy of accounts payable was critical—Pater had called it "very important. Actually, it's a key function."

Yet the general ledger balance did not match the journal payable balance, a critical defect underlying every prosecution accounting exhibit.

Because the prosecution had not wanted to risk doing a comprehensive government audit of Near North, it misrepresented preliminary work done by Deloitte & Touche as an "audit." Hogan told the jury that, "Christian Perez [of Deloitte & Touche] testified that he did the books and records for the audit."

But Perez had never testified that he performed an audit.

Hogan told the jury that Perez "testified repeatedly...that the books and records at Near North were completely accurate as far as he was concerned. Because why? He tested them. He did reconciliations. He went to the underlying accounting records. He looked at the general ledgers."

What Hogan didn't point out was that on cross-examination, Perez had testified there were *no* work papers associated with his work, that in fact *he did not do any reconciliations,* nor had he never looked at the payables—meaning that he didn't go into the "underlying" records. Hogan said Perez "looked at the general ledgers." What did that mean? Taking a look is not the same as performing a reconciliation. The fact that the defense objection to this falsehood was overruled particularly infuriated Segal, but he was no longer surprised by anything at this point.

The prosecution argued that Near North's conduct could have resulted in customers having their insurance coverage cancelled. "Picture the (Chicago Transit Authority's) insurance getting cancelled or other people as well, huge construction contracts, big municipalities, major casinos in Las Vegas and other places that Mike Segal wrote the insurance contracts for through Near North getting their insurance cancelled. No risk of loss? That's nonsense."

This was a misstatement of Illinois law, which says that when a customer pays a broker, the payment is attributed to the carrier. There is no risk of a customer having the insurance coverage cancelled—no matter what the broker does with the customer's money. This was a most crucial piece of evidence in that it basically nullified everything that flowed from it.

One of Hogan's craftier maneuvers came during his argument relating to the Premium Fund Trust Account. It was the key misrepresentation that the jury, the public, and eventually the Seventh Circuit U.S. Court of Appeals would buy into it. In fact, the appeals court would actually cite it to justify the denial of Segal's appeal. In the end, all believed that Segal had breached his fiduciary duty even though everyone had gotten paid and everyone had gotten insured.

"[It's] just like if you went to a lawyer and you said, you know... my grandfather died, and I'm getting a lot of money from his estate," Hogan told the jury, "and the estate is closing and there's going to be a disbursement from the bank, and I want you to hold the money. And you give it to your lawyer, and the lawyer puts it in a client fund trust account." In fact, an insurance broker's PFTA is not the same as a lawyer's trust account. A lawyer *does* have a duty to keep a client's money in trust and no disbursement is permitted unless it is for the benefit of the client. An insurance broker's PFTA, on the other hand, is a *fungible, commingled* account with accounting proscriptions to provide for an audit trail to establish a preference for paying insurance carriers.

Perhaps one of the more egregious arguments was Hogan's claim that Pater called Near North a Ponzi scheme.

"As Norm Pater told you, it was, in effect, a Ponzi scheme," Hogan said. "A Ponzi scheme takes money from one person and pays it out to another and to another and to another, and as long as you keep building up the pyramid and you have enough suckers on the bottom, the people at the top get the money, and then one day it stops. Sort of like a game of musical chairs."

What was wrong with that? Hadn't Pater used that term while he was testifying?

Well, yes, he did, but, as Hogan so conveniently left out, on cross-examination Pater retracted that statement as a mischaracterization. In fact, Near North generated real—not fake—multi-million-dollar profits annually.

Hogan also argued that Segal had improperly pressured the Illinois Department of Insurance to defer an audit of Near North's PFTA compliance, specifically claiming Segal used the influence of Illinois Governor George Ryan to pressure insurance officials into delaying such an audit. However, the testimony was that the audit was deferred because the insurance department did not have the manpower to conduct an audit immediately, and because the department did not perceive the situation at Near North to constitute a crisis demanding immediate intervention.

And then there were the members of the Takeover Group.

Hogan told the jury, "Devra Gerber, Jeff Ludwig, Dana Berry, Matt Walsh, all promised for years and years, lied to. I will fix it. They all quit. Is that the notion of somebody who's trying to take over Mike Segal's company—that they all walked out the door because they were so concerned about their own criminal liability?"

Not only did the Takeover Group members not testify at the trial, there was no evidence at all that they were concerned about their own criminal liability. In fact, the FBI knew—because they had the information in one of their own reports—that Gerber told them she had consulted an attorney who had assured her that she had *no* potential criminal liability regarding Near North's PFTA. The only criminal exposure for the Takeover Group was for their involvement in the illegal hacking of Near North documents and theft of Near North business on behalf of their new employer Aon.

After days and weeks of presenting false testimony, Hogan presented an argument that was the fruit of a bad seed.

Then it was the defense's turn to try to set the record straight.

Cognetti, representing Near North, went first and sought to defuse the wealth issue. "We've heard about wealth in this case many times," he said. "We have heard numbers that make my eyes roll. I'm a second-generation immigrant and our forefathers, as many of yours did, came to this country seeking wealth and opportunity. But there is a natural resentment, at times, against large corporations that make big profits, against people who have money and lead different lifestyles.

"Please do not stereotype any individuals or any corporations,"

Cognetti urged. "For stereotyping and prejudice and bias may be a cover for the lack of evidence…. Will *we* ever have the money that's mentioned in this courtroom? No. But don't resent those who work twenty-four hours a day or seven days a week to build something.

"There is a great danger when we give in to those biases and prejudices, and there's a great danger when we let those biases and prejudices become evidence."

Cognetti was at his most eloquent in addressing the issue of loss. "Now," he began. "Near North, as a corporation, we've been called thieves. We've been called racketeers, all sorts of things. Where is the person who did not get that which they were entitled to? When did you hear that person testify?

"Don't thieves take money and disappear with it? Do thieves try to correct problems? Do thieves mortgage their houses and put them into the business? Do thieves go out and borrow money?

"All those acts are inconsistent with criminal intent…and that's where the issue is going to be engaged—on criminal intent."

Cognetti paused and cleared his throat.

"And what should the government…to meet their burden…have said? Well, they should have presented a witness who took the stand, raised their hand and said, 'I'm an insurance company. Yes, we did business with Mr. Segal over there, Near North, and we didn't get paid. I'm Sal Cognetti from Scranton, Pennsylvania, and I took out insurance, and it was cancelled because of nonpayment, but I paid them.

"Isn't that the type of evidence you're entitled to hear? Or, how about the credits?" Cognetti continued, shifting gear. "I had a credit due. I paid, I canceled, there was an endorsement, and I never got my money. Isn't that what you're entitled to hear? Is that a reasonable doubt?"

Reidy struck a similar theme, reminding the jury that the prosecution had gone to extraordinary lengths to "separate you from Michael Segal so that you don't feel like one of his peers, so you feel like he's someone else, that he's apart, that he's rich, that he's a con artist. It's been a major effort [by the prosecution] in this case. If you look back at every time something was said, every chance there was to stick it in—it was stuck in."

Point by point, witness by witness, Reidy pointed out the lack of evidence—most notably the fact that there had been *no accounting evidence backed up by work papers or Generall Accepted Accounting Principles.* The accounting "evidence" was at the heart of the government's manufactured prosecution. Hearing this, Segal silently lamented the decision not to present any expert accounting witnesses to show the incompleteness and inaccuracy of the government's evidence.

"I think if you look at the evidence in this case, across all the counts and everything that's being discussed, there are substantial holes in the case," Reidy said. "Remember, they have to prove guilt on each and every count, and on each and every element of each and every count beyond a reasonable doubt, and that's a very tough standard. It's not supposed to be easy to convict somebody. You don't convict somebody because you *think* they're probably guilty.

"The government wants you to convict this man of fraud where there's no loss, where not a single victim has testified, nobody has said I lost a credit, no insurance company came in and testified about what they thought about the PFTA situation. A couple of the biggest insurance companies in the world loaned money into it. There's no intent to cheat anyone."

Polales, in the rebuttal argument—to which the defense cannot respond—came back to the April 20, 2001 email that McNichols claimed he sent to Segal—although the evidence strongly indicated it was never delivered and never sent. This letter was a blueprint, actually, because it covered up the first, unsuccessful attempt to force Segal to cede control of Near North to the Takeover Group. It also supported various misleading and false accounting exhibits, created the foundation for the character assassination of Segal, and the injection of political taint. In short, the Takeover Group had created a concise package to hand over to the prosecution.

Polales told the jury:

> *"That letter is a summary narrative of a historical set of events, which basically sets forth in a summary fashion all the stuff that you heard in the trial from the witnesses on the witness stand. It's a piece of evidence offered to explain what was going on internally in the company, what was driving the people at the point in time when they were really getting to the point where they couldn't put up with the risk of detection anymore, McNichols and the managing directors, and when they stood to lose all that they had worked for with Mr. Segal in terms of good jobs, good comrades, the collegiality, the joking, their life as they knew it, which was put at risk.*

Polales then added:

> *"[The] April 20th letter, 2001, signed by Dana Berry, Matt Walsh, Jeff Ludwig, Tom McNichols, cc: Sherri Stanton, general counsel, four pages. I'm not going to reread it, but if there is a written summary of the evidence in this case, this, ladies and gentlemen, is it. This is years and years and years of frustration by the top people at Near North putting in writing, in very specific terms, how fed up they are with Mike Segal."*

In reality, the so-called "blueprint" was a contrived piece of paper that the Takeover Group used to leverage the FBI into investigating Segal and Near North.

Polales couldn't resist a classic cheap shot, trying to suggest that Segal had a guilty conscience—in effect, that he knew he had done wrong—because he hired a lawyer. Everyone in the courtroom knew that crossed the line.

Polales told the jury, "Who does [Segal] run to after the misappropriation of trust funds through the fraudulent means is likely to be exposed if one wrong move is made? He goes to one of the best criminal defense lawyers in the city [referring to Reidy]."

Reidy bolted up from his chair. "Your Honor," he declared. "There's no evidence—"

Polales cut him off.

"That was in the evidence," he retorted.

"The objection is sustained," Castillo declared.

"I believe it was in the evidence," Polales persisted, as if by continuing to say so, it would magically appear in the evidence, and that even if it didn't, the jury would believe him and not Reidy.

"It's not in the evidence," Reidy said.

"All right," Polales said—and then gave it one more shot, unable to resist the opportunity to prejudice the jury. "And why does he do that?"

And then, the arguments were over. The judge instructed the jury on the law and the jury began to deliberate.

Chapter 21

The Verdict Is Guilty

On June 21, 2004, after more than two months of trial, the eight men and four women on the jury deliberated for a mere eight hours before filing back into Judge Castillo's courtroom and handing the verdict forms to Castillo's clerk.

In silence, Castillo reviewed the verdicts and handed the forms back to the clerk, who read them aloud. Segal was implacable as his lawyers tallied the results. The jurors, some of whom appeared variously through the trial to be bored, distracted or disinterested, were stone-faced. The trial had been a grind and some undoubtedly were not overjoyed about spending multiple months here, even if it was their civic duty.

On each of the twenty-six counts of mail fraud, racketeering, false statements, embezzlement, and tax conspiracy, the verdict was the same: Guilty.

The jury found Segal guilty of each and every one of the illegal acts charged in the indictment, although Castillo later dismissed sixteen of them as unsupported by the evidence.

Near North was also convicted on all of its twenty-one counts.

As the jurors were polled to affirm their verdicts, Segal flashed back to the day of jury selection, when Reidy had rejected a prospective juror who was an accountant—the only one in the jury pool. When Segal expressed concern about this, Reidy said he believed accountants were "too precise." Segal had understood then—and was reminded now—that more precision was *exactly* what the case had needed.

Castillo advised the jury that they were not finished with their service; a forfeiture proceeding would begin immediately. They would hear evidence and decide if Segal should forfeit as much as $35 million pursuant to the racketeering conviction. This clearly did not sit well with some jurors as looks of aggravation spread across their weary faces. Castillo sent them back to their deliberation room to decide whether they wanted to begin the forfeiture hearing immediately or to return the following day. Segal believed that despite Castillo's repeated denial of defense objections and motions, if he would have decided the forfeiture proceeding instead of the jury, Castillo would have seen through the accounting misrepresentations and the absence of defense accounting witnesses, and acted accordingly. But with a jury, Segal had little hope.

As soon as the last juror was out of the courtroom, Hogan was on his feet as if he had been salivating for the moment for years.

"We'd like Mr. Segal taken into custody immediately," Hogan declared. "I can't believe there's any doubt about the fact that he is a flight risk. His word is certainly, as the jury's determined, not worth very much, and we believe he should immediately be taken into custody. By our calculations under the [sentencing] guidelines, he's looking—depending on the amount of loss that the court finds—at a minimum of twenty years. He's sixty-two years old. I believe he has absolutely nothing to lose by fleeing this court's jurisdiction."

Hogan's request was extremely rare in a white-collar prosecution. Was this to twist the knife in retaliation for Segal's attempts to expose the government misconduct? On a more practical level, being incarcerated would make it difficult for Segal to consult with his attorneys in preparation for sentencing.

"What is the present bond, just for the record?" Castillo asked.

"I think it's a million dollars," Hogan said. "Mr. Reidy?" Castillo said.

Reidy rose. "Judge, this is the first I've had a chance to address this or heard about it, but I guess my position with respect to this issue, Judge— there's really no basis for putting Mr. Segal in custody immediately. He's not had any time to get his affairs in order. And, indeed, even from the point of view of the forfeiture…putting Mr. Segal in jail would be counterproductive.

"But I think, most importantly, Judge, Mr. Segal has always indicated his respect for the court and the law and the proceedings at every juncture and I think [he] is not a flight risk and [is] somebody who will proceed with respect to this thing in a legal fashion. And if he has issues, [he] will take them up on appeal… I believe the court or the court personnel have already acquired his passport, and his ties to the community—his ties to the things he cares about—are immense."

Segal sat in stunned silence.

"I believe that's true," Hogan said, "but, as the court's aware now, the situation has changed radically."

"Well, I do think that the situation has changed radically," Castillo said. "Let me take it under consideration. In the meantime, I would say this: Until we hear anything else, Mr. Segal should not go outside of this courthouse."

The jury returned and said they wanted to get on with the forfeiture hearing immediately.

Prosecutor Kendall—who would one day point to this case as the crown jewel in her career as a prosecutor and a primary reason for her nomination to a federal judgeship—stood up and addressed the jurors.

"No truer words were spoken in this courtroom than in the very first day when the defense argued to you that Mr. Segal wanted to expand into a nationwide network of financial service entities," Kendall said. "That is true. That was based upon greed. It was based upon a need for power. And it was based upon his desire to keep the wealth of that company for himself…. We are going to be seeking that you find $35 million is forfeitable from Mr. Segal—$35 million that he took based upon the violation that you have found unanimously that he committed."

The prosecution then summoned its first witness, Sue Prescott, a financial analyst for the FBI. Prescott testified that based on her "calculations" (none of which were true accounting procedures), Segal had diverted funds for personal and business use and left a hole in the company's finances equaling approximately $35 million. Her testimony was based on a list of bank deposits made during December 2000, January 2001, and February 2001. She had assumed that the deposits were made to plug a hole in the PFTA.

Prescott conceded that she did not know where those deposits were applied. Her testimony was designed to create an impression that she had performed an accounting reconciliation when in fact she never did. If depositing money was a crime, then no one was safe.

Hogan's last question to Prescott, in an effort to deflect the cross-examination he knew was coming, was, "Did you have documentation to try and calculate the disbursal of those funds out of the PFTA to see where they went?"

"No," Prescott replied. Hogan's purpose here, which he fulfilled handily, was to suggest that a lack of documentation was perfectly acceptable.

Reidy then began his cross-examination.

"I actually want to address first your statement right there at the end of your testimony that you did not track the money out of the old PFTA, is that correct?"

"No," Prescott said.

"So, your summary testimony here has to do with money coming into the PFTA, is that right?"

"That's correct," Prescott said.

"And, as you sit there, do you know what was done to the money that came into the PFTA?"

"No."

"And, so do you know how much of it was applied toward an existing PFTA deficit?"

"No."

"And, could you have done that analysis if you had taken the bank accounts and analyzed them further?"

"Probably."

"And, if you want to know how much money was necessary to pay premiums from old PFTA insurance…you want to look at how much money they spent on that, right?"

"Correct."

"And, you could have performed that analysis, right?" "Yes."

"But you did not perform that analysis." "No," Prescott admitted.

Prescott left the witness stand with her testimony in tatters. But in the end, either the jury didn't understand the evidence or they ignored it.

Then, a curious thing happened.

For the first time after weeks and weeks of trial, the defense finally called an accountant to the witness stand.

Reidy had put his associate in charge of the rest of forfeiture proceeding, saying that he had alienated the jury.

The defense initially planned to present an analysis by accountant Andrew Lotts showing that money Segal had borrowed was used to expand Near North and its subsidiaries and therefore that the forfeiture should be restricted to the amount of interest that would have been paid to a lender. But, in the end, this theory was abandoned.

Having done the comprehensive forensic work that no one else had attempted in reconciling Near North's accounting, Lotts was more than ready to testify that the government's numbers had absolutely no basis in fact.[49] Lotts and his accounting team had spent more than 14,000 hours reconstructing the books and records of Near North and con-

---

49   Lotts testimony at Forfeiture trial.

ducted a forensic analysis at a cost of $1.3 million. He and his assistant, Jill Skidmore, had tied out beginning and ending balances that reconciled the receivables and payables, examining more than one million transactions annually. They had concluded that the prosecution's accounting evidence was unreliable and based on computations that were impossible, incomplete, inaccurate, and false.

The prosecution's conclusions could not be verified because there were no working papers as required by the most basic accounting standards. In fact, according to Lotts, not a single prosecution witness who had testified at Segal's trial had provided a reliable computation of the records of Segal's insurance business. There was nothing that reflected the *origin* of accounting numbers *and the simple addition and matching of controlled accounting with detail and the aging of accounts payable.* Instead, the prosecution had presented the ginned-up spreadsheets of McNichols along with the misrepresented regulatory accounting methodology.

Lotts said there could be only one conclusion since it was a matter of mathematics. There was no $35 million hole—Near North was $5 million *to the good!*

Lotts testified that the accounting evidence recomputed from the prosecution's own record showed that the government knew or should have known that the $35 million evidence was "impossible, incomplete and inaccurate."

In Lotts' professional opinion—backed by working papers and based on Generally Accepted Accounting Principles—numerous prosecution exhibits had no basis in fact. On the contrary, the prosecution's "accounting evidence"—the sole evidence of the PFTA reconciliation deficit—was incomplete, inaccurate, and false.

Lotts prepared a simple chart to show a comparison of the prosecution's exhibits that purported to show the state of the PFTA and his own calculations, as follows:

Date	Exhibit #	Govt. calculation	Lotts calculation
12/31/1998	72	-$6,980,000	+$1,597,506
10/19/1999	81	-23,800,000	+$1,483,949
07/31/2000	108	-$6,918,000	+$638,350
04/30/2001	109/110	-$29,000,000	Inscrutable
06/30/2001	98	-$35,000,000	+$5,852,861

Lotts and his team determined that what the prosecution contended were the working papers from McGladrey & Pullen's engagement, actually were just status reports.[50]

"Nowhere in those work papers, at any level—audit, compilation, or review—was there substantiation for the PFTA reconciliation that was calculated here nor any of the numbers," Lotts testified.

Whether genuine working papers ever existed was doubtful. During the prosecution's case, Deloitte & Touche's Christian Perez testified that he couldn't find his working papers although he did not perform any reconciliations. An assistant to Hogan told the defense that the working papers were "lost."

Lotts said he had been suspicious of McGladrey & Pullen's report of a PFTA deficit ($23.8 million deficit, Exhibit No. 81, 10/19/01), so he went to the Near North accounting department and "asked them if it was even possible, being skeptical as an auditor that I am, (that) they could print a report mid-month…" as McGladrey & Pullen claimed.

"And the first thing they said is that would (have been) very difficult, if not impossible, because the computer system had been down," Lotts said. The numbers, he added, were "highly subject to error, given the fact that not only was the computer system down for that week, [but] the [computer] conversion…had completely failed."

---

50   Lotts Master Affidavit 10/17/13.

During cross-examination by Polales, Lotts went even further.

"I think their work was absolutely horrific, given the situation," he said. Polales suggested that Lotts was testifying negatively about McGladrey & Pullen because he had a poor opinion of the firm. "So, when I asked you the question, you didn't really like McGladrey & Pullen, you could have answered that with a yes, right?"

Lotts replied, "I have always regarded McGladrey & Pullen as a very fine accounting firm, until I saw the quality of the work that was performed on this engagement by them."

Polales wouldn't give up.

"So, I'll ask you again," he said. "When I asked if you didn't really like McGladrey & Pullen, you could have answered that with a yes, right?"

Lotts replied, "It's more detailed than that. It's not a like or a dislike. It's the quality of their work product in this engagement."

Polales appealed to Castillo. "Your Honor, I don't think his last three answers have been responsive, and I'd move to strike them."

"I'm not going to strike them," Castillo said. "I'm also going to ask you to refrain from argumentative questions."

Polales asked Lotts if he had his working papers, apparently hoping that Lotts would say he didn't have them. But when Lotts said his working papers were in his briefcase in the witness room, Polales abruptly changed the subject.

Lotts told the jury that the "numbers," which were prepared by and testified to by McNichols, were not even consistent within the exhibits themselves and there was no documentation to support them.

As for the exhibit that purported to show a $24 million negative reconciliation—the government's most important exhibit in the forfeiture—Lotts concluded that was false, too. Lotts's analysis showed that taking the prosecution's own acknowledgment of cash in the PFTA and subtracting the Illinois statute-required PFTA balance as of June 30, 2001, the resulting balance was a surplus of $5,852,861.

Lotts testified that the analysis was the work of a team of people, was supported by work papers, and fell within the requirements of the Illinois insurance statute.

This surplus stood in stark contrast to Poggenburg's claim of a $24 million PFTA-use deficit. The prosecution was asking the jury to order the forfeiture of $35 million, a figure Hogan reached falsely claiming that a $10 million escrow deposit was expended before June 30, 2001, which boosted the deficit to $35 million. He made that claim even though he had subpoenaed multiple bank records showing that the money was in the bank as of that date and the government's own Exhibit No. 550 also showed the money was in the bank.

As Segal listened to Lotts testify, he began to realize how different the outcome might have been had the testimony been presented during the guilt phase of the trial. Later, one of his lawyers commented that he admired Lotts's strong demeanor. Segal thought, *you might have realized this beforehand if you had shown serious interest in his work and taken the time to meet him.*

When Castillo recessed until the following day, Polales asked again that Segal be taken into custody, saying that the "likelihood of any relief that would get him out from under the exposure that he now has, he would have to be hoping for a miracle. And I don't think that's how a very smart, very business-savvy man will look at his odds in this case."

Reidy countered, "I think it's worthwhile to pay attention to Mr. Segal's faithfulness to the Court's orders through the proceeding and I think he has every reason to try and manage his way through this within the system, Judge, and I think that's what the Court should expect. He's never shown any desire to flee. You know, this possible result has been there for a very long time. And I would say...that the Court would be better off and acting more justly to allow him to have some time to deal with his affairs."

Reidy did not cite federal guidelines regarding bail for first-time, non-violent offenders, as Segal clearly was, but as even the judge knew, it is a rare defendant who doesn't get an opportunity to remain free before sentencing.

"There are a lot of factors to consider," said Castillo. "I think it's an understatement to say that Mr. Segal's world has dramatically and drastically changed after the jury's verdict and I have to take that into consideration. But I also have to take into consideration that Mr. Segal is still on trial with regard to this forfeiture and I am leery to interfere with Mr. Segal's ability to be able to consult and defend the forfeiture." So, while Castillo said he would not jail Segal during the forfeiture hearing, he would require him to wear an electronic monitoring ankle bracelet.

"I think the situation is dramatically changed," Castillo said. "I think there's every incentive for Mr. Segal not to stay here. I'm very familiar, in the course of my other full-time job, with what the sentencing guideline implications are. I am also very familiar that money does buy things like passports and means to move and it is a factor what age Mr. Segal is right now, given the potential sentence he faces."

The fact was, however, that all of Segal's assets were restrained. He had put everything he had into defending the company and its employees from ruin.

But then Castillo displayed the rest of his hand.

"And so, I will tell you, after tomorrow, it's going to take some mighty lawyering to convince me to allow Mr. Segal to remain free for an extended period of time up until his sentencing because I think time is a factor and time allows movement."

"Mr. Segal," Castillo said, "do you have any questions about this?" Rising from his chair, Segal said, "Not at this point, Your Honor."

"Do you understand that if you divert from your Lake Shore Drive place or your Highland Park place in any way toward O'Hare [International Airport] or Midway [Airport], you will be taken into custody by order of this Court? Do you understand that?"

"Yes, I do, Your Honor. That's the furthest thing from my mind," Segal replied.

And with that, court was adjourned.

Outside the courtroom, Segal's son Jonathan seethed. Approached by reporters, he responded to their questions with a question of his own: "You call that justice?"

There was no reply.

That evening, in a telephone interview with a reporter, Segal said he was disappointed at the swiftness of the verdict. Yet, he declined to criticize the jury's decision, saying the case was extremely complicated.

"Insurance is very esoteric. It's hard to get to the core of the evidence if you have all this other rhetoric," he said, referring to the "highly inflammatory" name-calling by the prosecution.

That wasn't the last interruption of the night. At 3 a.m., the monitoring center, in what Segal believed was intentional harassment, telephoned and falsely accused him of unauthorized movement.

Chapter 22

Forfeiture and End of Freedom

THE NEXT DAY, JUNE 22, 2004—the last day he would be a free man for the next eight years—Michael Segal appeared calm as he strolled into the Dirksen Federal Building. But inside, he was in tumult. The question hanging over him was life shattering: What would be his fate? He'd been one of Chicago's most successful businessmen—a man who had built Near North Insurance Brokerage into a firm employing 1,000 people with offices in seven states and the United Kingdom.

Just looking at Segal, it was hard to imagine that, altogether, he had just been convicted on twenty-six counts, including mail and wire fraud and racketeering. Despite the seriousness of the situation, Segal remained as garrulous as ever, chatting with a group of reporters outside the courtroom as they waited for Judge Castillo to take the bench. There was no doubt that Segal would be sent to prison, although for how long was still a matter of speculation. But right now, the press had another question: Would Segal cooperate with federal prosecutors in the hope of shortening a potentially lengthy prison term?

As one reporter put it, "Are you going to be a flipper?"

"I never worked in the circus," Segal retorted, smiling the smile that had charmed clients and friends for more than four decades. What he wanted to ask in return was how the reporter could actually believe a crime had been committed and what about the attorney-client privilege violations, the massive hacking of Near North emails, and the taping of his own attorney?

Lotts resumed the witness stand and continued dismantling the false accounting claims of the prosecution. Lotts's analysis actually prompted the prosecution to abandon its supposed evidence of a PFTA deficit and shift to unsupported theories in order to arrive at the $35 million loss claim.

Lotts pointed out the implausibility of the prosecution's $35 million deficit claim by noting that a prosecution exhibit reflected a $7.7 million PFTA surplus *just three months later, on September 30, 2001.* Additionally, another government exhibit showed that as of August 31, all of Near North's insurance premium payment obligations were current. This exhibit along with an affidavit had been submitted to the Illinois Department of Insurance to show that there was no PFTA deficit of $35 million as of June 30, 2001.

Lotts shredded Poggenburg's testimony. "Government witness Poggenburg, through a series of leading questions by Hogan, avoids the complete recognition of all the PFTA bank accounts as of June 30, 2001," Lotts declared. "Poggenburg does so by stating that he did not perform bank reconciliations nor did he review Near North's bank reconciliations. Poggenburg had direct knowledge of the $10 million bank account balance when he conducted his review in August 2001." Through Lotts's accounting reconstruction, Segal had finally exposed the flaws in the prosecution's accounting exhibits.

But would this matter? Segal wondered. *It should,* he thought, *because it is rare that the government's own records and exhibits prove that statements made under oath were false. But would the jury listen to a defense accountant at this stage of the proceedings? They were tired and worn down and wanted to go home. They already voted to convict. Was there any amount of new testimony that would change their minds?*

During jury selection, an IRS agent had worked closely with the prosecution, frequently leaving the courtroom and then returning. Segal believed at the time that the agent was conducting background checks on prospective jurors so that those selected would be people with little accounting backgrounds so they would be more easily swayed by the prosecution evidence. Now, Segal wondered, *would these men and women be subconsciously prejudiced against a man of his wealth?*

Ironically, the prosecution's claim that Segal had raided Near North's assets to the tune of $35 million, and that the jury should claw it back through forfeiture, could have been foreclosed or mitigated had the prosecution not torpedoed two proposed pretrial escrowed sales of Near North. If these sales had been allowed to go forward, the true value of Near North would have been established through an arms-length deal with a disinterested third party.

Prior to indictment, Near North had been worth approximately $250 million, but after Segal was arrested, the value of the company decreased by more than $100 million. At a pretrial meeting between the prosecution and attorneys from Winston & Strawn regarding a proposed sale of Near North assets, the prosecutors made it clear they had no interest in the actual economic value of the corporation. According to a Winston & Strawn memorandum of the meeting, Polales said that the government would "go to war" if the company did not obtain permission for the proposed sale of assets and would seek to force any new owner to forfeit the company as part of the RICO proceedings—an outlandish assertion without a legal basis. Polales had smirked that the prosecution really didn't care about insurance producers in the John Hancock Building. Any pretense of protecting the public interest, as well as the jobs and livelihoods of company employees at Near North, had been cast aside in the zeal to obtain a conviction.

Subsequently, when the defense presented evidence that the government blocked efforts to sell the firm it had seized, Hogan claimed that there was no real sale opportunity because no letter of intent had been signed. However, Winston & Strawn had sent an email to Hogan with a letter of intent to purchase Near North. This was not the last time Hogan would make this misrepresentation.

The government had warned Segal that he needed to understand that—like the total annihilation of one-time accounting giant Arthur Andersen in the Enron scandal—he would suffer severe consequences if he chose not to cooperate. Polales actually said that the government was prepared to take a "scorched earth" approach to dealing with Near North—that U.S. Attorney Patrick Fitzgerald was an aggressive prosecutor who "wouldn't bat an eye to do another Arthur Andersen." In fact, that had been a baseless threat since, in the wake of the Enron affair, Justice Department guidelines had been amended to ensure a more judicious approach when investigating and prosecuting a corporation.

Hogan had said that if Segal would agree to plead guilty—an offer that was immediately rejected—the likelihood of a sale of Near North would increase. In the end, however, by blocking the sale, the prosecution passed up $90 million in escrowed cash that would have been paid to the U.S. Treasury, as well as the chance to save the jobs of hundreds of people. That was all in the past, though.

The closing arguments began with Kendall making an impassioned plea, entreating the jury to decide that Segal should forfeit $35 million. She repeatedly referred to a $35 million "hole" in Segal's insurance business, created by his burning desire to build a national network. "He put the money in his pocket. He lived a life of excess. He lived the life of the hotshot around town. And you know what? He was the emperor with no clothes. He was spending other people's money."

This analogy, which the prosecution had used several times, was a clear attempt to divert the jury's attention from the fact that there were no victims and no actual losses.

Kendall ignored the only forensic accounting evidence and belittled

Lotts's analysis as essentially too little and too late. She repeated the prosecution theme that had been repeated for months, day after day, week after week: Segal was a thief and a crook.

In the defense closing statement, McNulty countered by saying a $35 million deficit did not exist and the number was fabricated. "The $35 million deficit in the PFTA that they're referring to is not something that was ever received by Mr. Segal," he said.

What would the jury believe?

Shortly after 5 p.m., the jury filed silently back into the courtroom. The clerk read the forfeiture verdicts: Segal and Near North were to forfeit $30 million. Segal was to lose 60 percent of his interest in his company. (Castillo later amended that to 100 percent.)

The jury was dismissed and Hogan stood up and demanded that Judge Castillo order Segal taken into custody immediately. This was highly unusual—years later when Illinois Governor Rod Blagojevich was convicted and would ultimately get a 14-year sentence, he was allowed to remain free pending sentencing.

Hogan claimed that Segal was probably still in possession of considerable liquid assets and was a flight risk because of his age and the threat of a significant prison sentence.

"He is the quintessential person…with every incentive in the world to flee," Hogan argued. What went unsaid was that by incarcerating Segal immediately, the government would severely curtail his access to his lawyers, limit his ability to work on the accounting for his appeal, and deny him access to a computer. Where Segal would get any assets was puzzling—his assets were about to be restrained.

It really didn't matter what Reidy said in response—that Segal had been respectful and had always shown up, even returning from an overseas trip and surrendering his passport; and that he could use the time to assist in the orderly distribution of assets to satisfy the forfeiture—the judge already had made up his mind.

"I think today we've come to the end of the line for Mr. Segal," Castillo said. "And I'll tell you why."

"I think Mr. Segal faces a substantial sentence in this case...I think at his age, any sentence would be seen as substantial," Castillo said. "Then, add to that the forfeiture determination that was just made, and then I look at what are the prospects of some other change in this outcome...and I think those prospects are nil."

"Mr. Segal has every incentive to flee. If I looked at the situation from the category of someone who's always followed the law for his whole life from day one until the last day, I think that *that* person would have an incentive to flee," Castillo said. "But then when I add to that the fact.... that Mr. Segal is not one to take the law very seriously, he comes nowhere close to even making it a tie, let alone meeting his burden of [showing] that he will stay here and face the music...Mr. Segal is remanded into custody," Castillo declared.

These statements were extremely prejudicial to Segal since he had never before been accused of any crime, let alone of any state insurance violation.

At a later hearing for bail, the prosecution was so determined to keep Segal locked up that when Reidy subsequently said that friends of Segal were willing to cover a $5 million bond, Kendall made the unsupported argument that the people posting the money were so wealthy that even if Segal fled and the bond was forfeited, the $5 million would not be missed.

Segal believed that Kendall was adamant about him being taken into custody because it would enhance her chances of being nominated as a federal judge—a nomination that was made just a few months later, in September 2005. The delay of about eighteen months until Segal's sentencing would hamper his ability to connect with his lawyers because of the restrictive conditions at the Metropolitan Correctional Center (MCC) where Segal was housed. Segal believed that Kendall wanted him locked up to hamper his efforts to expose the government's evidence as false, which would reflect adversely on her.

Calmly, Segal rose from his chair at the defense table. He was determined not to show emotion. With steady hands, he removed his wristwatch, pulled out his wallet and his ever-present medications. He handed them to a paralegal and turned to face two deputy marshals who were waiting patiently. Gently and quietly—almost apologetically—they escorted him through a side door to the lockup. One bailiff, who had been in the courtroom throughout the trial, had a hard time looking Segal in the eye. "I feel sorry for you and for what has been done to you," he said.

Soon after, Segal was at the MCC. When he first arrived, through the kindness of the intake supervisor, Segal was allowed to call his family briefly to assure them he was okay and to apologize for what had happened. His first stop was a holding cell and that's when the reality of what was happening—a cold reality—began to truly sink in. He could not step across a threshold without permission. Segal was given a snack—fruit and potato chips, but the empty feeling growing inside wasn't hunger. As the cell door closed behind him, Segal noticed that a white man, perhaps in his 20's or 30's, also was in the cell. In seconds, scenarios flashed through Segal's mind. Should he say something? What would it be? Will he be a target?

He noticed the man eyeing the food.

"Hey, you want this?" Segal held out his hand. "I'm not hungry."

"Sure, thanks," the young man said. "I just got here."

"Why are you here?" Segal asked.

"I got arrested," he said. "They say I robbed a bank this afternoon. What about you?"

"It's complicated," Segal said. "They just took my company away from me."

The young man sat quietly, save for the crunching of the potato chips. He asked no more questions.

So passed Segal's first moments of confinement. It would be a long time before he would be free again. Right now, there was almost too much to process. He concentrated on presenting himself as confident and self-assured so as not to suggest weakness.

The first day he was in his cell, several guards barged in and tossed everything. Somehow a newspaper columnist learned of the call he made to his family and reported it, prompting officials to suspect Segal had a cell phone, which is a prohibited item. Of course, no cell phone was found.

After weeks of hearing false accusations, Segal tried to comprehend the loss of his business and his freedom. As Segal had said to a reporter weeks earlier: "We are destroyed."

At the time he said those words, Segal was referring not just to himself, but also to his family, friends, and all of the people who had helped build Near North. They all had to watch it disappear because of the greed and self-interest of a handful of former employees.

Chapter 23

Attacking the Verdict

*"The Fifth amendment is…one of the great
landmarks in men's struggle to be free of tyranny,
to be decent and civilized."*

—Justice William O. Douglas

TWO MONTHS LATER, IN AUGUST 2004, Segal's lawyers filed a post-conviction motion asking Castillo to overturn the convictions on numerous grounds—some of which had been argued prior to and during the trial, but previously rejected by Castillo.

The motion contended that Segal had not written off any credits: "No customer who is alleged to have lost credits testified that he or she was deceived about anything. None of them even took the witness stand. The prejudice resulting from the improper submission of this charge as part of a single scheme or artifice to defraud fatally tainted the jury's verdict on the mail fraud, wire fraud, and RICO counts."

The defense argued that mail fraud was different from theft or stealing, and that the government included the premium credit evidence as a course of conduct because it was easier for the jury to grasp, even though no customer had suffered a loss. However, the jury instructions did not require the jurors to specify which course of conduct had occurred.

Segal himself had found a significant ruling by the Seventh Circuit U.S. Court of Appeals in 1995, *Richards v. Combined Insurance,* which held that return premium credits *cannot be subject to RICO prosecutions.* "The evidence of record shows only that the defendants said that they would return the premium and that they did return premiums," the court ruled. "Such evidence hardly supports a case for mail fraud and certainly does not support one for RICO convictions."

The post-conviction motion also asserted that the prosecution had failed to present any evidence that supported counts sixteen through twenty-two, which alleged that Segal and Near North had made false statements to the Illinois Department of Insurance in connection with financial reports or documents.

These counts also charged Segal with violating federal statute 1033, which prohibits anyone engaged in the business of insurance whose activities affect interstate commerce to knowingly, with intent to deceive, make a false material statement or report or willfully and materially overvalue any land, property or security. But there was no proof that Near North and Segal were "engaged in the business of insurance." As defined by the U.S. Supreme Court, Near North was a broker and did not underwrite risk—a fact that had been conceded by the prosecution during the trial.

Secondly, the motion pointed out, "the government offered no evidence that Mr. Segal or Near North submitted any records to the Illinois Department of Insurance (or any other regulatory body) which might arguably qualify as 'financial reports or documents' within the meaning of the statute." This was something that Reidy had not pointed out during the trial. The seven Near North license renewal applications to the Illinois insurance department, which were the basis of the charges, were not in Segal's handwriting.

"The government's flip-flopping on this issue speaks volumes as to the weakness of its case," continued the motion. At one point, the prosecution said the false statements were in financial reports Near North was required to keep under state insurance law. At another point, the prosecution said the false statements were in applications filed for state insurance licenses.

Segal advised his lawyers that this license-filing claim was far-fetched because no financial records were required and there was absolutely no proof at trial that any financial records were ever presented to any insurance regulatory official or agency as required by law. In fact, Castillo had ruled as such in response to a defense motion for acquittal saying there was no misrepresentation or nondisclosure.

The motion noted that the legislative history of the enactment of the false report statute confirmed that the law was not intended to apply to insurance broker license applications.

"In sum," the defense motion said, "the indictment failed to allege and the government failed to prove that Mr. Segal or Near North made a false statement 'in connection with any financial reports or documents presented to any insurance regulatory official or agency.'"

The motion said that Castillo had erroneously barred the defense from presenting evidence that Near North—as a brokerage firm—was not in the business of underwriting insurance or underwriting risk. "At trial, the Court barred defendants from arguing that any statements made in the license renewal applications were not 'in connection with any financial reports or documents,' and that defendants were not engaged in 'the business of insurance.'"

The motion cited defense attorney Donna Walsh's request, prior to the closing arguments to the jury, that the defense be able to argue those points to the jury.

"You are not permitted to make those arguments to the jury," Castillo had said. "The next place you'll make those arguments, if you're not successful, will be somewhere else. That's what I can say about that."

The motion asserted that Castillo's denial had prohibited the defense from challenging the prosecution's proof relating to an essential element of the offense.

The motion also attacked the tax conspiracy conviction relating to Watkins's embezzlement. "Mr. Segal should be acquitted of Count 28 because the government presented no evidence of an agreement between Mr. Segal and Mr. Watkins to defraud the United States. Despite Mr. Watkins's plea agreement that compels him to cooperate with the government and places him under the government's control, the government never called Watkins to testify at trial," the motion said. "Instead, to satisfy the agreement element, the government relied entirely on a single 1989 memo purportedly drafted by Mr. Watkins to Mr. Segal.

"The Court erred in admitting a substantial amount of hearsay that did not fit within any exceptions to the hearsay rule," the motion said. "For instance, the Court admitted hearsay from several Near North employees who never testified at trial and whom defendants never had an opportunity to cross-examine." The list included Watkins, as well as Takeover Group members Berry, Ludwig, Walsh, Gallagher, and Gerber. In addition, the motion contended that Castillo had erroneously allowed into evidence out-of-court statements from several outside consultants of Near North. Under the Sixth Amendment, a defendant has a right to confront—cross-examine—his accusers.

Furthermore, the motion said that Castillo had mistakenly refused to bar the government from suggesting that a PFTA deficit placed customers at risk of loss.

"In Illinois, once insurance is bound through a broker like Near North, the insured customer is covered whether the broker forwards the premium to the carrier or not," the motion declared. Castillo, the motion said, was incorrect when he said he was "not convinced" that the state law eliminated the possibility that any of Near North's customers would suffer a loss.

The defense additionally said there could be no violation of the law without a scheme to deprive someone of money or property. This was not a matter of ignoring case law, the defense said. Rather, Castillo ignored the state statute, the defense said. There had even been a 1993 Illinois Appellate Court decision, *Scott v. Assurance Company of America*, which upheld the statute.

The motion renewed the defense argument that Castillo had erroneously denied the pretrial motion for an evidentiary hearing relating to the cyberhacking. The motion also noted that the defense had presented evidence that cooperating witnesses had "advance notice of certain FBI witness interviews, and, in turn, used this knowledge as leverage in urging *at least* one Near North business partner to leave Near North."

The defense raised, once again, their claim that the prosecution had not turned over any written record of hundreds of phone calls placed to the FBI by McNichols, Walsh, Berry and Gallagher during the investigation and prosecution.

"In its effort to secure a conviction, the government thwarted the truth-seeking process, stretched the rules of evidence, and exploited every opportunity to portray Mr. Segal and Near North as wealthy, powerful, and thereby deserving of punishment, all in violation of basic notions of fundamental fairness and due process." Among other things, the motion also noted that the government:

- Followed through on a threat to file additional charges if Segal continued to press the civil lawsuit against the government's cooperating witnesses which is a separate constitutional right to address our federal courts.

- Poisoned the jury with its accusation that Segal had lied to federal investigators, only to withdraw the charge during the trial.

- Offered inadmissible lay opinions concerning alleged violations of state law even though those crimes were not charged.

- Exploited Segal's relationship with local politicians and other well-known customers to portray him and Near North as "politically connected" and therefore unsavory.

- Knowingly accepted information that had been unlawfully hacked from Near North's computer system.

"Each of these abuses prejudiced the defense; viewed in their totality, they deprived defendants of the right to a fair trial guaranteed by the Fifth Amendment," the motion concluded.

Four months later, Castillo agreed that the prosecution had failed to present any evidence that the license renewal applications were financial reports or documents. "Given the complete absence of evidence establishing that the license renewal applications were financial reports or documents, we conclude that no rational jury could have found that defendants made a false statement 'in connection with any financial reports or documents presented' to the Illinois Department of Insurance," the judge declared. "Furthermore, no testimony established that the license renewal applications had any potential influence on any state official."

So, Donna Walsh had been right when she brought up that very issue during the jury instruction conference. But it was too late now to know whether this issue had any overarching prejudicial influence on the jury regarding the rest of the case. Judge Castillo overturned the convictions on counts sixteen through twenty-two and granted a judgment of acquittal.

Castillo then rejected the remaining defense arguments. "Defendants…asserted that we should have barred the government from arguing that defendant's abuse of the PFTA placed a risk of loss on consumers. They assert that under Illinois law the customer is afforded coverage from the carrier even if the broker does not pay the customer's premiums," the judge said. "We remain unconvinced that this state law provision eliminated the possibility that one of these Near North customers would suffer a loss as a result of defendant's abuse of the PFTA." This ruling signaled that Segal would be facing a lengthy prison sentence. Castillo said there was "overwhelming evidence" of Segal's guilt. He then set sentencing for February 23, 2005.

Chapter 24

Eighteen Months in Jail Before Sentencing

Designed by noted architect Harry Weese, the Metropolitan Correctional Center in Chicago opened in 1975. Standing twenty-seven stories tall, the "Prison in the Loop," so called for its location inside the elevated train tracks that loop around the city's central business district, was built in the shape of a triangle. The jail, which houses all levels of security, was designed to hold 440 inmates, but on any given day the population exceeded 600. The cells are separated into self-contained modules designed for forty-four inmates. Each module has two floors with single-room cells around a perimeter and a common area in the middle, as well as a guard station. Each cell has a slit window—bars were added after an escape in 1985—five inches wide and seven feet high. The cell doors are metal—no jail bars—and are locked at night and opened in the morning. There is a daily head count at 4 p.m. and anyone not in his cell is punished.

After Segal was convicted and the prosecution was arguing that Segal should be incarcerated until his sentencing, a member of the defense team heard prosecutor Kendall say, "Whatever we do, we must keep Segal here."

During his incarceration there, Segal avoided looking out of the narrow window of his cell. It was too painful to see the buildings of many of his insurance customers. It reminded him of the unfairness of what had happened.

Some windows looked out onto a parking lot, where prisoners' girlfriends or wives occasionally put on dance or strip shows. Anyone whose window provided a good view of these festivities was subject to takeover through polite intimidation by inmates.

Technically, the MCC is classified as an "administrative security facility," because defendants are held there while awaiting trial. It typically holds inmates accused of a wide array of crimes ranging from white-collar fraud to drug dealing, bank robberies, and contract killing. To handle the highest-risk inmates, the MCC is, in reality, a high-security institution. All inmate telephone calls are recorded except for conversations with attorneys. Visiting is tightly controlled and visitors—including lawyers—have to wait endlessly before even getting to the only elevator. Credentials are strictly checked. This onerous process discourages visitation.

In Segal's case, every visit concluded with a strip search. He was not allowed to pass any paperwork to his lawyers and could not receive any from them.

On his first day, Segal tentatively walked into the area where lunch was being served to about seventy-five prisoners. Cautiously, he selected a seat near the guard's desk. He ate quickly and quietly and returned to his cell, intending to attract as little attention as possible.

Ultimately, Segal met an array of characters there, including alleged members of organized crime and street gangs. He discovered that his media notoriety earned him some respect. Other prisoners considered him a "neutron," meaning he was not connected to any gang and was not perceived as a physical threat. On occasion, he saw verbal and physical confrontations, which were quickly broken up. He never felt in jeopardy. Segal developed a rapport with his MCC case manager, Charvella Christmas, who was the supervisor of all case managers and whose office was on the seventeenth floor, where Segal was housed. When Christmas learned that Hogan had been one of Segal's prosecutors, she went out of her way to allow Segal to use a private, unmonitored telephone—which was highly unusual. It turned out that years earlier, she had disapproved of El Rukn gang members getting preferential treatment in the prosecution overseen by Hogan, which had led to his firing.

Segal would always credit Christmas with helping him survive his initial confinement. When he first arrived, one of her assistants took him aside and advised him that if anyone threatened him or acted improperly, Segal should let them know. While he never felt the need to complain on his own behalf, he did speak up when an abusive inmate forced another inmate to give up his cherished once-a-week hamburger. Within days, the abusive inmate was transferred to another floor. Segal saw that Christmas spoke the inmates' language and could not be intimidated. She managed to keep inmates in place in a respectful way. She did not express favoritism and kept a watchful eye out for any signs of trouble.

Meanwhile, Reidy bowed out of the defense team for the sentencing and appeal. This was disappointing because Reidy knew the case and because he had successfully obtained a reversal in the case of Chicago alderman Larry Bloom, who had been convicted under a similar honest services theory.

At the recommendation of his friend Jerry Solovy, a well-respected attorney at Jenner & Block, Segal hired Marc Martin for the post-conviction proceedings. Martin, in turn, made a strong pitch for Segal to bring in attorney Jeffrey Steinbeck, a sentencing expert who shared an office with Martin. Bringing in Steinbeck, Segal later said, was his worst decision of all.

Segal would learn that Kendall had mentioned during a presentencing hearing that Steinbeck was coming into the case. This was before

Segal even had hired him, which Segal saw as evidence that his lawyers were talking behind his back.

It was hard enough to try to constructively contribute to his defense efforts given the MCC restrictions, but Segal's plight became exponentially more difficult after prison officials refused him access to Provigil or a similar medication, which he had taken daily for many years to combat his attention deficit disorder. The chief psychologist at the Federal Bureau of Prisons did not approve of the use of such medications by inmates, and when the defense raised the matter, Castillo declined to intervene.

Segal had not raised ADD as part of his defense during the trial, although that hadn't stopped the prosecution for ridiculing him about it. Polales had asked Mandi Miglets, who was a college student working part-time at Near North and had no medical or psychological training, if Segal had "any functional business disability" and she had said, "No, and the ADD wasn't a disability."

During closing argument, Hogan as part of his barrage of sarcastic cheap shots, said, "Now, this isn't somebody with an attention deficit disorder. This is somebody with an insurance premium deficit attention disorder."

Segal found the testimony and comments hurtful and insulting because he had worked with many young children to help them understand the strengths and weaknesses inherent in the disease. Near North employees were aware of his challenges with ADD, as well as his longtime support of charitable organizations associated with it. He had established a special in-house program, run by Joy, for employees and their family members similarly afflicted.

Segal also suffered from dysgraphia, a disability that often overlaps other disabilities such as ADD, which affected his ability to write things down coherently. For that reason, he'd customarily dictated his emails and correspondence. These handicaps had created major burdens for

Segal in communicating with his lawyers when he was free, let alone when he was in the MCC. His new lawyers—Ed Joyce, Martin, and Steinbeck—had to rely heavily on Segal for information.

In November 2004—after five months of confinement—Segal's lawyers filed a renewed motion for release on bond, arguing he had no way to obtain funds if he were to try to flee. A trustee had assumed control of Segal's business and the prosecution was seeking to freeze all of his assets. After years of scrutinizing Segal, if Segal had any hidden funds, the prosecution would have found them. The motion described Segal's close family ties and the fact that he had become a grandfather in recent months and had only seen his first grandchild while in custody. The motion also noted that Reidy had not fully described Segal's significant community ties. Numerous letters were attached from people of influence in the city of Chicago, including former Chicago School Board president George Munoz; Monsignor Kenneth Velo, principal aide to the late Joseph Cardinal Bernardin; retired Chicago Police Superintendent LeRoy Martin; and Jerry Reinsdorf, owner of the Chicago Bulls and Chicago White Sox. All of them said Segal was not a flight risk.

Family members and friends offered to post property and cash totaling more than $5 million so Segal could be released on bail to get his affairs in order.

"We believe it is safe to say, as a general proposition, defendants convicted of non-drug and non-violent crimes have been permitted to remain on bond pending sentencing and thereafter self-surrender at the designated institution," the motion said. Segal's attorneys could find not a single case in which someone convicted for the first time of a financial violation with no loss and no victims was denied bail before sentencing. Most urgent, though, was Segal's medical condition. The defense noted that Segal entered the MCC with four prescriptions, but the MCC only allowed one. As a result, Segal's ADD had "not been adequately controlled…and Mr. Segal's ability to focus and to communicate with counsel" had diminished.

"Mr. Segal's physical condition has recently taken a turn for the worse. His body is covered with hives and rashes. Some of them have become bloody (and susceptible to infection) due to an incessant need to scratch. Medical attention at the MCC is scarce. Mr. Segal has been required to wait weeks at times to see a doctor." As proof, Segal unbuttoned his orange prison jumpsuit and showed the rash on his chest to Castillo. *Chicago Tribune* columnist John Kass used that moment to ridicule Segal as a once-powerful political figure reduced to whining about his medical condition.

Castillo declined to release Segal on bond, but he did order the MCC to review Segal's medical condition and make sure he received the proper medical care "ASAP."

No medication, however, was forthcoming. Castillo's order gave the jail officials wiggle room to do nothing.

First, Segal was taken under guard to a government-funded psychologist at the University of Chicago. That evaluation was inconclusive and quoted Segal as saying things he later denied he said. A month later, he was taken again under guard to a court-appointed psychologist in downtown Chicago. Based on Segal's responses, the psychologist suggested that he ask one of his lawyers to file a motion to allow the MCC to modify conditions so that Segal could work more effectively. Segal shared this suggestion with Steinback, but nothing was done. Although the report that was issued said Segal understood the purpose of sentencing and that he was fit to be sentenced, it did not mention that Segal felt he had been cut off from his defense.

Then Segal was sent to a psychiatrist at the federal medical prison in Springfield, Missouri. He wondered whether this was an attempt to delay his sentencing. In the bizarre world Segal now inhabited, while Castillo could not get the MCC to allow Segal his medication, Kendall was able to get court approval for a private plane with two guards to take Segal to the facility, which housed federal prisoners with mental disorders. Segal was sent on a holiday weekend, resulting in a stay of five horrendous nights in maximum security. During that time, he met an inmate who nonchalantly admitted that he had threatened to kill two U.S. presidents.

Segal participated in two, forty-five-minute sessions with a psychiatrist. The doctor told Segal that he understood his circumstances and how anxious he was, and that he was doing a remarkable job of controlling his emotions.

Upon his return, the prosecution filed a sentencing memorandum outlining its version of the proof in the case. Kelly Rice, Segal's probation officer, suggested he prepare a "defendant's version" as a "valuable complement" to the probation department's presentencing report (PSR). A PSR documents the history of the person convicted of a crime—favorable and unfavorable—which the sentencing judge can consider in crafting a sentence. Segal greatly appreciated Rice's advice and attention.

Working from the 6,000-page trial transcript, Segal compared the prosecution's sentencing memorandum to what had actually been said at trial.

Painstakingly, he began assembling a document in rebuttal. Hour after hour, day after day, week after week, and month after month, Segal labored over his response. Steinback assured him that he could present it at sentencing.

Segal developed a good relationship with the MCC warden and during an interview with the media he spoke favorably about the MCC's operations. Subsequently, Segal asked the warden for permission to bring in a court reporter to assist him in preparing his sentencing appeal. The request was referred to Castillo, who said he had no objection, but had no jurisdiction. Although the warden was optimistic, the jail's legal counsel rejected the request. Segal later was informed the denial came after Kendall objected.

Ever resourceful, Segal used his commissary funds to hire inmates to type up his response. Ultimately, this document totaled one hundred fifty-four pages and itemized the false testimony and unsupported evidence relating to the PFTA deficit.

Segal pointed out numerous facts that were asserted as occurring at trial, but in fact did not. And meanwhile, Segal's lawyers (without the participation of Steinback and without any input from Segal) filed their own response to the prosecution's sentencing motion, attacking it for including summaries of statements from numerous people who had not even testified at the trial. This included Takeover Group members Dana Berry, Devra Gerber, Jeff Ludwig, and Matt Walsh, as well as Daniel Watkins.

"First, the government has failed to demonstrate that the out-of-court statements are sufficiently reliable," the motion said. "Second, the use of hearsay information at sentencing, or to calculate the advisory guideline range, violates the Sixth Amendment right to confrontation." That argument was based upon a 2004 U.S. Supreme Court ruling, *Crawford v. Washington*, which held that cross-examination was required to admit prior statements of witnesses who were not available. Justice Antonin Scalia, writing for the majority, said that defendants have the right to live testimony from the witnesses against them, even if the accusations could be presented in other forms.

After months of research and study, Segal was ready. Martin and Steinback told him that they would present Segal's document as well accounting testimony to rebut the prosecution claims.

Chapter 25

Sentencing Debacle

SENTENCING DAY—NOVEMBER 30, 2005—FINALLY ARRIVED, eighteen months after the jury's verdict and three weeks before Kendall would be confirmed as a federal judge by the U.S. Senate. Segal would forever believe that his sentencing had been delayed so that Kendall's background investigation could be completed before there was any investigation of defense claims of misconduct during the investigation and trial.

Segal, clad in an orange jumpsuit, was grim-faced as he took his seat at the defense table. He had just learned that his 154-page version of the evidence was not going to be presented. Even more distressing, there would be no accounting testimony. There would be no witness to testify about premium credit write-offs. Segal was floored.

Months earlier, Martin and Steinback had told Castillo they would present accounting testimony and Castillo had agreed to allow them as much time as they needed. And, indeed, on this day, accountant Andrew Lotts and his assistant Jill Skidmore were in court, ready to be called.

When Martin first suggested Steinback be hired, he told Segal, "No one is as good as Steinback when he is at his best."

But it appeared to Segal that this was not the Steinback he got. Segal probably shouldn't have been surprised. In the weeks prior to this day, Steinback had scheduled and cancelled numerous meetings and failed to respond to more than fifty telephone messages. Segal had harbored the feeling that Steinback was too cozy with prosecutor Kendall. At the moment when his freedom and the work of a lifetime were hanging in the balance, Steinback, Segal felt, had sold him out.

Castillo started by denying the defense motion to strike the unreliable hearsay testimony from the Takeover Group and others that was included in the PSR. The judge then granted *all* of the prosecution's objections, *without giving any reasons*. Incredibly, Steinback had not filed any objections to the prosecution's PSR.

Moving briskly, Castillo turned to the sentencing guidelines.

Federal sentencing guidelines, which went into effect in 1987, were intended to bring uniformity to sentences across the United States. Based on a mathematical formula and stated in months, each offense carries a base level and additional enhancements are applied, depending on a number of factors.

The judge rejected the defense argument that the revised (and more severe) guidelines, which went into effect after November 1, 2001, should not apply to prior offenses. This decision automatically would translate to a longer incarceration. Castillo adopted the prosecution's argument, saying, "I believe that enough facts have been proven to me either by way of trial testimony or by way of reliable hearsay…to use the sentencing guidelines that went into effect after November of 2001." Never mind that the hearsay from the Takeover Group was anything but "reliable" and had been shown to be false by Lott's analysis.

Turning to the issue of loss, Castillo said. "I am adopting the government's position in this case…we have a loss here that matches the forfeiture requested—that is, a loss that is in excess of $30 million. And I think that the arguments that were made in the government's submission really hit the nail on the head, and that is that the view of the defendants in terms of Mr. Segal's conduct is over-simplistic and that this was a straight theft from the PFTA."

Although Castillo praised the presentencing report as one of the finest he had ever seen while on the bench, he ignored the portions that said Segal and Near North had no fraudulent intent regarding the PFTA and that combined with no losses, should result in a sentence of about 18 months. Segal could hardly believe what he was hearing. Both the presentencing report and the judge's final written opinion had acknowledged that there was "no loss." How could Castillo claim that this was a case of "straight theft" when the prosecution had offered no evidence of a single improper disbursement or even one unauthorized check to Segal?

Years later, Segal recalled that moment. "It felt like I was in a tribunal in a corrupt Third World country, where the judge automatically accepts claims by prosecutors while ruling out any attempt by defense attorneys to insist on actual facts."

Segal wanted to leap up and shout that there was nothing close to a theft in the record. He wanted to remind Castillo of his prior ruling that there were no misrepresentations to clients by Near North and that the PFTA was not a conventional trust account and therefore could not have victims. Castillo was simply wrong to speak of a "risk of loss," and ignored the state insurance statutes and supporting case law which provided that "customer payments to an insurance broker are deemed received by the carrier."

The only genuine "loss," as far as Segal was concerned, was his $250 million company and $50 million worth of assets.

Castillo then declared, "I also believe the government has met its burden to use the sentencing enhancement…that this offense involves at least twelve victims with regard to the credit write-offs." This statement also seemed untethered from reality given that the government never produced a single client who testified to an improper write-off.

The judge agreed with the prosecution that the offense involved sophisticated means, citing the prosecution statement that, "For over twenty years, Mr. Segal operated a large enterprise comprised of multiple entities in violation of the law." This, too, ignored the trial record, which stated that Near North of Chicago was the only entity involved. Moreover, defense attorney Ed Joyce had filed an affidavit from the Department of Insurance saying that Near North *had never had a violation.*

"[Segal] did so," Castillo said, "through a sophisticated scheme that included the manipulation of top managers, the refusal to allow outside auditors to release public information regarding his books and records, his control over those in the accounting department, his intentional maintenance of inadequate computer systems, and his bold refusal to permit anyone to tell him how to operate his business legally. Nothing could be more sophisticated than this practice.

"Completely matches my view of the testimony, having reviewed the transcripts," Castillo said.

Segal believed that none of Castillo's statements were supported by the trial record, except by hearsay from McNichols.

Castillo did reject the prosecution's claim that the sentence should be increased for affecting a financial institution. "I am giving the benefit of doubt to Mr. Segal and will sustain the objection that has been made by defense counsel and I will not use this enhancement," he said. The charge never should have been brought in the first place because the statute referred to stockbrokers, not insurance brokers.

At the outset, the prosecution had called for an enhancement figure of forty-two, representing a factor in determining the time of incarceration, which would result in a minimum sentence of thirty years in prison and a maximum of life in prison. Castillo's rulings cut the enhancement figure to thirty-eight, which meant that the sentencing range was nineteen years and seven months to twenty-four years and five months. Segal felt this was a meaningless gesture by Castillo to appear to be compassionate.

Castillo then turned to the defense recommendations and reduced the enhancement for loss from twenty-two to sixteen, thus cutting the overall enhancement to thirty-two, which put the sentencing range at ten years and one month to twelve years and seven months. The problem, Segal realized, was that the judge did not follow his commission's own guidelines for the starting point for determining his sentences. By using a "risk of loss," Castillo had erroneously inflated the enhancement figure. In making the downward departure by rejecting some of the government's extravagant claims, he was making himself seem fair, but was really just gaming the numbers. Worst of all, the judge and the prosecutors completely ignored Lotts's forensic testimony at the forfeiture trial that the five government documents on which the case was based were in fact false.

So, even before a single word of argument, Castillo had set the stage. Unless he could be convinced by Segal's defense to make an additional downward departure and impose less than the minimum, Segal would face at least ten years in prison. At the same time, unless the prosecution could convince Castillo to depart upward, Segal would face no more than twelve years and seven months.

Before the sentence was formally imposed, Segal lawyer Edward Joyce rose to point out errors in the PSR based on Near North records that were unreliable. The result, Joyce said was that "many of the people who testified in this case were using less-than-reliable data, and when you use less-than-reliable data, you get a less-than-reliable answer."

Joyce said that after spending considerable time with Lotts, it was clear that the PFTA deficit "is based on testimony at trial that the witnesses acknowledged was pretty much of a guesstimate, that they didn't have the opportunity and didn't go back and review the underlying entries. They didn't review the underlying supporting schedules. They didn't review the underlying accounts."

Joyce continued, "And consequently, the number they had was—we think was incorrect...Mr. Lotts's firm spent a great deal of time, looked at...the underlying schedules, the canceled checks and the payments and they came up with a number ...which is radically different." In fact, Lotts determined there was a surplus of $5.8 million.

"But, again, I believe that that's sort of a red herring because the issue here to me is who lost money other than Mr. Segal's loss of a very valuable brokerage business," Joyce said. He cited affidavits from Lotts as well as the Illinois Department of Insurance that "no insurance company ever wasn't paid their premium; that no brokerage client of Near North ever was denied coverage; and in terms of loss, I would submit that's the loss we should focus on."

"In addition, there's no evidence anywhere, to my knowledge, that suggests that Mr. Segal took the deficit from Near North Insurance and put it in his pocket," Joyce added.

Castillo became testy at that suggestion and lost patience with Joyce altogether. The judge appeared to have already made up his mind.

"So," said Castillo, "you're saying that if I'm a bank president and I can walk into the vault and get $3 million, I can go and invest in whatever I want, as long as I don't lose the money—take it to Vegas and lose it—I'll be okay?"

"Absolutely not, Judge," Joyce said.

These are not the facts of the case at all, Segal thought. *There wasn't one dollar of one transaction submitted into evidence that was unauthorized by the statute.*

Castillo cut him off.

"That's the equivalent of what you're arguing here," the judge said. "I'm not going to sit here and just stay quiet because I presided over this trial, and now what is going on is sort of a revamping of what occurred in the trial testimony," he said. "So, you can keep going, but my question to you, Mr. Joyce, is, given the ruling that I've made to adequately reflect what is in my view a loss, a ruling that is favorable to Mr. Segal, what are you doing? Are you just making your record?"

At the defense table, Segal looked on in disbelief. *Of course, that's what Joyce was doing. Isn't that what he was supposed to be doing?*

In an attempt to pacify Castillo, Joyce said, "I was going to segue immediately to what I think is a loss that Your Honor addressed and I think possible the government misstated."

Joyce said that the prosecution had identified 12 customers who were entitled to premium credits totaling $542,000.

"We went out and contacted people listed on that list of folks," Joyce said. "The most significant person was Waste Management. They were allegedly entitled to $357,000. There's an affidavit from a Waste Management executive saying they're not entitled to that credit.[51] Second, we approached Ticketmaster—"

Again, Castillo interrupted. "Isn't that more accurately an affidavit indicating they don't believe they're entitled to it?"

Castillo is playing word games, Segal thought. *The majority of the credit write-offs were to Waste Management, which had provided an affidavit that it was not owed a credit.*

"That is correct," Joyce said.

"And isn't it more accurate to say that this trial record reveals much more than just 12 potential rip-offs of customers for purposes of these write-offs?" Castillo asked.

Even without the inflammatory language, Castillo was mistaken. *He's got this wrong, too,* Segal thought. Both the trial record and the sentencing report said that the total entries made on the books relating to credits equaled $106 million. Segal had issued $28 million worth of credits to clients, and that there was no evidence of any other credit write-off issues.[52]

"Well, when it comes to credits, there were millions and millions of credits that were applied to customers of Near North," Joyce replied. "If Mr. Segal was attempting to steal vast amounts of money...from credits, they wouldn't have applied millions and millions of credits, and we wouldn't be focusing on twelve."

---

51   Waste Management Haufe Affidavit.
52    $28M of credits returned to clients.

Castillo was perturbed. "I'm not focusing on twelve.... I am obligated under the sentencing guidelines to make a reasonable estimate of what I believe the losses are."

"I'm not second-guessing you—" Joyce began.

"I think you are, Mr. Joyce," Castillo retorted. "I think you are. And the problem is, I sat up here during the trial every day, every minute, and you, sir, respectfully, did not."

Castillo was in no mood to be challenged any further. He was sticking to a loss of more than $1 million by more than ten victims to justify the sentence he was about to impose. "So," he said. "Right now, your argument, boiling it down to its essence, is you believe the evidence at trial...does not establish a loss of over a million dollars?"

"That's correct," Joyce said.

"I totally reject that, having reviewed your affidavits," Castillo said.

Segal wondered, *Has he actually read the affidavits? If so, does he imagine that these people are lying under oath?*

And with that, Joyce sat down.

Prosecutor Kendall then began the prosecution argument on how long Segal's sentence should be.

"He stole the money and he used power and clout to cover his tracks. This is a quarter-century of crime," Kendall declared, even though the Illinois PFTA statute was less than 10 years old at the time of the alleged crime.

"People need to know that their money will be secure," she said. "They need to know that it will be safe. It is going to send a strong message to the insurance industry that you cannot gamble away other people's money, and promoting that respect for the law is critical in this case. And the fact that this one, this crime, went on for [a long time] is a factor that you should take into account as well."

As for sending a message to the insurance industry, a different message was already present. Every major insurance carrier had provided letters of support to Segal.

Now it was Steinback's turn, and he focused a plea for mercy based on Segal's attention deficit disorder. This statement had been provided in writing by Segal's family, who had been led to believe it would helpful. But in fact, it didn't matter, which Steinback and certainly Castillo knew.

Years later, Segal would look back at Steinback's performance and regard it as little more than an attempt to create sound bites. Steinback's speech couldn't make up for his refusal to present Segal's response to the presentencing report. Steinback had scared Segal's family prior to sentencing by saying that if he argued too aggressively, Castillo would retaliate and sentence Segal to thirty years in prison.

Segal later said, "In his own way, I would say Steinback was worse than Hogan, who at least acted as a prosecutor seeking a conviction even if he engaged in prosecutorial misconduct. Steinback seemed to go out of his way to disrupt and undermine any defense on my behalf at sentencing and it became clear that it was not an oversight. I was unaware at the time of allegations that he had traded off clients in deals with prosecutors. In my case, he avoided every professional responsibility he had as an attorney, including the failure to point out the facts that there were no losses to clients, no false credits, and that any loans were fully collateralized. He became a part of a wrongful prosecution based on manufactured evidence." (Segal later was told that Steinback subsequently left his law practice for a year to take a job working for a car dealer.)

Steinback told Castillo that Segal's life at the MCC had been an "absolute living nightmare" because his medications had been denied. He portrayed Segal as a generous man who made many charitable contributions and helped the less fortunate.

"Mike never passed a homeless person without reaching into his pocket and giving them money," he said. "The fact is that he lived sixty-two years of his life without even a single charge or arrest, much less a conviction, and that is mitigating. He overcame this level of ADHD to become a lawyer and a CPA, and that is mitigating. The fact that he lost those degrees and can never retrieve them is of some moment; the fact that no one handed him a thing, that he worked his way up through the industry for over forty years, that is mitigating. And the fact that he made his own breaks, he created his own opportunities, he took a temporary accounting job, which had him randomly assigned at some fledgling business called Near North while he was working his way through law school. There he worked, he struggled, he climbed the ladder of that company until fifteen years later, he could buy it," Steinback said.

"Then, he made new inroads in the insurance industry, and these can't be ignored—products such as movie business insurance. He grew the company from three employees to over nine hundred; grew the premiums from $700,000 to a billion; and he became the largest independent insurance broker in Chicago. And this was not job spoon-fed to him by some kindly uncle. He built it nearly from scratch and at one point, it was preeminent nationally in seven different states. And because mistakes were made does not undo forty years of hard work and they cannot boil it away. It's not fair."

Steinback went on to quote Segal's wife, Joy, as saying that many times Segal "couldn't sleep at night because he knew he had so many people who were counting on him. She speaks about the fact that he loved the insurance business. He wanted to treat his company like a family business. It is especially excruciating for Mike and his family to read that the government's identification of a class of victims in this case are the employees of Near North who either had to find other jobs or were dismissed because of the ruin of Near North. A lot of these people are in this room. They're here because they care about him. They're out of a job and they still care. Those jobs, that family business, it's all but gone and with it an entire life's work.

"The Moody Bible Institute has expressed a debt of gratitude to Mr. Segal for a two-hundred-fifty-unit building that it has and one person from that institute said that...[Segal] 'made Moody Bible possible for the city,'" Steinback said. "There are some twelve hundred senior citizens in section eight housing because of Mr. Segal. There has been for years funding to the battered women's homes through the Chicago archdiocese because of Mr. Segal. Michael Segal's family prays this Court tempers justice with mercy, prays this Court finds Michael Segal to be unique, prays this Court gives him full measure because he is a fundamentally good man, not a fundamentally bad one. And right now, Your Honor, he clearly is in his most dire of need," Steinback said.

Finally, Segal rose to address Castillo himself.

"I stand here a man of different circumstances," he began. "My family has different circumstances. A thousand and plus people who relied on me have different circumstances. I have a tremendous amount of remorse. I'd like to spend some time and discuss that with you."

Segal looked directly at the judge.

"I believe in our system and the system said that the jury found me guilty," he said. "I can't do anything about that in front of you at this point and I respect that."

Castillo interrupted.

"But you disagree with the verdict, fundamentally, Mr. Segal, right?"

The interjection seemed a cheap shot to Segal and unsettled him in what was already a difficult situation. Of course, he disagreed with the verdict, but he was attempting to speak in a measured way. The "remorse" he'd referred to was because he'd hired a number of employees who had betrayed him and because he had not presented the defense he'd wanted.

"Yes, I do disagree with the verdict, and I don't know whether it's a good thing or a bad thing to explain why I do or not," Segal replied.

"You can proceed," Castillo said. "And let me just tell you, this is your time at this point, so you can take all the time you need. But I do find that you disagree with the verdict, and I find that troubling because you say you have remorse. But I think it's more the remorse making yourself out to be a victim of some elaborate scheme to take away your company, prosecute you, send you to jail, and I just don't believe that's what happened in this case."

"I respect you're sitting there," Segal said.

It was difficult to control his tongue, since Castillo, with those words, essentially rejected the defense, including the actions of the Takeover Group, including the group's attempt to extort control of Near North from Segal, the hacking, the surreptitious recording of Segal's attorney, and the theft of Near North documents for the benefit of Near North's competitors.

"But you can go ahead," Castillo said.

"I want to talk a little bit about my cooperation because that's important for you to understand," Segal continued. "The day I was arrested, which I thought was a little unusual, even though I asked for an attorney, I sat for two-and-a-half hours, and I answered every conceivable question that was put to me.

"I'm supposed to be so smart or—as a lawyer, I didn't say I must have my lawyer, I must not talk any further.... I answered every question that... I found out subsequently was in my arrest warrant. And... what the public doesn't know, for whatever reason...I'm cast...in a particular role as a powerful, wealthy, political-type figure, and I just want you, the Court, to know that for three-plus-hour additional proffer sessions, I sat...under oath."

Segal was referring to sessions prior to the trial during which he met with the prosecution without an attorney and answered their questions. At the time, Segal was attempting to rebut the false implication, leaked to the media by the prosecution, that he was not cooperating with the investigation.

Segal told Castillo that when his attorney, Daniel Reidy, asked why he would do something like that, he replied, "Mr. Reidy, I have nothing to hide...I'll answer those questions."

"I want you to know that," Segal said. "There's a tremendous amount of speculation…that I'm here for other reasons. I don't want to hide behind that. I've attempted to sit down with my lawyers and to be able to explain, Your Honor, to be able to explain that insurance is very complicated. Accounting is very complicated."

Segal paused and went on.

"Let me just ask you a question: Why me? Why was I arrested first? Why is this—I believe—not a federal issue?… It's straightforward—there's no loss."

What he didn't say was how he was still bewildered that the federal government, which had no jurisdiction in regulating insurance, would arrest him six days after he filed a lawsuit against former employees who were hacking and stealing his business on behalf of their new employer. "So, I have remorse for not being able to be in a position to discuss this with you. I have a tremendous amount of remorse and bad feelings—how I disappointed people," Segal continued. "That's in the past. I just have to ask the questions…to place in the record so that my grandchildren someday could read this record, okay—I don't point aspersions to any individual who, from the government or anyone else or the media, but there's another side of the story.

"I was unfortunate—and I will say this: I have respect for Mr. Reidy over there, but I didn't learn until the day before the government rested its case that we weren't going to put one defense witness on. I wanted to testify. I wanted to explain. I'm an accountant. That shouldn't be used against me. That should allow me to articulate that numbers have to be numbers and there's a precise science and generally accepted accounting methodologies. I never stole one penny from this company. The only money that's missing was embezzler's money…I was accused that I looted, I was pilfering and it's just not right.

"I am somewhat disappointed, you know," Segal said. "I am a lawyer. I've never practiced extensively. I've learned a lot about the federal system. I have to respect it because that's the only system we have. And

I'm not getting into the prejudices of how that works, but there's a couple things here that really have to be laid on the line."

Segal thought about how Castillo had played to the media to justify a prosecution for a victimless crime and glossed over government misconduct. He implored Castillo to view things in a different light.

"I am not a bad person," Segal declared. "I never intended to hurt anybody. I am only hurt. My family is hurt. They've sacrificed my time with them for forty years. We did something that people perhaps should applaud me for doing. I put people to work.... We're not a financial institution, Your Honor. I didn't speculate this money in Las Vegas. I just want to take a minute to show how things could be perhaps viewed from a different perspective. There's a charge here...that I put $500,000 to purchase the Kaercher Agency in Las Vegas. The record is replete [that] the Zurich Insurance Company loaned us the money. I didn't take that money from the PFTA. And not one penny after that loan was taken to pay for Kaercher. It was a great deal and it was a legitimate deal and it was a deal not using any (PFTA) money, but I have a wire fraud charge on it."

Segal was attempting to respond to Castillo's analogy that he had taken money from the PFTA and gambled it in Las Vegas.

"It's my fault that I didn't adequately defend myself, and I can't ask you to go backwards. That's not my point, okay, but I am disappointed here that I studied the [presentencing report], and, I don't know—I went through every line on it. In accounting, the loss has to be proven... I felt there were a lot of obvious things that I would have liked to have got my point across because I didn't testify. It's my problem. It's too late, but I'd just like to let you know. You said, 'Your two loans are not collateralized.' I understand you've covered this issue, okay, and I don't want to go further, but they were collateralized."

"I do like to fight back," Segal declared. "I don't say I meant it that way, but if you worked for forty years and...you never hurt anyone."

Noting that he paid himself less money than some of his employees until he could get the accounting straightened out, he said, "I have never stolen a dime in my life."

He paused to gather his thoughts one last time, then expressed his tremendous remorse for allowing himself "to get in this situation."

He paused again.

"And I believe in the judicial system."

He then walked to the defense table and sat down.

Castillo asked Kendall whether he should take into consideration Segal's difficult time at the MCC, particularly since he was denied his medication.

"It's of his own making, Your Honor," Kendall replied.

"That's the government's view?" Castillo asked.

"That is the government's view, Judge," Kendall said. "He has fallen hard because his way of life—his lifestyle—was so grand and he was not motivated to do these tasks before by some impulse behavior. He was motivated by pride and greed. He should get no benefit because he suffers from—not even a psychological disease—which the Bureau of Prisons is perfectly capable of treating. If he is suffering in prison right now for the first fifteen months and may continue to do so, it's because he is the person who is now living a lifestyle that is so drastically different than the one that he lived in the past."

What Kendall did not say was how hard she fought for that most unusual presentencing incarceration.

"Well," Castillo said, "It's finally my turn to speak. This is a tragic case of epic proportions, as far as I'm concerned. You can see two sides to Mr. Segal. There's the nice, the charming, the brilliant side. That same good side is a charitable side who's done good things, no question about that.

"But, I have to say, there's testimony in the record and there's evidence of a dark side to Mr. Segal, one that is mean-spirited, one that is immoral, one that is unethical. And I will tell you from the minute that I was assigned to this case, everything I tried to do was to give you, Mr. Segal, a fair shake in this federal judicial system."

Segal was baffled. What sort of "fair shake" was Castillo referring to, given the judge's denial of a pretrial hearing on misconduct as well as the multiple examples of false testimony by prosecution witnesses?

Castillo said he had excluded prejudicial evidence and praised Segal's legal team as well as the prosecution lawyers as an "all-star lineup" and an "outstanding group of advocates."

"But I'll tell you one thing, Mr. Segal," he said, "even if the best attorneys who ever practiced in this city—and I'll name two—even if Abe Lincoln and Clarence Darrow came back from the dead to represent you, they wouldn't have saved you."

That comment was just too good for the media to ignore. Segal had to shake his head at the outrageous nature of it. *Since this was an accounting case, Lincoln and Darrow would have brought in accounting evidence,* he thought.

Castillo then excoriated Segal, saying the case was "a rip-off of trust fund money.... And yes, this was an accounting case, but I would say this is creative accounting at its best."

It was clear Castillo rejected the forensic accounting evidence presented by Lotts in the forfeiture hearing.

"There's nothing that could have saved you from your conviction in this case—not your cooperation or your attempts to blame everybody else, substituting invective to deflect from the failure to recognize the facts of the case. There's an old saying that power corrupts and absolute power absolutely corrupts. Well, Mr. Segal, you had absolute power over Near North and you absolutely corrupted Near North. They now stand convicted alongside you.

"So, your life's work was a corrupt insurance entity and it was made that way by you as you kind of ran around like an emperor with no clothes. However, in this case, it was an emperor of an insurance agency with no PFTA. You totally commingled it from beginning to end, just using this money for all kinds of inappropriate things, no ethics to it at all—by a CPA and a lawyer," the judge continued. quoting Kendall nearly verbatim. Segal found this to be a particularly ugly and hurtful statement, because the government had not presented one check disbursement that was unauthorized under the Illinois statute.

Castillo continued castigating Segal for several more minutes before he got to the bottom line. This, including the comment that Near North was a "corrupt insurance entity," Segal thought, was hyperbolic rhetoric employed to further justify the harsh sentence that was coming.

"And so, at the end of the day, I am sentencing you to one hundred twenty-one months," Castillo said. He also ordered Segal to pay restitution of $841,527.96 for the credit write-offs, in addition to the $30 million the jury had ordered forfeited.

So, there it was: Ten years and one month in prison, a severe sentence. The fact that the prosecution had sought thirty years camouflaged the fact that even ten was harsh.

In the fiscal year ending in September 2004, the average term of imprisonment in all federal cases was just under sixty months. The average length of prison sentences for violent offenses, including murder and kidnapping, was about ninety-six months and for drug offenses, it was about eighty-four months. Segal was paying what's commonly known as the "trial tax." Defendants who go to trial get longer sentences than those who plead guilty. And accusing the prosecution of committing misconduct certainly didn't help

The list of sentences imposed for major thefts by fraud offenders who caused losses of more than $30 million in actual economic harm shows the anomaly of Segal's sentence. Conrad Black was convicted of stealing millions of dollars from shareholders and sentenced to six-and-a-half years. Eric Stein got eight years after being convicted of stealing perhaps as much as $50 million from nearly 2,000 investors. Currency trader John Rusnak caused $691 million in losses before he was convicted of bank fraud and got a sentence of seven-and-a-half years. In Illinois in 2004, two grain-elevator officials were sentenced to forty-six months and thirty-seven months respectively, despite defrauding more than three hundred farmers out of more than $30 million.

As a member of the national sentencing commission, Castillo had to have been aware of the excessiveness of Segal's sentence, but for now, the proceedings were over.

As Castillo left the bench, deputy U.S. marshals escorted Segal out of the courtroom and into the lockup. The prosecutors and defense lawyers stacked their papers, packed up their boxes, shut their briefcases, and walked out.

The courtroom was silent. But questions remained.

Was the prosecution of Michael Segal about seeking justice or was it about taking down a businessman in the mistaken belief that if squeezed hard enough, he might help take down others? Was this a case built on illegal cyberspying carried out by a disgruntled former employee who sought to bring Segal to his knees and steal his business? And, after Segal fought back, did the case become a matter of the prosecution protecting its own conduct and witnesses? And why did the defense wait until *after* Segal was convicted to present its own analysis of the finances of his businesses?

The next step?

The Seventh Circuit U.S. Court of Appeals.

Chapter 26

Rejection

IN THE SPRING OF 2007, Albert Alschuler, one of Segal's appellate lawyers, stood before a three-judge panel of the Seventh Circuit U.S. Court of Appeals to deliver his oral argument on why the convictions of Segal and Near North should be reversed.

"Good morning, and may it please the Court," Alschuler began. "At the beginning of 2002, the Near North Insurance Brokerage, or NNIB, was a business valued at $250 million. They brokered more than a billion dollars' worth of insurance per year. Its revenues had grown from $70 million to $119 million within the past four years. It employed more than 1,000 people. NNIB had been in existence for forty years and in all that time, no NNIB customer had failed to receive insurance he had purchased, and no insurance carrier had failed to receive a premium it was due."

Alschuler paused, but just briefly.

"Today, NNIB is forfeited to the government. Those 1,000 jobs are gone. But they vanished because federal prosecutors, in effect, anointed themselves Illinois insurance commissioners and convinced a federal judge and jury to impose a penalty for the violation of Illinois state insurance regulations that greatly exceeded the penalty the Illinois legislature and Illinois administrators considered appropriate.

"This case turned federalism on its head. In essence, the federal government tried NNIB and its owner, Michael Segal, for state crimes in a federal court. Worse, the government used the federal mail fraud statute to bootstrap minor state violations into a twenty-year federal felony. Then the government bootstraps some innocuous mailings in furtherance of the regulatory violations into a RICO violation requiring a forfeiture of the company and $30 million besides.

"The mail fraud statute outlaws schemes to deprive people of the intangible right to honest services. So, what's the deprivation of the intangible right to honest services? Well, it's a violation of fiduciary duty for personal gain. And what's a violation of fiduciary duty? According to the government, it's any violation of a duty imposed by state law.

"So, the government told the district court in effect, we get to try state crimes in the federal court. The district court accepted the government's theory and spent fifteen pages of its instructions detailing Illinois insurance regulations. Then, it added some baffling boilerplate. The defendants were not charged with state crimes, and it's not enough to find that they violated a state law. The jury was left to go, 'Huh, how's that? What else has this case been about?' The Court [Judge Castillo] refused to instruct the jury [that] the required intent was not an intent to violate state insurance regulations, but an intent to defraud.

"When the mail fraud statute forbids fraudulent deprivation of property, the Supreme Court gives the term property a uniform national meaning. Confidential information is property throughout the United States and state licenses aren't. The Court should give the intangible right to honest services a uniform national meaning as well. It would be as if the state of Iowa were to declare next year that lawyers have a fiduciary duty to tell their clients their bar examination scores.

"The violation of fiduciary duty is bribes, kickbacks, self-dealing, and we can give those terms uniform national meaning. The alternative is—as I say—to bootstrap every little violation of what the state calls a breach of its fiduciary duties for its purposes into this 20-year federal felony. I don't think that's the way to give content to this extraordinarily vague statute.

"And then this trial illustrates a second reason why prosecutors call the mail fraud statute our Stradivarius, our Colt forty-five, our Louisville Slugger. Prosecutors used this statute to make an end-run not only around rules of federal jurisdiction, but around rules of evidence and joinder. From the beginning to the end of a two-month trial, they presented evidence with one central theme: portray Michael Segal as an unattractive person. The government's evidence tended to show that in violation of Illinois law, Segal and NNIB failed to maintain adequate funds in a Premium Fund Trust Account or PFTA. Insurance carriers got their premiums but the premiums were not in the place Illinois law required them to be. No creditor testified that NNIB failed to pay its debts."

Segal was not present for the arguments. He still was confined to the federal penitentiary in Oxford, Wisconsin. He was particularly frustrated because he had labored hard and long to prepare a document requested by Alschuler outlining false information that Hogan had inserted into the prosecution's appellate brief. But by the time Segal completed his analysis, he was told not only that it was too late, but that appeals courts do not rule on factual issues, only on legal ones. For Segal, this was yet another defeat in his attempt to inform the court of the false information. In August 2007, the long-awaited decision was finally issued and it was a huge disappointment to Segal and the defense team. The ruling essentially rubber-stamped the prosecution's version of the facts and rejected the defense version.

Written by Appeals Judge Terence Evans from Wisconsin, the decision rejected all of the defense arguments save one—that the $30 million ordered forfeited could have been the result of a miscalculation. The decision was joined by appeals judges Kenneth Ripple and Diane Sykes, a former law clerk for Evans when he was a U.S. District Court Judge in Wisconsin.

In some ways, the decision was not a surprise to Alschuler because of an exchange he'd had with Evans as he began his rebuttal. "Let me ask you a question," Evans said. "I've always assumed that lawyers kind of lead off with their strongest argument, unlike the manager of baseball team, where you don't put your best hitter on the first bat. But your lead-off argument here in your brief was 'vindictive prosecution' and I didn't hear one word about that from you."

Alschuler said that after much discussion that issue was put first "not because it was our cleanup but because it was our first chronologically. This was the first error that occurred in the case. This occurred even before it went to trial. These charges were added for no reason other than to retaliate against Mr. Segal and NNIB for filing a civil lawsuit."

He explained how that was followed by Castillo conducting what essentially was a long smear of Segal in a trial where the prosecution was permitted to toss in everything but the kitchen sink based on the pretense that the PFTA deficit, the unreturned premium credits, insurance discounts, and campaign contributions were all part of one twelve-year-long fraud scheme.

And then, Alschuler explained that the jury instructions had failed to explain that state law violations don't establish federal honest-services fraud and that mailings don't establish a pattern of racketeering activity. All of that was followed by a forfeiture proceeding that was conducted almost as an afterthought and, he argued, got everything wrong.

The Appeals Court ruling did not address in any way the misconduct exposed in the defense pretrial filings.

When Segal was briefed about the oral arguments, he wasn't surprised. By that time, he'd concluded there was a culture of protecting prosecutors.

In his decision, Evans said that, on a claim of vindictive prosecution, the appeals court reviewed Castillo's legal conclusions and his findings of fact for "clear error" and found none.

"The Constitution prohibits initiating a prosecution based *solely* on vindictiveness," Evans said. Quoting prior case law, he noted that,

"[F]or an agent of the [United States] to pursue a course of action whose objective is to penalize a person's reliance on his legal rights" is "a due process violation of the most basic sort. "

"After a trial, in very limited circumstances, courts have applied a burden-shifting presumption of vindictiveness where prosecutors have pursued enhanced charges after a defendant successfully challenged a conviction and was awarded a new trial. Our precedents do not provide for the application of such a presumption before trial. It remains a fact that a pretrial claim of vindictive prosecution is extraordinarily difficult to prove. To prevail on this sort of claim...a defendant must affirmatively show that the prosecutor was motivated by animus, 'such as a personal stake in the outcome of the case or an attempt to seek self-vindication.'"

Of course, the defense believed that this was precisely the case. In fact, in the superseding indictment, the prosecution alleged that the "methods and means to [further the criminal enterprise] included the use of substantial economic resources to threaten to and to conduct expensive retaliatory litigation against those who would oppose his will. "

When the defense requested that the prosecution identify "each instance of the alleged 'expensive retaliatory litigation,'" the prosecution responded by identifying the lawsuit filed against Aon, the Takeover Group and Cheley.

Evans cited case law stating that prosecutors have a right during plea negotiations to threaten additional superseding indictments. But Hogan's threat was made at a time when no plea negotiations were taking place. Four superseding indictments followed, including the RICO indictment—all for a non-violent case based on an alleged violation of a state insurance regulation.

What was the root of the prosecution's animus? In part, it was Segal's refusal to wear a wire, but it also must also have stemmed from exposure of prosecutorial misconduct, starting with the knowledge of the cyberhacking and passing of stolen emails to the Takeover Group and the FBI.

This was different from the typical pretrial allegations of vindictiveness, which relate to accusations that prosecutors attempt to coerce guilty pleas by bringing superseding indictments. Segal's defense contended that Segal and Near North were exercising their constitutional right to go to court to try to stop the destruction of Near North. The defense believed that had Segal and Near North been allowed to continue with its civil lawsuit, the evidence would have shown the prosecution was engaging in improper use of stolen attorney-client emails, failing to document conversations with witnesses, and taping of Segal's defense attorney—which could have caused the prosecution to be exposed to potential liability under the McDade Act, the potential collapse of the criminal case entirely, and the exposure of potential ethical violations—all of which are damaging to legal careers.

In finding that the actions of the prosecution were proper, Evans noted that that prosecutors have "wide discretion over whether, how, and when to bring a case."

Judge Evans accepted the prosecution claim that the civil suit "intimidated" Takeover Group "witnesses," who were never called to testify at the trial in any case. "A prosecutor cannot be said to act vindictively by taking into account a defendant's perceived efforts to intimidate witnesses. In short, defendants have not made out a claim for vindictive prosecution, nor have they shown sufficient evidence to warrant a hearing on the claim."

In effect, the ruling was a protective cloak for the government. It is difficult to imagine a more direct threat than the one that was made and acted upon. Did the prosecution's claim that its witnesses were being threatened justify doubling down on Segal and Near North with a RICO indictment?

Evans ruled that it was.

In 1989, the Sixth Circuit U. S. Court of Appeals, in *U.S. v. Adams*, noted, "It is not only the inexperienced and the overly ambitious who may be tempted to misuse the prosecutorial power, although they are certainly subject to that temptation. There are times when the judgment of even the most highly qualified and virtuous of prosecutors— perhaps especially they—will yield to an excess of zeal. One thinks of the Massachusetts men who, in an age not so very far removed from our own, prosecuted witches."

The defense had contended that the second superseding indictment contained no new facts, but rather repeated verbatim the charges in the previous filing. No new facts supported the new criminal allegations, the defense said, just a new, closely related corporate defendant and additional pressure on Segal.

Essentially, the appeals court agreed with the prosecution's argument that the RICO charge was brought because the charge that had been pending against Segal *before* the threatened superseding indictment did not reflect the entirety of the prosecution's evidence of wrongdoing.

"That the initial charges may not reflect the extent of a defendant's wrongdoing is clearly illustrated by the evidence in this case," the appeals court said. "It is hard to imagine that any prosecutor would fail to find [Near North] a proper defendant or fail to conclude that Segal's wrongdoing extended far beyond one fraud count. The evidence supports the indictment, and Segal and [Near North] have not made a showing of vindictiveness."

The appeals court also accepted Hogan's contention that the allegations in the amended civil complaint relating to the hacking and sharing of documents with the Takeover Group were intended to harass and intimidate the Takeover Group, even though the lawsuit had been filed not by Segal but by his independent board, which consisted of a former U.S. Attorney and a former FBI supervisor concerned about protecting the assets of Near North from the hacking. The appellate court referred to some of the Takeover Group documents in supporting the decision, but failed to take note of the demand by each member of the Takeover Group of a payment of $5 million to each of them. The defense had considered this to be extortion.

In essence, the court said that even if Cheley had been illegally hacking into Near North's computers and stealing emails and documents protected by attorney-client privilege, and even if Cheley had been passing the documents—about a thousand of them over eight months—to prosecution witnesses Walsh, Berry, and Gallagher, any action Near North might have taken to defend itself in court was an act of intimidation.

Moreover, the court held that the evidence of the hacking and sharing of the documents wasn't sufficient reason for an evidentiary hearing. One had to wonder what evidence *would* be sufficient.

The appeals court rejected the argument that insurance carriers were at little or no risk based on the prosecution's assertion that Near North was "often late in paying carriers and held checks to carriers until it came up with sufficient funds to send them out." This statement ignored the fact that all carriers were paid, there was no evidence that Near North was ever late in paying a carrier, and under the law, payments made to a broker are deemed to be paid to the carrier, so there was no risk of loss.

The restitution order was upheld, despite the affidavit from Waste Management that the $357,079 that the prosecution claimed was owed in fact was not owed. The appeals court dismissed the affidavit, saying, "But given other evidence, it was certainly possible that Waste Management didn't know it had credits coming." That was a preposterous claim. Any business that thought it was somehow shortchanged more than a third of a million dollars would never state in a sworn affidavit to a federal court that they were not owed such a large sum of money.

In ordering the remand to Castillo to reconsider the forfeiture issue,

Evans said that it was unclear how much of the $30 million that had been ordered forfeited had gone to Segal personally as net proceeds and how much of it had either been reinvested in the company's subsidiaries or simply left in the company.

"Without that information, we cannot determine whether at least part of the $30 million forfeiture would constitute double billing, given that the amount that went back into the company will be forfeited through the forfeiture of the enterprise. Double billing…cannot be the intent of Congress…. Accordingly, we will remand the case to the district court for a determination of what portion of the $30 million was not reinvested in the enterprise, but rather went to benefit Segal personally and is subject to forfeiture as proceeds of the illegal enterprise."

Despite the best efforts of Alschuler and Martin, the appeals court declined to overturn any of the nineteen guilty verdicts.

Alschuler later reflected on the nature of the prosecution of Segal and Near North. "I had the clear impression that Judge Castillo simply did not like Mike Segal," he said. Segal's arrest and the original federal charge of violating a state insurance statute were "highly unusual. There's really no way the federal government would be arresting Mike on some minor state violations, even if true, and asking him to wear a wire unless they believed he was politically connected and thought he would be able to deliver a mayor or some city councilmen. Of course, they were wrong in thinking he could do that."

Chapter 27

Segal Battles Back— from Prison

On December 1, 2005, the day after he was sentenced to prison, Segal boarded a bus in Chicago with other soon-to-be inmates of the Federal Correctional Institution in Oxford, Wisconsin. Known as FCI Oxford, this would be his home for the next several years. He settled into his seat, still wearing handcuffs, and tried to make the best of the four-hour drive to rural Wisconsin. As the bus chugged past rolling hills, dairy farms, and deer stands, he noted the few leaves that still clung tenaciously to the stands of oak and other hardwood trees that flanked the now-harvested fields of corn, beans and hay. Momentarily, viewing the open space was a balm for his troubled mind. He managed to get freed from his handcuffs for a short while by volunteering to pass out food when the bus stopped at a roadside oasis.

Despite his legal travails, Segal was still optimistic that justice would prevail at some point as long as he continued to fight as best he could from behind the prison walls. *They will never break my spirit*, he vowed internally, although he remained shaken and angry.

He recalled his occasional chats with thirty-four-year-old Markel Johnson, a fellow inmate at the Metropolitan Correction Center, a father of three children who had agreed to cooperate against members of the Mickey Cobras street gang, but had come to regret his decision.

Segal found him to be articulate and well-mannered—not a stereotypical gang member. In their last conversation, Johnson said prosecutors pressured him to cooperate and he had done so. Before being sentenced on gun and narcotics convictions, he was being offered an additional sentencing reduction if he agreed to cooperate against others with whom he had no prior dealings.

Segal related to Johnson's situation, even though he had been convicted of a white-collar crime and Johnson had not. Listening to Johnson evoked memories of the meeting with Polales and Murphy in the Westin Hotel and how he was pressured to wear a wire. Johnson was worried. If he agreed, he would be in physical danger once he was released and, even more so, his family would be in danger. At the same time, Johnson told Segal that if he refused, he didn't think he could survive much time behind bars. Segal did not offer any advice; he was struggling with his own case.

Not long after, Johnson hanged himself in his cell.

For most of the other inmates at the MCC, Johnson's death had been just another day, another bed opening up. Now, as the bus neared the end of its journey, Johnson's dilemma and death were a reminder of the bleakness Segal would face for the next several years. Johnson became a touchstone to remind him of what might happen if his spirit faltered.

At Westfield, Wisconsin, the bus left Interstate 39 and headed west on County Road E. The trees loomed closer to the road. Segal leaned into the left turn onto County Road G and then abruptly the bus made a right turn onto Elk Avenue. It seemed aptly named, located as it was in the middle of a hardwood forest. As he disembarked, he noted that the prison looked a bit like a junior college. It housed a thousand inmates, some convicted of white-collar crimes, as well as various other non-violent offenders, including some public officials convicted of corruption and an array of drug dealers. It once had been home for Harry Aleman, the most prolific mob hitman in Chicago history, whose paintings of pastoral scenes created here once adorned the walls of a restaurant in Chicago's Little Italy neighborhood.

"*No Fences, No Violence, No Privacy*" was the heading of a *Chicago Tribune* article about the minimum-security facility. Some called it "the university," a reference to the name it shared with the vaunted institution of higher education in England. It didn't cross his mind right away, because his brain was often racing with so many thoughts and apprehensions, but it seemed more than likely that he may have been the only Oxford inmate who actually also spent time in Oxford, England. He'd gone to attend the graduation of the daughter of a good friend. How his fortunes had changed.

On arrival, Segal went through the now-familiar rituals of processing. Some friends of his friends who'd been unfortunate enough to find themselves there knew he was coming and greeted him. It was surreal. Upon arrival, one of the first things he noticed was a salad bar. He was fortunate to be assigned to a room that faced the woods. Like everyone else, Segal was housed in a module for four inmates with two sets of bunk beds. He used his commissary funds to negotiate for a lower bunk, but didn't see the need to get a better mattress—the upgrade inmates referred to as a "Cadillac mattress."

Segal spent most of his time in the library where he met some inmates who seemed decent people. Most faced shorter sentences. Many were serving time for drug-related crimes. He learned early on to stay away from the braggarts. About half of his fellow inmates were African-Americans from Chicago or Milwaukee. He earned grudging admiration as a business executive who was continuing to fight the government. One man noted, "You had a lot to lose and you fought back. Some of us had nothing to lose and we caved in."

When he could, Segal counseled them on life as well as their vocational interests. Many were vibrant and surprisingly upbeat. Some of the bonds he made lasted for years beyond his release.

Segal also developed a rapport with most of the correctional officers and quickly became known as someone who was not violent and followed the rules. But just like on the other side of the walls of Oxford, there were jerks on the inside as well.

A guard Segal knew only as Montez seemed to have it in for him, putting him in solitary—the hole—three times. He was locked in a cell with no contact except for one hour every other day. The light was on constantly and the result was sleep deprivation. Segal learned from others that in solitary, the days were meant for sleeping, while the nights were for staying awake.

The first time Segal was placed in the hole was after he filed a writ of certiorari he had prepared with friends, asking the U.S. Supreme Court to review his case. His case manager at Oxford arranged for Segal to use the fax machine in his office to send and receive documents to his attorney Joshua Muss in Washington, D.C. to get them properly formatted. Muss was one of Segal's closest friends in D.C. and who, like virtually all of his friends, continued to support him. Years later, when Segal finally was released, a good number of people apologized for not coming to visit him. Segal assured them that he was not hurt. Privately, he preferred not to have visitors, as he was embarrassed about where he was and wanted to spend his time sorting out what had happened to him as well as fighting back.

There came a day when Segal found out that a fax was supposed to arrive at a time when the case manager was not in his office. Segal called the law office and tried to get it delayed, but it was mistakenly sent anyway. Montez intercepted the faxed document, declared it unauthorized, and sent Segal to the hole.

There were times when Segal had visitors and Montez would order Segal to mop the floor in front of them. Segal realized Montez was someone who had to exert control. Segal was thankful that Montez was the exception. The other officers treated him professionally.

There was a daily routine. Each morning, Segal was required to make sure that the phone stations were clean. He took pride in doing the job well. Then, he headed to the library to bury himself in his research. His past experience as the owner of a restaurant paid off when he became the risk manager of the prison kitchen. Some inmates were suspected of taking advantage of the privilege of working there and he stepped in to keep an eye on things. There were perks—he was able to eat early with the cooks before the other inmates and the food was acceptable. Segal adapted. He considered this a balancing out—he had eaten enough "fancy food" to last a lifetime.

Maneuvering through life in prison requires some of the same skills needed on the outside world—patience, the ability to sense what others are thinking, and a willingness to make concessions—particularly when the possible repercussion is physical injury. He witnessed some loud confrontations and a few physical assaults—inmate on inmate. Segal did his best to stay clear.

But above all, being a skillful negotiator and a good listener were keys to achieving one's goals in a setting where leaving is not an option. Segal listened when fellow inmates wanted to talk about their lives and their cases. And he came to know inmates who had suffered some of the same injustices that he had faced and he empathized with them.

Although it was difficult, Segal also tried to stay abreast of current events in the outside world—something that many inmates were beyond caring about. The television was a link to that outside world, but who got to watch what channel was usually tightly controlled by whoever was bigger, stronger, and louder. In the common area where inmates watched television, there were four screens and a limited number of channels. Inmates watched with earphones so that all four screens could be in use constantly. Typically, one television was turned to a Spanish language channel. Another was usually devoted to sports and another to the Black Entertainment Television. The fourth seemed to be devoted constantly to Jerry Springer reruns. Through polite persuasion, Segal convinced inmates to allow him to turn on CNN nightly for one hour so that he could watch the news.

Privileges can be a moving target, though, and preserving them sometimes depends not on negotiation, but rather pure muscle. There came an evening when 9 p.m. rolled around and Segal, as was his habit, changed the channel to CNN. This prompted a new inmate—a formidable man with a very foul mouth—to erupt in rage. He demanded to know who changed the channel and then began moving in a threatening fashion toward Segal. Clearly, this new inmate didn't know the "agreement" that was in place. As Segal began to back up, suddenly, several other inmates, many just as physically formidable, closed ranks in front of him and confronted the inmate. Thereafter, Segal tuned in CNN without concern.

In April 2009, nearly four years after his arrival, Segal filed a motion under federal statute 2255, which allows those convicted of crimes to challenge their conviction and sentence. Such a motion is one of the last legal avenues to a defendant and the most common issue raised is that the trial defense attorney provided an inadequate legal defense, which resulted in a constitutionally unfair trial.

The legal term is ineffective assistance of counsel (IAC) and was set out in a 1984 U.S. Supreme Court decision titled *Strickland v. Washington.* In its ruling, the Supreme Court held that two conditions had to be met in order to prove an ineffective assistance claim against a trial lawyer (Reidy) or a sentencing lawyer (Steinback). He had to show that their performance was below an objective standard of reasonableness and he had to show there was a reasonable probability that but for the deficient performance, he would have been acquitted.

It is an extraordinarily high threshold. If a defense lawyer can show that his actions were the result of a reasonable strategy, the motion is defeated. But, as hard as this might be, thousands of convictions across the United States since 1984 have been overturned on this basis.

Segal mailed his thirty-two-page motion, along with 3,242 pages of exhibits, on April 20, 2009. The motion said trial lawyers were deficient in several areas, including the failure to argue that the mail and wire fraud charges were barred by the McCarran-Ferguson Act; the failure to call any accounting experts, the failure to call witnesses to rebut the prosecution claim of a PFTA deficit, and the failure to investigate or challenge the IRS agent's account of how he said he discovered government exhibit No. 5—the document that purported to have Segal's initials squiggled on it.

"Either by cross-examination or through the use of an accounting expert, (Reidy) could have shown that the bulk of the evidence against Segal was unreliable because it did not come from the books and records of the company, was not reconciled, was inconsistent, and/or was nothing more than conjecture," the motion said. "Instead of pointing out the fundamental flaws in the evidence, Segal's lawyer sat by while his client was buried by what can only be called accounting garbage."

The motion said that, prior to the trial, Reidy "knew of major infirmities in the government's financial theories and evidence. Counsel was aware because…accounting experts hired by Segal presented their work and findings to him." Over Segal's objection, the defense did not work with accountants and did not present any of this evidence in Segal's defense at trial.

Segal warmed to the argument, believing that while many defendants raise these issues, it's not often that a defendant has the proof, such as the failure to present Lotts's testimony.

"An expert would have made it clear that, contrary to the government's repeated assertions, no audit was ever performed. By using the word 'audit' in connection with financial information and results, the government falsely suggested that such information and results were reliable from an accounting perspective…. In short, Segal's lawyer had plenty of ammunition to shoot down the case against Segal. Sadly, counsel did not fire a shot."

Two months later, Castillo dismissed the petition without even asking the prosecution to respond. In a one-paragraph order, he said that he had completed a careful evaluation of the petition and concluded that it "must be dismissed because it does not establish any constitutional violation that was not addressed in Mr. Segal's direct appeal. Mr. Segal's attack on the inadequacy of his multiple counsel is not supported by the record and does not meet the *Strickland* standards or its numerous progenies. Mr. Segal's belated attempt to reargue his innocence is simply not supported by the record. Finally, the Court expressly finds no evidence of prosecutorial misconduct."

This was not surprising, considering Castillo's comment at sentencing—that even Clarence Darrow or Abraham Lincoln couldn't have helped him.

Segal's only recourse was to ask Castillo for *permission* to appeal Castillo's ruling. While it would seem logical and fair, if not a Constitutional right, to be able to automatically appeal an adverse decision, that is not the case. Under federal law, a defendant cannot appeal unless the same judge who denied the petition grants a "Certificate of Appealability" (COA). A defendant is required to make a "substantial showing" of the denial of a constitutional right.

In August 2009, Segal filed his request for a COA. He had the advice of Paul Schlieve, a fellow inmate who had been studying the law and was filing his own 2255 motion. Schlieve was a former professor at the University of North Texas with a Ph.D. in math and library science who got tangled up with some folks who were cooking and selling methamphetamine and wound up with a thirteen-year sentence. Schlieve said that he was trying to help one of them get out of the drug milieu, but a jury voted otherwise.

Based upon conversations with Schlieve, Segal changed his strategy to focus on going through the trial record and providing more explanation and proof of constitutional violations as well as the failure to present Lotts's forensic analysis at the trial.

Segal contended that Castillo's summary dismissal of his 2255 appeal was a "draconian measure" that courts are cautioned against using except in rare circumstances. He asserted that he had received ineffective assistance of counsel at his trial, his sentencing and on appeal. The issues were the same—failure to present accounting evidence, failure to invoke the McCarran-Ferguson Act, failure to call witnesses to rebut the prosecution's false claim of stealing customer credits, failure to adequately challenge Exhibit No. 5 and failure to call Illinois insurance regulatory experts.

In conclusion, Segal argued, 'When you strip away the political taint and mischaracterization, Segal's case is an accounting and regulatory case that only lends itself to finite accounting evidence. Once the 'central scheme' of this goes away, all of the remaining counts of the indictment, including the RICO count, disappear as well."

In January 2010, Castillo denied Segal's request for a COA, again ruling that there were no constitutional violations and that Segal had received an adequate defense. *Clearly*, thought Segal, *checks and balances are illusory if a judge can deny my right to an appeal.*

Segal's only remaining option was to ask the Seventh Circuit U.S. Court of Appeals to grant him a COA. That, too, was denied.

Chapter 28

Prosecutorial Misconduct Rampant

"Obviously, even one example of real misconduct is too many.... If you've engaged in misconduct, the response of the department has to be swift and strong."

—Lanny A. Breuer, Assistant Attorney General in charge of the U.S. Justice Department's Criminal Division, September 23, 2010.

NEARLY FIVE YEARS INTO HIS incarceration at Oxford and while his request for a COA from the Seventh Circuit was pending, Segal shifted the focus of his efforts from the courts to the upper levels of the U.S. Department of Justice. One of the biggest challenges, as so many other victims of federal courts have learned over the years, is that the Office of Professional Responsibility (OPR), which is supposed to investigate cases like Segal's, is an arm of the Justice Department and cannot realistically be expected to investigate itself. In the view of its many critics, it is an understaffed, toothless organization where well-documented cases of misconduct go to die and be buried.

The Justice Department's U.S. Attorneys' Manual provides: "Evidence and non-frivolous allegations of serious misconduct by Department attorneys that relate to the exercise of their authority to investigate, litigate, or provide legal advice shall be reported to OPR."

For decades, OPR has been criticized for failing to act on misconduct allegations. In 1998, William Moushey, an award-winning investigative journalist and professor at Point Park University in Pennsylvania, wrote a series of articles about misconduct in federal cases. Moushey reported that he had uncovered more than 1,500 cases in which federal agents and prosecutors were accused of engaging in misconduct to obtain convictions. As he put it, "Little oversight is happening. The office opened official investigations into only nine percent of the 4,000 complaints filed against federal law enforcement officials during the past twenty years. The office found that only four percent of those complaints had merit. Since the office only discloses specifics of its investigations on rare occasions, it is not clear what punishment was meted out."

Year after year, decade after decade, legal commentators have criticized the system designed to investigate and discipline federal prosecutors. Bruce A. Green, in his 1995 article, "Policing Federal Prosecutors: Do Too Many Regulators Produce Too Little Enforcement?" wrote that the "process for sanctioning wrongful conduct of federal prosecutors is structurally inadequate.... There are certainly enough authorities—federal and state, external and internal—overseeing federal prosecutors. Yet, commentators have uniformly lamented the lack of effective discipline of prosecutors who violate standards of professional conduct."

In 1984, Walter W. Steele, Jr., in an article titled "Unethical Prosecutors and Inadequate Discipline," wrote, "The public record suggests, however, that federal prosecutors are rarely, if ever, referred to federal grievance committees....Without a doubt, the dearth of reported disciplinary proceedings brought by state authorities against federal prosecutors reflects that not only are they rarely reported, but such proceedings are also rarely initiated."

One of most frequent criticisms is that the Attorney General appoints the OPR lawyers. As a result, they are essentially charged with investigating and disciplining their own. If OPR does find evidence of misconduct, the file is adjudicated by the Professional Misconduct Review Unit (PMRU). If the PMRU agrees with the OPR finding, it makes a disciplinary recommendation.

In Segal's case, misconduct could be seen in plain view and heard on tape, such as when FBI Agent Murphy advised embezzler Daniel Watkins on how to change his sworn affidavit from a truthful one, which would have exculpated Segal from the IRS charge, to the false scenario that added years to his incarceration. And there was evidence of government collaboration with the hacker and the members of the Takeover Group.

Segal now pinned his hopes on sending a document detailing this litany to Lanny Breuer, the head of Justice Department's criminal division. And, thanks to a fellow inmate who had experienced a similar injustice, Segal had reason to believe that he had the right attorney to do the filing.

James Cole, of the law firm of Bryan Cave LLP, was a highly regarded attorney who had worked previously with then-Attorney General Eric Holder. By coincidence, Segal knew Cole's family, as Cole had represented another of Segal's closest friends. Segal's friend, in fact, agreed to cover the substantial cost of Cole's services. He did so after asking Cole for his opinion of Segal's case and whether the Justice Department had the authority to do a review that might lead to overturning a wrongful conviction. Segal's friend reported that Cole said Segal's case was "one of the worst cases" of misconduct he had encountered in his legal career and that he "failed to see where there was a crime."

So, in early 2010, Segal retained Cole, as well as fellow Bryan Cave attorney Will Olsen. They assembled a powerful package of documentary proof of prosecutorial misconduct. Unfortunately, in May 2010, Cole and Olsen stepped off the matter when they were nominated to join the Justice Department—Cole as First Deputy to Holder and Olsen in the civil division. Cole said that if confirmed (and he was), he would be required to recuse himself from any matter involving Segal or Near North.

As a result, the package was submitted by Washington, D.C. attorney Stanley Brand, who from 1976 to 1983 had served as general counsel to the U.S. House of Representatives under Speaker Tip O'Neill. Brand had also been the House's chief legal officer.

In June 2010, a 122-page presentation[53] requesting an investigation of the prosecutors and FBI agents in the Segal case—accompanied by a twenty-three-page letter from Brand drafted by Cole and Olsen—was hand-delivered to Breuer, who had recently been quoted in a *USA Today* article about prosecutorial misconduct as saying that it should be met with a "swift and strong" response. Segal was extremely hopeful that with a new administration in place under President Barack Obama, and because Cole and Brand had praised Breuer as non-political, he finally might get an independent review of his case.

Brand's request was quite straightforward.

"I am writing to request that the Department of Justice conduct a review of apparent misconduct by members of the U.S. Attorney's Office for the Northern District of Illinois and the FBI Chicago Field Office (collectively 'the Government') during the investigation and prosecution of our client, Michael Segal. The most serious of this misconduct involved the Government's interaction with sources who provided the Government with evidence illegally obtained by a computer hacker and the Government's actions to protect these sources after the discovering of the hacking."

"Finally, after Segal's conviction, the Trustee for Near North stopped discovery and then dismissed the civil suits against Aon, the Government's sources, Kemper, and Cheley regarding the hacking. The

---

53   Stan Brand and Jim Cole letter to DOJ - June 2010.

Trustee stopped discovery the evening before the deposition of Walsh that would have explored, for the first time, details about Walsh, Berry, and Cheley's relationship and the Government's knowledge of, and involvement with, the hacking. Based on information and belief, Segal submits that the [U.S. Attorney's Office] directed the Trustee to stop discovery and dismiss these civil suits.

"We believe that this analysis raises serious questions about whether the Government engaged in misconduct during the investigation and prosecution of Segal that deprived him of constitutional protections and undermined the integrity of the Department of Justice."

In closing, the letter said, "We believe the facts described...raise serious questions about whether the prosecution team in this matter engaged in misconduct that violated Segal's rights and tainted his trial. In particular, the Government's knowledge of Cheley's hacking, the interaction between the FBI case agents and Walsh and Berry who received the hacked material, and the Government's misstatements and other conduct that prevented Segal's discovery of the Government's full involvement with the hacking may have deprived Segal of his Fourth Amendment right against unreasonable search and seizure and violated his right under *Brady v. Maryland* and its progeny to receive all exculpatory evidence, including impeachment evidence. Moreover, the Government may have violated Segal's Fifth Amendment right to due process and his Sixth Amendment right to counsel in engaging in conduct that disregarded Segal's attorney-client privilege."

Two months later, the American Bar Association House of Delegates, in an unrelated action, approved a recommendation directed to the Justice Department to "release as much information regarding completed individual investigations as possible." They added, "In recent years, too little public disclosure has been made regarding OPR's investigations and the DOJ disciplinary determinations predicated on them in cases involving alleged professional misconduct."

Despite Breuer's comment to *USA Today,* the response to the letter was neither swift nor strong.

Four months later, Mythili Raman, Principal Deputy Assistant Attorney General and Chief of Staff for Breuer, dismissed the letter, saying the issues raised were the subject of ongoing litigation in the Seventh Circuit U.S. Court of Appeals.

In December 2010,[54] Brand responded, "That is incorrect. The issues we have raised regard prosecutorial misconduct by the U.S. Attorney's Office in Chicago that has caused a grave injustice to Mr. Segal. Those issues are not currently before the Seventh Circuit. Additionally, *it is meaningless to suggest that Mr. Segal should have to rely for relief on the very office that engaged in the misconduct against him.*

"We request that you reconsider our concerns, as laid out in my letter to you of June 8, 2010…and provide us with an opportunity to discuss this matter more fully with you or an appropriate member of your staff. In addition, we request that our concerns be submitted to the Office of Professional Responsibility for consideration."

That last request may have been the match that lit the fire of retribution against Segal. How dare he take on the prosecutors of his case? At a subsequent forfeiture hearing before Castillo, Hogan approached members of Segal's legal team and said Segal would regret filing his complaint with the Justice Department and OPR.

In May 2011, nearly a year after Segal's complaint to Breuer, Robin C. Ashton, attorney for OPR, issued a two-page letter saying no action would be taken.[55]

"OPR has jurisdiction to investigate allegations of misconduct involving Department of Justice attorneys or law enforcement personnel that relate to the exercise of an attorney's authority to investigate, litigate, or provide legal advice. It is, however, the policy of this Office to refrain

---

54   Stan Brand response letter to DOJ, 12/10/10.
55   DOJ letter to Stan Brand, 05/06/11.

from investigating issues or allegations that were addressed or that could have been addressed in the course of litigation, unless a court has made a specific finding of misconduct by a DOJ attorney or law enforcement personnel or there are present other extraordinary circumstances. Based on our review of your correspondence and the pleadings filed in *United States v. Segal and Near North Insurance Brokerage, Inc.*, we have determined that your allegations fall into this category," Ashton wrote.

If these weren't extraordinary circumstances, Segal thought, what would it take?

The last sentence seemed particularly disingenuous: "We regret that we can be of no further assistance to you."

After the rejection, Segal wrote a letter to Cole asking why he believed his filing had been ignored and why the response consisted of just one-and-a-half pages—particularly in light of what had occurred in Miami two years earlier. It was there, in the spring of 2009, that U.S. District Judge Alan Gold found that the federal government had acted deceptively and "in bad faith" in the case of Dr. Ali Shaygan, who was acquitted of 141 counts of illegally prescribing painkillers. Gold criticized the multiple prosecutors in the case and fined the government more than $600,000. Evidence showed that while Shaygan's case was pending, the prosecution had begun a secret investigation of Shaygan's legal team allegedly because the defense was tampering with witnesses. The prosecution had taped the defense attorneys' conversations and offered bribes to a defense attorney, which were rejected, Ultimately, the federal government had apologized for the misconduct.

Now, Segal was left to ponder whether he had been rejected because of a fraternity of protection or because of Chicago politics and bad timing—that his claims could cause embarrassment to U.S. Attorney Patrick Fitzgerald, who was then prosecuting another high-profile political case—that of Illinois Governor Rod Blagojevich which had tendons to other Chicago and national politicians.

However, further efforts to engage OPR or the Justice Department were put on hold because the U.S. Supreme Court had tossed Segal a potential lifeline.

Chapter 29

Honest Services
and Freedom

"There are 150 million workers in the United States. I think possibly 140 [million] of them would flunk your test."

—Supreme Court Justice Stephen Breyer, describing the Justice Department's test for violation of the "honest services clause."

HIGH ON THE LIST OF vague catch-all statutes that Harvey Silverglate cited in his book, *Three Felonies a Day: How the Feds Target the Innocent,* is the "honest services" statute—a very elastic rule. Segal's prosecutors stretched it to the breaking point to obtain a conviction of Segal and Near North for engaging in a fraud that deprived insurance carriers and customers of their right to "honest services."

About halfway through the 20th century, prosecutors began using the mail and wire fraud statutes to charge fraud involving "intangible harms." The statutes, prosecutors contended, implied that these harms included a deprivation of "honest services" by a defendant—most often politicians and public employees. The practice was temporarily halted in the 1980s, when the U.S. Supreme Court found that the term "honest services" did not appear anywhere in the United States Criminal Code. Although Congress passed another honest services law, the statute remained controversial. At one point, a Justice Department spokesman said, "Prosecutors can take differing views on what a person's honest services should be. There is prosecutorial discretion." This was the same old story—prosecutors asserting that they know it when they see it.

As the *Wall Street Journal* opined in 2011: "That's great for prosecutors, who can employ the statute to fit virtually any business practice. But it's not so great for business folks who find themselves caught in high-profile scandals in which prosecutors want a scalp. 'Honest services' is a catch-all statute that can catch just about anyone."

That editorial could have been written with Segal and Near North in mind. The newspaper went on to note that in 1925, Judge Learned Hand had called the conspiracy charge "the darling of the modern prosecutor's nursery." The honest services theory, the newspaper said, was the "new darling.... With Congress unlikely to admit its mistake and define the statute any more precisely, the Supreme Court may have to weigh in again."

On June 24, 2010 that's just what happened when the Supreme Court reversed the conviction of Jeffrey Skilling, the former chief executive officer of Enron, who had been convicted—along with other executives, including the prominent accounting firm of Arthur Anderson—of what the court called "an elaborate conspiracy" to prop up Enron's stock prices by overstating the company's financial well-being. The indictment had accused them of engaging in a scheme to deceive investors about Enron's true financial performance by "manipulating its publicly reported financial results and making false and misleading statements" that deprived Enron and its shareholders of their honest services.

The decision gave Segal new hope, a feeling that was boosted when Brand said his case fit precisely within the boundary of the Skilling decision.

The Supreme Court held that honest services encompasses only bribery and kickback schemes. In the decision, Justice Ruth Bader Ginsburg specifically referred to an amicus brief filed in the honest services case of Alaska Congressman Bruce Weyhrauch. The brief, crafted by Segal appellate lawyer Albert Alschuler, said that the governing standard for honest services prosecutions "should be no broader" than the one that the Second Circuit U.S. Court of Appeals approved in 2003 in *U.S. v. Rybicki:* "a standard that (at least for defendants other than public officials) limits honest-services fraud to schemes to obtain bribes or kickbacks or to engage in undisclosed self-dealing capable of causing economic detriment." Alschuler had taken a similar position in Segal's case, but Appeals Judge Terence Evans's opinion had summarily dismissed his argument, saying it was foreclosed by an earlier decision that, in Alschuler's view, did not address the question at all. Alschuler's annoyance with the rejection of his argument in Segal's case was one of the reasons that Alschuler filed his amicus brief.

Segal's lawyers immediately returned to the appeals court to overturn his conviction. The honest-services issue had been on the defense radar from the beginning and lawyers for Near North had argued unsuccessfully to Castillo that the charge of honest services was wrongly applied. Segal, the defense noted and the prosecution conceded, was not a public official and had not taken bribes or kickbacks.

Finally, in May 2011, the Seventh Circuit issued its ruling. Judge Evans wrote that Segal had "received what we suspect he must have viewed as a ticket to a do-over of the whole shebang…Why is that? Well, the alleged scheme that ran through the indictment against him claimed that Segal was involved in garden-variety mail fraud along with fraud involving the deprivation of his 'honest services.'" Evans said: "The evidence fails to suggest that Segal was involved in either bribery or a kickback scheme. So, the instructions given to the jury regarding honest services fraud were wrong."

It wasn't a win yet. Evans said that if the prosecution could support the verdict with an alternative and valid legal theory "such as money/property fraud," the conviction would stand.

"So, the issue here boils down to this: Would the jury have still convicted Segal had it not been told that in addition to the valid money/property fraud allegations, an allegation of honest services fraud could also be taken into consideration? We conclude that the jury would—and most certainly did—convict Segal for money/property fraud, irrespective of the honest services charge."

The court agreed with the prosecution's argument—though it was as contorted as a circus acrobat—that they never meant a deprivation of honest services.

The court remanded the case to the trial court for resentencing because Castillo may have increased Segal's sentence because Castillo might have believed that Segal committed honest services fraud *and* money and property fraud.

Segal's lawyers petitioned the appeals court to rehear the case "en banc"—before all the appellate judges. Although such appeals are rarely successful, Segal was pleased to be able to address in the petition the false statements in Hogan's filings. The defense believed that the conflict between their version of the facts and the prosecution version was sufficient to merit overturning Segal's conviction—or, at the very least, to get the case remanded to Castillo for a hearing to determine whether Segal had been convicted of regular mail fraud or honest services fraud. The petition said that in denying Segal's appeal, the panel had essentially "converted the violation of Illinois insurance regulations, which, after *Skilling*, should not ever be an indictable offense, to money/property fraud without any evidence that Segal lied to any insurance client of Near North or any insurance company that provided coverage for Near North's clients."

Further, the petition noted that at sentencing, Castillo had concluded there was "no evidence that [Segal] intended to defraud either the insurance clients or the insurance company."

"Post Skilling, it is not a federal crime to violate a state insurance regulation," the petition said. "The only scheme Segal was charged with was a scheme to violate the State of Illinois insurance regulations. Absent a violation of these regulations, Segal did nothing wrong."

Moreover, the defense said, an honest services mail fraud prosecution must be based on a uniform national standard and the prosecution of Segal was based upon an Illinois insurance statute that is in place in just half of the states—hardly a national standard.

Segal's petition, prepared by Alschuler, Edward Joyce, and Marc Martin, noted that the appeals court had held that the word *defraud*, as used in the mail and wire fraud statutes, meant *fraud* as it was understood in common law. In effect, it required proof of the essential criminal elements of regular mail fraud to deprive money and property.

"Moreover, after recognizing that materiality was an element of pecuniary mail fraud, the panel did not address Segal's argument that the jury might have resolved this issue in his favor. The panel maintained that Segal 'represented to the insureds and insurance carriers that he would hold the insurance premiums in trust' but instead used PFTA money to expand his business. Not one single witness testified that either Segal or Near North represented to an insured or a carrier that Near North would hold insurance premiums in trust."

These comments were based on the appeals court's conclusion—which relied upon Hogan's misrepresentations and the deletion of the second part of the District Court's opinion—that Segal and Near North had lied in license renewal applications filed with the state. The petition said, "This conclusion is surprising because Segal and Near North not only did not lie in those applications, but Castillo...found that the jury's guilty verdict with respect to seven counts of false statements in the indictment was not supported by the evidence and acquitted Segal and Near North of that violation."

Segal's lawyers were shocked by the prosecution's misrepresentation and the appellate court's acceptance of Hogan's argument that Segal wasn't convicted of dishonest services fraud.

This was hardly the first time that Segal's lawyers accused the prosecution of filing briefs that misrepresented facts. However, the courts repeatedly rejected these claims. Indeed, the defense contended that Hogan's filing to block Segal from relief under the Skilling decision intentionally deleted part of the district court's written ruling which had eliminated the essential element for the regular mail fraud charge. Misrepresenting the record can be considered a fraud upon the court, although it rarely results in relief.

For example, in the initial appeal of the convictions, the prosecution argued that the Segal case was similar to the federal prosecution of Mark Vincent, an Illinois lawyer. Vincent set up a clients' trust account so that their funds could be deposited and he could purchase real estate on their behalf. Instead of buying property, Vincent paid his business expenses and bought himself a car, jewelry, and other luxury items. When the funds began to run out, Vincent applied for a loan and then lied about why he needed the money. Hogan argued that the PFTA was the same as Vincent's trust fund—an argument that Evans adopted. But Segal's lawyers pointed out that the Vincent case was about a lawyer's trust fund for client funds. Segal's defense contended there was no similarity, under Illinois insurance law, between that kind of account and a PFTA, which allows commingled funds. Evans should have known better, Segal speculated, since he was one of the judges in the Vincent decision.

The request for an *en banc* hearing was denied, so Segal turned to the law firm of Mayer Brown to file a petition with the U.S. Supreme

Court. Before filing the petition, the lawyers at Mayer Brown were so convinced that an injustice had been done that they asked the Solicitor General's office to confess error and agree to overturn Segal's case. And although there was hope of success, ultimately, the request was denied. The petition to the Supreme Court argued there were no misrepresentations to the alleged victims and that none of the alleged victims suffered even a temporary deprivation of money or property. The petition noted that the prosecution claimed the appeals court affirmed that Segal "was taking [his victims'] money," when in fact the Seventh Circuit had said only that he was taking "the money," without assigning ownership to either policy holders or carriers.

The petition noted that "the harm contemplated by a scheme to defraud 'must affect the very nature of the bargain itself,'" but that in Segal's case "there was no evidence that maintenance of the PFTA was material to any customer or carrier." Instead, customers and carriers got what they bargained for.

"The government shamelessly seeks to void this issue by invoking the court of appeals' statement that [Segal] 'fraudulently represented to the insureds and insurance carriers' that 'he would hold the premiums in trust.' But as the government just well knows, the record is utterly devoid of any evidence supporting this assertion."

The petition also noted that the mail and wire fraud convictions were predicated on conduct that violated Illinois law, "but would have been perfectly legal in many other States. The untenable effect of this approach is to criminalize Segal's conduct in those States—and only those States—that impose PFTA rules, which nearly half of all States do not."

The petition was denied. What was next?

Segal then filed a request for a sentence reduction that would end his incarceration. Hogan filed a motion in opposition, which the defense characterized as "an inaccurate and unsupported summary of the factual record based on false facts and misstatements."

This was no surprise. Hogan had fought every step of the way to try to prevent this high-profile prosecution from turning into a high-profile embarrassment. He was involved in all of Segal's post-trial efforts, which was unusual since trial prosecutors customarily hand over the duties in cases after sentencing to prosecutors in the appellate, forfeiture and restitution divisions.

With the assistance of Jennifer Doherty, a smart and detail-oriented associate of defense attorney Joyce, Segal took advantage of his analysis of the 6,000-page transcript he'd spent so much time on—the analysis that had been ignored at his sentencing. Now, it wouldn't just be Segal venting to his lawyers while incarcerated.

The subsequent motion declared, "When Segal was convicted, there was no doubt that 'honest services' mail fraud was the foundation of his conviction. *Skilling* has demonstrated that the honest services foundation of Segal's conviction was fatally defective. Consequently, Hogan has recast the entire trial as a prosecution based on pecuniary fraud. To do so, the Government has to rely on the false facts that previously were only a distraction to the issues then present. These false facts and misstatements, including the Government's misstatement relating to accounting and regulatory evidence, are not supported by the record." The motion said that the prosecution had alleged "without any support," that Segal's sentence had not been imposed because there was a deprivation of honest services, but rather, because "the defendant stole a staggering amount of money from a trust." Paragraph by paragraph, the defense attacked the prosecution's motion.

Castillo denied the petition.

However, on May 29, 2012, Segal was back before Castillo again and this time his prison sentence was reduced to time served.

At last, he was free.

Clad in slacks and a blue blazer, Segal hugged friends and relatives. He had seen the last of Oxford. His original release date was

October 2012, so he was released about five months early after serving nearly six-and-a-half years. Segal did appreciate this, of course, but it felt somewhat anti-climactic after waiting for so many months following the appellate court's decision.

He wasn't fully freed, though. Castillo ordered him to be on supervised release for three years during which he had to complete 120 hours of community service and his travel was restricted. His probation officer, Teressa Zammuto, made unannounced visits to Segal's home, typically parking in his driveway and entering wearing an over-sized, bullet-proof vest.

And when Segal sought to open a business, Zammuto at first said she had no problem, but then changed her mind and said Segal had to go to court to get approval, even though court approval was not required. Why she changed her mind was anyone's guess, but Segal suspected the change came after she discussed the matter with someone in the U.S. Attorney's Office (Hogan was out of town). In January 2014, Castillo not only found no problem with it, but said that he also would contemplate an early termination of the supervision. In October 2014, Castillo did just that because Segal had met all of the conditions imposed upon him.

He was free in all respects.

While Segal's prison ordeal may have been over, his financial ordeal was not. And neither was his effort to persuade the Department of Justice to investigate the prosecutorial misconduct.

Chapter 30

DOJ Still Ignores
the Evidence

In May 2013, Near North's attorney Sal Cognetti took a stab at persuading Attorney General Eric Holder to examine Segal's case. He composed a two-page letter to Holder and attached a thirteen-page summary. Cognetti was the only lawyer from the trial who hadn't abandoned Segal, and they'd become friends. Segal appreciated Cognetti's diligence, as well as the fact that he had lobbied successfully for the passage of the McDade Act.

Cognetti previously had worked closely with Holder and when Cognetti was in Washington DC for a meeting, Cognetti left the letter and case summary for Holder. Holder promised to read it and respond.

Cognetti's summary, titled "The Government vs. Michael Segal—Manufacturing a Financial Crime," was an eloquent treatise that detailed the rise and fall of Near North and Segal, and the misconduct behind it. "The enclosed documents summarize a particularly brazen case of prosecutorial overreaching and misconduct that suggest repeated violations of federal law and DOJ procedures," Cognetti wrote. "The facts surrounding the conviction of Michael Segal, a prominent Chicago insurance executive, and the destruction of his business, Near North Insurance Brokerage, strike an ominous tone in the role of prosecutors in our democracy."

Cognetti pointed out Cole's comment that Segal's case was "one of the worst" examples of misconduct he had encountered and that he could not see where there was a crime. Cognetti laid out the history of Segal's prior attempts to engage the Justice Department.

"In response, an assistant to Mr. Breuer sent a lengthy letter in May of 2011 stating incorrectly that the abuses and constitutional violations had already been litigated," Cognetti explained. "Mr. Segal's attorneys followed up in November of 2011, respectfully pointing out the unresolved issues and leaving no doubt about both the extent of the misconduct and the issues that were never litigated. A year and a half later, that letter has never been answered by the Department of Justice.

"Mike Segal has been on a crusade for over thirteen years to expose the manufactured and false facts that gave rise to his conviction. His persistence and dedication to truth and justice should be admired and a review should not be prejudiced by his questionable conviction. Neither the time spent over the last years in prison by Mike Segal nor the fortune lost by the destruction of Near North can be regained, but a fair evaluation will reflect the truth. That truth can educate others and improve the entire criminal justice system. A tidal wave of the government's power can overcome most if not all individuals; the only defense we have is our belief in honest prosecutors," Cognetti said.

"Carol Marin, a well-respected reporter for *NBC News* and *Chicago Sun-Times* columnist, once compared the saga of Michael Segal and Near North Insurance Brokerage (NNIB) versus the U.S. Attorney's Office to a Hollywood movie, one that she would 'pay to see.' She got her wish, though she did not need to purchase a ticket. The titanic bout between William Hogan, a controversial prosecutor from the U.S. Attorney's Office, and Michael Segal, a successful, self-made Chicago businessman, is probably fodder for such an exhibition. The story is an incredible one and, like most real-life dramas, contains twists and turns that put a fictitious court thriller to shame.

"The story of the federal prosecutors…is well-known and easy to find. The media, ever more interested in a melodrama that ends with the downfall of a powerful man than in the strange circumstances surrounding his demise, made sure of that. There is a second side to the story, though; one based on documented facts that were buried, or simply not told loud enough. It is a tale of the damage done by a few in the U.S. Attorney's Office's scorched earth campaign, a course of action that affected thousands of people and annihilated multiple companies, all to punish a man for supposedly violating a non-criminal Illinois statute—a charge which the state in question had already refused to levy—from which the District Court ruled no party suffered an economic loss.

"All of this was done to take down a man with no criminal history, running a company that, in its forty-year existence, had never been the subject of customer complaints or regulatory violations. This farce would engulf Mr. Segal and his company, Near North. It resulted in Mr. Segal's harassment, conviction, and imprisonment. It also brought about the indictment, a legal fiction, and the destruction of NNIB. Near North Insurance Brokerage was one of the only companies to be treated in this manner since the Arthur Andersen debacle brought about a self-imposed DOJ ban on such tactics as a material DOJ violation of procedures in itself.

"This is Michael Segal's story, a story backed up with reams of court documents and the work of legal scholars, computer experts, and certified forensic accountants.

"Segal is seeking redress in a case where constitutional protections have been willfully violated for 12 years and injustices are piled on top of injustices. He is seeking an answer to the well-documented filings sent to the head of the Criminal Justice Division in November of 2011, but never answered as of May 2013."

While waiting for Holder's response, Segal sent a letter of his own in July 2013 to Robin Ashton at the Office of Professional Responsibility

(OPR) which contained a summary filed with the Internal Revenue Service Inspector General based on the participation of IRS agents in his case. "The key misconduct in the original case—illegal cyberhacking of documents, the wiretapping of a defense attorney, the creation of false evidence, the interference with exculpatory evidence—was at the heart of events.... Unfortunately, William Hogan's misconduct, which remains ... uncorrected, continues to dominate current forfeiture and restitution proceedings. Most recently, he has sought to influence the current IRS civil tax court proceedings by stating the need to find additional tax civil liabilities to IRS attorneys.

"Given AUSA Hogan's...well-documented misconduct in my case, it is inappropriate that he remains in the position of handling government filings and negotiations in forfeiture and restitution hearings that would not normally be his area of responsibility.

"I strongly urge your office to investigate the past undisclosed misconduct and due process violations and to help stop their continuation in current court proceedings and negotiations. Unless corrected, the reputation of the DOJ is stained by the professional misconduct. Public confidence in the DOJ requires an accounting and appropriate action regarding this case. My attorneys, accountants, and forensic investigators would be happy to assist you and your staff in achieving a global solution."

The response?

William J. Birney, associate counsel for Office of Professional Responsibility, wasted no time, emailing Cognetti to say the matter was closed and that his allegations did not warrant further inquiry. He suggested that Cognetti was free to direct his complaint to Judge Castillo or to Gary Shapiro, Acting U.S. Attorney in Chicago.

Cognetti never received a direct response from Holder, despite the previous public statements Holder had made about the need to end the delays in dealing with prosecutorial misconduct after the wrongful conviction of U.S. Senator Ted Stevens. As Sidney Powell wrote in *Licensed to Lie*:

> "Not only has Mr. Holder failed to make any of the reforms he promised in the wake of his forced dismissal of the indictment against former Senator Ted Stevens, the changes he has made have been for the worse. Absent a dramatic about-face, Holder will leave the Department of Justice littered with corrupted prosecutions and prosecutors, his own contempt of Congress, numerous Supreme Court reversals, and scathing rebukes from federal judges....
>
> "We now have confirmation that Mr. Holder is protecting and retaining prosecutors whose intentional or reckless prosecutorial misconduct has been confirmed. Indeed, he has refused repeated demands to release the names of the lawbreaking prosecutors or identify the cases their misconduct infected. No one is holding Holder accountable."

Cognetti emailed a response to the OPR. "Misconduct at any time by a representative of the Department of Justice should be evaluated and considered based upon the facts presented," he said. "Whether a defendant or his attorney under the pressures of a prosecution had the information, knowledge, or ability to raise the misconduct during the proceedings is of no moment.

"The policy of the Department of Justice should hold wayward prosecutors accountable. If the OPR needs a court finding prior to initiating any action, then what purpose does OPR serve? It is actions and decisions like this that give rise to the Hyde Act and the McDade Act. The issues raised in the Segal case are serious and are continuing today. Your decisions sanction vindictiveness by the prosecutor and reward him for his actions. Unfortunately, your decision only continues this saga."

In September 2013, Cognetti duly wrote to Shapiro (with a copy going to Holder), "concerning the actions of Assistant United States Attorney William Hogan in his ongoing vindictive attacks against Michael Segal." Shapiro had been First Assistant U.S. Attorney when Segal was arrested and now was in charge of the U.S. Attorney's Office. Cognetti told Shapiro, "One of my fears in highlighting the misconduct of Mr. Hogan to the Attorney General was that Mr. Hogan would retaliate against Mr. Segal. Unfortunately, this fear has become a reality." Mr. Hogan continues at every turn to act in bad faith, blocking or delaying implementation of a settlement of the government's claims against Mr. Segal. These actions, coupled with prior actions outlined to the DOJ, highlight the need of immediate corrective action by you and the DOJ. Mr. Hogan's totalitarian actions, reflected in his treatment of Mr. Joyce, are totally inappropriate, as is his constant invocation of your name in threatening a further delay through appeals. I am unsure of the depth of your knowledge concerning those actions.

"Hopefully, this letter provides you an opportunity to ensure the public is protected by an effective United States Attorney's Office that is made up of honest and conscientious attorneys and does not permit misconduct to go unanswered."

Shapiro responded by calling Cognetti's letter "intemperate" and an "ad hominem" attack on Hogan. "I suppose one man's vindictiveness is another's negotiation or, put another way, another's advocacy of his client's interests (here, the United States) and those of the victims of Segal's fraud. None of the positions you so blithely accuse Mr. Hogan of taking in bad faith are the positions of a rogue prosecutor. Quite the opposite; they are the views and negotiating positions of the team handling this litigation, all of which I have approved. They are the result of a careful analysis of the facts and law as we know them, and are positions we believe to be in the best interests of the United States and the victims of Mr. Segal's fraud. So, if that's not clear enough, I reject the premise of your letter that anything untoward has occurred in our handling of this litigation. Of course, as always, you may take your complaints to the district court judge presiding over this matter, if you believe any of them worthy of further airing."

In signing off, Shapiro took one final shot, labeling Cognetti's effort a "baseless, out-of-court vituperation."

Cognetti fired right back, quoting the case of *Berger v. United States*, in which Supreme Court Justice Robert H. Jackson wrote:

> "The United States Attorney is a representative not of an ordinary party to a controversy, but of a sovereignty whose obligation to govern impartially is as compelling as its obligation to govern at all; and whose interest, therefore, in a criminal prosecution is not that it shall win a case, but that justice shall be done. As such, he is in a peculiar and very definite sense the servant of the law, the twofold aim of which is that guilt shall not escape or innocence suffer. He may prosecute with earnestness and vigor, indeed, he should do so. But, while he may strike hard blows, he is not at liberty to strike foul ones. It is as much his duty to refrain from improper methods calculated to produce a wrongful conviction as it is to use every legitimate means to bring about a just one."

Cognetti also cited a 2012 decision by the Seventh Circuit U.S. Court of Appeals in Chicago that said, "The Department of Justice has an obligation to its lawyers and to the public to prevent prosecutorial misconduct. Prosecutors, as servants of the law, are subject to constraints and responsibilities that do not apply to other lawyers; they must serve truth and justice first."

Cognetti wrote, "Hopefully these principles and values are not foreign to you in the operation of your office and the people you supervise. Your letter reflects a complete lack of understanding of the facts and the proceedings. One could conclude that Bill Hogan wrote it.

"Your letter refers to 'victims of Mr. Segal's fraud,' but the court record and presentencing report...state that there is 'no evidence the Defendant intended to defraud either the insurance clients or the insurance carriers' and that Segal's management 'did not result in a loss to his clients.' In other words, there are *no* victims, *no* fraud, *no* losses to clients. Neither was there evidence of non-disclosure or fraud to the Illinois Department of Insurance."

Cognetti sharply criticized Shapiro for referring to the "looting of Near North Insurance's premium trust fund account." He wrote, "Let alone that the Illinois Statute makes it clear there is no conventional trust provision that was misrepresented as such. Instead, both the District and Appellate Court cited violations of the 'honest services' provision by Segal, a legal theory which was invalidated by the Supreme Court....

"The only victims in this case, as a result of Mr. Hogan's unlawful exertions—his collaboration with and protection of illegal cyber-hackers, the wiretapping of Segal's defense attorney Harvey Silets, the myriad violations of attorney-client privilege, and the interference with exculpatory evidence—were Mr. Segal himself, who spent seven years in prison for a manufactured crime, and the nine hundred employees of Near North Insurance Brokerage who lost their jobs.

"It is not our purpose to relitigate Mr. Segal's trial or appeal. Mr. Segal cannot get back those seven years of his life or the company he built that never had a regulatory violation in its forty-year history. I wrote to you in the hope that by pointing out Mr. Hogan's recent repeated violations of the forfeiture settlement, you might assist and help bring an end to the numerous delays, the endless wasting of court assets and the continued misrepresentation of accounting evidence used vindictively to harm Segal and his family. Your letter avoided any response at all to the specific examples of the forfeiture misconduct I cited, including Hogan's repeated failure to unblock funds that were due to Segal's ownership or properties, the blocking of Segal's ability to purchase NNIB insurance policies for his family or exercise his option to purchase from the government his half share of Chicago Bulls ownership.

"As recently on October 1, 2013, AUSA Hogan had threatened to cancel Segal's family life insurance as part of the ongoing vindictive threat."

Cognetti referred Shapiro to the June 2010 filing prepared by Cole and Olsen and submitted to Lanny Breuer. "You can also call Mr. Cole to confirm his co-authorship of the filing and get his insights into how that misconduct led to a major miscarriage of justice, ruined lives, and destruction of a $250 million company.

"The prosecution of this case began with a scheme to use an alleged regulatory state violation to force Mr. Segal to record in the future unknown parties at issue. I am sure you were not aware of this initial strategy and to counter the false innuendoes given to the media Segal had cooperated fully with the government on the day of his arrest and subsequently sat through three proffering sessions with your AUSAs to show his cooperation and truthfully answered all questions under the law of perjury."

Cognetti attached numerous documents that contained references to the trial record and forensic accounting affidavits to provide further detailed evidence that there were no victims owed restitution.

"Knowledge of misconduct carries an obligation to investigate and bring this disgraceful chapter to an end. Given the nature of your supervisory relationship with Mr. Hogan, reflected in your response to my letter, it would make a lot of sense to arrange for appointment of a respected, independent-minded DOJ official to review the well-documented due process issues in this case, or you can arrange to meet with Mr. Segal's attorneys to learn additional facts as a step toward finally resolving these issues. Mr. Segal has not yet taken these issues public, but given the overwhelming evidence of egregious prosecutorial misconduct, I would urge you to take prompt action to enable a measure of justice after Mr. Segal's long ordeal.

"At some point this injustice will be unearthed," Cognetti concluded. "The question is—will you be part of unearthing the wrongs that have been committed—or part of the cover-up?"

The answer?

There was no response. Nothing was done. Again.

Chapter 31

IRS Vindicates Segal

THE CIVIL TAX ASSESSMENT CASE that the Internal Revenue Service pursued against Segal in the U.S. Tax Court was a circus separate from the forfeiture proceedings. Instigated by Hogan while Segal was still in prison, it was a civil fraud proceeding designed to collect back taxes and a 75 percent penalty and interest for company payment of personal expenses. It was also meant to collect money that Hogan claimed Daniel Watkins had given to Segal that was not recorded as income or reported on his income tax returns.

Segal represented himself and flatly rejected an IRS suggestion to settle the case out of court. Instead, he spent countless hours in the prison library learning how to conduct a U.S. Tax Court proceeding.

The civil tax case was predicated on the same facts as the Klein Tax Conspiracy criminal charge—that Segal and Watkins had conspired to prevent the IRS from collecting taxes.

When Watkins pled guilty, the government stated that Watkins regularly provided cash from Near North's petty cash fund to Segal to pay for Segal's personal expenses. Watkins claimed he'd concealed the payments by labeling them as postage and repairs or maintenance expenses.

Once Segal was freed and began focusing on the tax case, Hogan, although he was not involved in the case, demanded meetings with the IRS attorneys and claimed he had even more evidence for them. One of the IRS lawyers whom Hogan met with told him to send them any additional information he had, but nothing ever arrived.

When the IRS again raised the possibility of settling the case, Segal requested the documents backing up their case. Two young IRS attorneys, who may well have seen the case as a career booster, responded with a host of demands for admission of facts and the production of documents. Segal responded in kind, making multiple requests to them. As the proceedings moved along, the senior IRS attorney in charge told Segal that in the beginning, he'd thought that Segal was blowing smoke and that he believed Hogan. Ultimately, however, the IRS counsel's office actually began to help Segal, providing explanations and guidance about how to deal with the sometimes arcane and confusing procedural aspects of U.S. Tax Court.

In February 2014, the truth emerged when Segal sat down to take Watkins' deposition under oath. Watkins, who said that his current job was delivering newspapers, appeared with a criminal defense lawyer, who was clearly not working pro bono. Segal asked Watkins where he'd found the lawyer and Watkins said, "in the yellow pages." Segal wondered who had bankrolled his defense.

During questioning, Watkins admitted he had worn a wire to a meeting with Segal's defense lawyer, Harvey Silets, under the guidance of Agent Murphy.

But most striking were Watkins's responses to questions from IRS attorney John Comeau.

"In 1999, any other money that [Segal] received from Near North that was not his salary, do you know whether he used it for his personal benefit?" Comeau asked.

"No, I don't know if he did," Watkins said.

"Did [Segal's wife] Joy receive money from Near North, other than direct deposit salary?"

"I don't recall any."

"So, Joy received a salary that was direct deposited?" "Yes."

"Mr. Segal received a salary that was direct deposited?"
"Yes."

"And the two of them also received money—cash—from Near North that was not direct deposited, but given to them personally?"
"Yes."

"And, do you know, when you gave them that money, whether they used it for a business expense of the company or a personal expense for themselves?"

"Generally, I didn't know."

"You didn't know? Did Mr. Segal ever say to you: 'The money that you're giving me, that isn't my direct deposit salary now, I want you to hide that money so that it doesn't like look like it came to me?'"

Here was Watkins's golden opportunity to bury Segal—to confirm that they were, as the prosecution had contended for more than a decade, engaged in a conspiracy to cheat the IRS. But that wasn't the truth.

"He never said that to me," Watkins said.

Comeau pressed Watkins: "Did he ever say to you: 'The money you're giving to me, that is not my salary—now, I'm talking about the years 1999, 2000, 2001—did he ever say to you, 'Don't post that money to my draw account, post it to something else, whatever you like?'"

"No. He never said that."

"Did he ever say, 'Don't post it to my draw account—put it—call it postage?'"

"No."

"Did he ever say to you, 'I don't want to pay taxes on the money that I'm receiving that's not my salary, the additional money?'"

"No."

"Did he ever say to you, generally at all, during the years 1999, 2000, 2001: 'You know, I really don't want to pay tax on the money I receive from Near North?'"

"No," Watkins said.

"Did he ever ask you to help him conceal the money he was receiving from Near North?"

"No."

"Did he…conspire with you to somehow defraud the government when it came to taxes?"

"No."

"Did you ever overhear him conspiring with anyone during those years?"

"No."

"To evade taxes?" "No."

"Did you know that one of the counts that he was indicted for was conspiring to defraud the government and filing false returns?"

"No."

"Did the government, prior to Mr. Segal's indictment, ever come to you…and say, 'One of the things we're going to charge this man with is cheating on his taxes or conspiring. Do you have any evidence relevant to that?'"

"No."

"They never asked you questions about that?"

"No."

"And if they had asked you questions about that, if they had, would you have been able to provide them with evidence that would show he was conspiring to defraud on his taxes?"

"No, I don't think so," Watkins replied. This admission refuted the government's Exhibit No. 5, a document Segal believed had been fabricated.

"Did the government ever tell you why it was they didn't call you as a witness in Mr. Segal's case?"

"Dean Polales…said, 'The case is going so well against Mr. Segal, we don't need you to testify, so we're not going to call you,'" Watkins said.

"They never said anything to you like, 'We don't think you would make a good witness—that you would fall apart?'" Comeau asked.

"I don't recall that, no." (Of course, if he had been put on the witness stand, Watkins would have been forced to admit he knew nothing about Exhibit No. 5.)

Watkins told Comeau that he was responsible for providing the financial information to the individuals who prepared the tax returns for Segal and his wife.

"Did Mr. Segal ever say to you, 'Don't tell them about the money I received other than my salary?" Comeau asked.

"No," Watkins said.

"Did Mr. Segal ever say to you, 'Don't give the return preparer the postage account because they might inquire what all that money is there for?"

"No."

"If Mr. Segal never told you to post an item to postage, why did you ever post items to postage?"

"He did one time, many, many years ago," Watkins said. "He just came and he got a small amount and he said put it to postage. And then, many times after that, when he would come, he wouldn't say what it was for, I didn't know what to do with it."

"So," Comeau asked, "You thought: 'Well, I don't know what to do with this. I'll put it to postage?'"

"Correct," Watkins said.

"And the only time he ever said to you, with a very small dollar amount, put it to postage was many, many years prior to 1999, 2000 and 2001?"

"Yes."

"He had never, ever, ever said that to you again?"

"Never verbally said that to me, no."

Watkins went on to explain that Segal didn't know that he was embezzling from Near North and when confronted by Segal, Wish, and Silets, he was scared of getting into trouble.

"I guess it would be fair to say Mr. Segal never came to you and said, 'Hey, why don't we embezzle some money from this company together?'" Comeau said.

"No, he never said that," Watkins replied.

"Would you think that when Mr. Segal took money out of the accounts, other than for his salary, that he was— Did he say to you, 'I'm doing this because I'm embezzling from the company?'"

"No."

"Did he say, 'I'm doing this because I'm trying to conceal it from my income taxes'?"

"No."

"Do you remember the day you were fired?"

"I don't remember the day."

"Do you remember why you were fired?"

"I believe some changes were made to my initial statement or something that [FBI agent] Pat Murphy suggested, and then [Segal] didn't approve of those, and so he fired me."

"Do you remember Mr. Segal...yelling at you...about why you would have posted items to postage?"

"I don't recall him ever yelling at me for that," Watkins said.

"Can you think of anything that would indicate in any way that [Segal] wanted to cheat on his taxes in 1999?" Comeau asked.

"No," Watkins said.

"2000?"

"No."

"2001?"

"No."

So, there it was.

Watkins affirmed under oath that he'd never conspired with Segal to defraud the IRS and had no knowledge of Segal ever cheating on his taxes. It was inconceivable to Segal that the prosecutors who owned Watkins could not have known that to be the case. A failure to disclose it to the defense certainly would have been egregious prosecutorial misconduct. And now it was patently clear why the prosecution had never called Watkins as a witness at the trial.

Days later, Segal got a call from IRS counsel, who suggested that the government was prepared to drop the case. Segal told the official that while this was great news, he would prefer to continue on with his discovery. He had already served subpoenas on McNichols and other government witnesses who had lied during the criminal trial, including Agent Rogoz, who had given the questionable testimony about Exhibit No. 5.

The IRS attorneys initially did not object to Segal's request to depose Hogan and Polales, but then insisted that Segal petition the court for an order. Before things went any further, however, the IRS sidestepped the issue entirely and did something what would have been inconceivable before Watkins was questioned. The case against Segal was dismissed and closed.

The order, filed in U.S. Tax Court, said, "There are no deficiencies in income tax due from the petitioner for the years 1999, 2000, and 2001" and "the petitioner is not liable for the fraud penalty...for the years 1999, 2000, and 2001." As a result, a $1.1 million tax lien was vacated and Segal received a refund of more than $25,000.

The tax case had been based on the exact same facts and evidence that had been presented by the prosecution during the criminal trial. Now, the IRS had determined that evidence was not enough to sustain a civil judgment which carries a lesser burden of proof than the beyond a reasonable doubt standard of a criminal proceeding.

As much of a victory as it seemed, Segal regretted there would be no sworn depositions of McNichols or Rogoz.

Segal later was informed that Hogan had gone to the IRS counsel's office to challenge Segal's intention to take those depositions. After the Tax Court dismissal, Segal learned that Hogan was so enraged that he filed an internal complaint accusing Comeau of failing to do a proper job and implying that he'd taken money from Segal. As a result of that act—which, to Segal, seemed just another example of Hogan's vindictiveness—Comeau was told to stop talking to Segal.

This prompted Segal to fire off another letter to J. Russell George, U.S. Treasury Department Inspector General for Tax Administration, saying that he understood that an investigation of the IRS and prosecutor misconduct had been opened.

"This ruling adds urgency to the investigation of wrongdoing by IRS agents that was outlined in my previous letter," Segal wrote. "The deposition and other facts submitted to the IRS Counsel goes to support the knowledge and cover up of multiple exculpatory evidence that was misrepresented and interfered with.

"As much as I was pleased, after my long ordeal, that the U.S. Tax Court had dropped the civil tax fraud charge and penalties, my concern is that the Tax Court had ordered depositions of several agents who had aided Hogan in manufacturing the…Klein Tax Conspiracy charge. Had the proceeding continued, I believe statements the IRS agents would have made under oath would be truthful and would establish the crucial facts that would aid your investigation. Truthful statements would confirm that exculpatory evidence was covered up and that the prosecution manipulated IRS agents to assist them in their goal.

"The actions of these IRS agents under pressure and misdirection (by) AUSA Hogan and ex-AUSA Polales added years to a prison term that was based on a wrongful conviction, which extensive evidence showed misused the IRS to pile on vindictive punishments after I exposed related misconduct that led to my wrongful conviction.

"The manufactured…Klein Tax Conspiracy charges and conviction were but one example of Hogan's vindictive actions involving the IRS. In recent months, it is my belief that AUSA Hogan has inserted himself into the Tax Court proceedings, demanding that IRS counsel increase the proposed penalties for the civil charge, which the IRS and the Tax Court now acknowledge had no basis in fact.

"To cover up the previous misconduct that led to my...Klein Tax Conspiracy conviction, Hogan attempted to interfere with the recent court-ordered depositions of IRS agents and other witnesses involved in my case, such as telling the IRS legal counsel's office that Segal's subpoenas could be invalid. Hogan summoned IRS counsel to meetings in his U.S. Attorney's Office on multiple occasions to urge them to find more tax liability in my case and he berated IRS counsel for allowing discovery in the deposition of IRS agents. It is my belief that at the most recent meeting, when IRS counsel was called to Hogan's office, the IRS agents who were scheduled to be deposed were already seated in his office, no doubt having received instructions from the prosecutor. With IRS counsel present, Hogan raised the issue that the IRS agents who testified at my trial had information that they learned through the grand jury and should not have to be deposed. For multiple reasons, this argument is not valid.

"Your decision to open up an investigation has been further validated by the actions of the IRS counsel's office who followed the evidence and ignored the pressure from AUSA Hogan and followed the evidence to drop the manufactured civil charge. I will provide a copy of the deposition of Daniel Watkins and share other evidence as to the issues of the IRS agents and the order of the Tax Court, for I have requested to meet with the two investigators who met with me last year when your office began looking into these matters. I would hope that under this recent development, your investigators would meet with me at any time.

"Given recent allegations and questions raised about the misuse of the IRS for retaliatory or political purposes, it is crucial that the investigation continues and establishes how the IRS will not be allowed to be misused to aid misconduct in a wrongful prosecution. Your respected office is charged with holding the IRS accountable for their actions and several news organizations have had an ongoing interest in how my case has been handled. It is important for your office to maintain the confidence of the public and the reputation of the IRS."

Finally, Segal urged, "Now is the time to enable the IRS agents who were manipulated in my case to come forward and provide a truthful account of how its processes were misused and to ensure that what happened to Michael Segal will not happen to others, and provide support for those agents and IRS attorneys who would stand up and repudiate such unlawful conduct."

And so, at least in one segment of the prosecution's case, Segal's assertion of innocence was vindicated. But as of this writing, no one in the IRS had been publicly disciplined nor had there been any explanation coming from the Inspector General's office.

Although the IRS, by dismissing the civil tax case, had acted to correct an injustice, the failure of the Inspector General of the IRS to hold accountable those involved, including Hogan and Rogoz, was, Segal believed, another failure of checks and balances at the federal level.

Chapter 32

Forfeiture — Will it Ever End?

"Jarndyce and Jarndyce drones on.
This scarecrow of a suit has, over the course
of time, become so complicated, that no
man alive knows what it means."

FIFTEEN YEARS AFTER THE SEGAL'S forfeiture trial, the case had become a modern day true-life parallel to the fictional court case that Charles Dickens conjured up in his 19th century novel *Bleak House* to ridicule England's chancery court system.[56]

Segal was indicted in 2002, convicted of racketeering in 2004, sentenced to ten years in prison in 2005 and ordered to forfeit $30 million as well as his company, Near North, valued at more than $250 million, costing one thousand people their livelihoods, although no customers lost a nickel, all got their insurance and the court ruled there was loss and no fraudulent intent. Segal was released in 2012 and seven years later, in 2019, the case was, as Dickens put it, still droning on.

On the surface, it was about money—how much did Segal have and

---

56   Jarndyce v Jarndyce Wikipedia, Jarndyce v Jarndyce Encyclopedia

what were his personal assets and investments, how much did he owe
to the government for his civil forfeiture, and what did he agree to pay?
The intricacies of this financial dust-up were buried in hundreds and
hundreds of pages of legal briefs, but it basically boiled down to this:

At the conclusion of the forfeiture hearing the prosecution per-
suaded Judge Castillo to freeze *all* of Segal's assets, as well as his
family's, to ensure that the $30 million judgment was satisfied. So,
when Segal was sent off to jail with no bail before sentencing, he
essentially had no assets and those members of his family who were
working for Near North immediately lost their jobs. Since more than
$30 million was frozen, Segal asked for the release of funds suffi-
cient to pay for family medical needs and legal fees and other pending bills, but after Hogan objected, Judge Castillo denied the request.
It was the first of several such denials.

Segal's lawyers appealed and in May 2007, the Seventh Circuit U.S.
Court of Appeals ordered Judge Castillo to hold a hearing to determine
an accurate accounting. The appeals court said it could not determine
whether the $30 million forfeiture was fair because it might have been
the result of double counting and that such double counting "cannot
be the intent of Congress."

There seemed an end in sight.

But it was not to be because Hogan changed the prosecution strategy to get around the Seventh Circuit's mandate. Properties and assets
that Hogan once had argued belonged to Segal, such as his investments
and retirement accounts and his Highland Park home,, Hogan now
claimed actually had been owned by Near North all along and therefore were forfeited under the jury's decision that Near North and all
its holdings were to be turned over to the government. The net effect
would be that Segal would continue to be denied assets. Segal saw this
as a Hogan plan to try to preserve the $30 million forfeiture judgment.

It came as no surprise that Hogan continued to fight all efforts to return any of Segal's assets. Year after year after year, despite the best efforts of Segal's lawyers to expose misconduct, Hogan had continued to find new ways to punish Segal. What was surprising was that Hogan—who had been the trial prosecutor—remained the driving force in the forfeiture litigation instead of sticking to his trial duties. It was highly unusual for a trial prosecutor to spend such a long time involved in the forfeiture. By 2019, he had been at it nearly fifteen years after the conviction. It seemed as if Hogan was devoting his life to pursuing Segal. How, Segal wondered, did Hogan's actions not raise eyebrows in the Justice Department?

There was no doubt in Segal's mind about Hogan's motivation. When Segal had filed a complaint with the Department of Justice Office of Professional Responsibility, Hogan told his lawyer that filing the complaint was a mistake. The implication seemed obvious—he would get even. And when one of Segal's lawyers contacted Hogan about getting involved in the forfeiture proceedings, Hogan shouted, "I'm not going to give Mike Segal or his wife one nickel."

Hogan first sought to overturn the appeals court decision by filing a motion for reconsideration. When that was denied, he initiated a series of pleadings containing an amalgam of conflated trial record and extra/non-record evidence designed to persuade Castillo that what the prosecution previously said were Segal's personal assets were really corporate assets which would be forfeited under the corporation's separate civil forfeiture judgment, not Segal's. Hogan argued that Segal owed the entire $30 million, based on a finding by the jury that as of June 30, 2001, the PFTA had a $30 million deficit—even though Segal's accountant, Andrew Lotts, had concluded that the PFTA had actually had a $5.8 million surplus. Additionally, Hogan refused to acknowledge Segal's personal infusions of cash into Near North over the years which amounted to at least $17 million and as much as $22 million.

The defense challenged Hogan's reference to non-record evidence, noting: "It has been over a year and a half since this issue was remanded by the Seventh Circuit and it is time for this Court to enter judgment."

Segal's attorneys Edward Joyce and Jennifer Doherty said the prosecution's claims were based on the following misrepresentations and false evidence:

- An "authenticated" summary series of documents labeled Trial Exhibits SES containing non-trial record evidence sandwiched between actual trial evidence.

- That Angela Amaro had given Segal at least $1,000 a week in cash, although there was no support for that in the trial record.

- A figure of $667,845 in unreported income for the final three years prior to Segal's arrest. That figure had been conceded as wrong on the witness stand and the concession was later supported by the IRS.

- That Segal did not own certain partnership interests when ownership of the partnerships had never been determined by the jury or Judge Castillo and trial and government records showed the opposite.

- That Norman Bobbins, the chief executive officer of LaSalle Bank, had testified that he would not approve a loan directly to Near North—when in fact Bobbins had not testified at all.

- That Segal's Highland Park home belonged to Near North. The government kept the proceeds from the sale of the Highland Park property, even though the property belonged to Segal personally.

Segal's lawyers filed a motion to strike the government's facts that were not in the record or were misrepresented, but Judge Castillo did not rule on it. The defense asserted that the total payments representing salary, benefits and perks from Near North to Segal, based upon the record, were at most $1,598,626 and that figure "should be reduced to zero by the credit to which Segal is entitled because he invested at least $17 million in NNIB. Even the government admitted, the defense noted, that Segal "poured millions of dollars into the enterprise."

The defense contended that "the government's submission demonstrates what all its submissions to this Court following the remand have shown—it does not take seriously the mandate of the Seventh Circuit. For the fifth time, the government has selectively reviewed the evidence incriminating Segal, denounced his crimes, and addressed every phantom issue in the case while at the same time it ignores the one issue that is before this court: 'How much of the $30 million [in racketeering proceeds] was not reinvested in the enterprise, but rather went to benefit Segal personally.'"

As the forfeiture proceedings continued to play out, Segal was under financial duress. He was denied money for lawyers and accountants, asset representatives would not to talk to him, and the trustee refused to turn over information.

Meanwhile, Hogan continued to file motions filled with what Segal's lawyer saw as misrepresentations. It was a war of attrition as Segal wore down and his legal fees piled up.

For example, when the defense noted that if the prosecution had not blocked the sale of Near North prior to the trial, the enterprise would have sold for more than $100 million (which would have been put into an escrow account), Hogan asserted in a court filing that there was no such sale because the offer documents were never signed. However, that was just false. An email dated January 31, 2003 showed that Hogan had received three copies of a signed letter of intent from Winston & Strawn attorney Howard Pearl.[57]

Over the years, a series of fire sales needlessly dissipated Near North's assets. For example, Near North National Title, a commercial title insurance company that Segal had started from scratch, was sold

---

57   Signed Letter of Intent from Frontenac for Near North, 013103.

for $700,000, even though one of the largest title insurers had offered to purchase it for $10 million just before Segal's arrest and even though another group offered a substantially higher price. That group was blocked because one of the buyers allegedly had a prior relationship with Segal.

A similar fate befell Near North's International Film Guarantors, another of Segal's start-up companies. Even though it was the largest film guarantee company, was earning as much as $5 million a year and had $16 million in the bank, the government agreed to sell Segal's interest for what amounted to $3.5 million while Segal was in prison. Segal's lawyers filed an objection, but Castillo rejected it after the government and the buyers' lawyers claimed that the $16 million was set aside for claims, even though there was reinsurance covering any potential future claims and there was a history of no claims being filed. This ultimately reduced the proceeds the government could have obtained by several million dollars. Segal's lawyers appealed and the government, as it did in in the district court, made the same misrepresentation to the appeals court.

Perhaps the most damaging, however, was the forfeiture trustee's order to dismiss the civil lawsuit that Near North had filed against the Takeover Group and the admitted hacker, David Cheley as well as Kemper Insurance—where Cheley did much of his hacking—and Aon. The lawsuit, which had been put on hold prior to Segal's trial, was a significant potential asset of Near North in that the defendants all had significant liability exposure. When the lawsuit resumed after Segal's trial and the first member of the Takeover Group, Berry, was deposed, the trustee ordered the lawsuit dumped. Although the trustee conceded to Segal's defense lawyers that the lawsuit likely had merit and could have resulted in a substantial financial recovery for the government, the trustee said the decision to dismiss the litigation was out of his hands. Segal believed the order to discontinue the lawsuit came from the U.S. Attorney's Office, although one of his lawyers later reported that Marsha McClellan, the prosecutor from the forfeiture department, said no such instruction had been given.

Ultimately, the prosecution claimed that Segal owed $18 million with little or no supporting records. The defense, meanwhile, argued that, at most, Segal owed $1.5 million and more likely, the prosecution owed Segal money instead.

Finally, in August 2009, after more than 20 briefs had been filed, Judge Castillo rejected the prosecution's attempt to introduce new evidence that had not been presented during the trial.

Unfortunately for Segal, Castillo sided with Hogan, relying primarily on the testimony of Takeover Group member McNichols. Castillo said it was impossible to trace "each dollar from the enterprise into Segal's pocket, or anywhere else for that matter," and despite his own previous ruling that there was no loss and no victims, cited the appeals court ruling that Near North's "lackluster accounting system" was "a deliberate attempt to conceal his fraudulent conduct." The appellate court had chosen not to rely on a document in the trial record, supported by witness testimony, that had been prepared by Deloitte & Touche which set out the ownership of the assets.[58]

Castillo's bottom line: Segal personally owed $15 million. The judge did not address the differences between the prosecution's accounting arguments and Segal's accounting arguments and chose to ignore evidence of proceeds remaining or reinvested in the enterprise. Segal was devastated by Judge Castillo's rejection of trial evidence that Segal had loaned or otherwise personally contributed more than $17 million in cash to Near North for corporate expansion. Had Judge Castillo accepted the trial record, Segal's lawyers believed this would have covered the judgement and Segal would not have owed anything pursuant to the appeals court's remand ruling.

---

58   Exhibit 41 D&T, Affidavit of Larry Boysen

Both the prosecution and Segal appealed.

In May 2011, the appeals court upheld Castillo.

"We remanded the case to the district court in 2007 to determine if there was any double-counting when Segal was forced to forfeit his enterprise and $30 million—some of which Segal may have reinvested in his enterprise," the Court said.

This was a crushing blow to Segal because the court was ignoring its own mandate to determine the net proceeds *based on the trial record* and Hogan's filings showed that there was an excess of $17 million in funds that Segal had put into his own company.

"On remand, the district court did exactly what we asked of it," the appeals court said. "Using the evidence that was available, it cogently explained the amount of money that Segal took for personal use. None of the shortcomings alleged by the government or Segal rise to the level of clear error. Setting a restitution figure in a case like this is akin to hitting a zone rather than a point. The zone the district court ended up in seems eminently reasonable to us."

The case bounced back into Judge Castillo's courtroom where he set a two-phase hearing to determine which of Segal's restrained assets would be used to satisfy the $15 million judgment. The first hearing was to determine ownership of the restrained assets; the second was to determine the value of all assets owned by Segal. Segal would then use $15 million of his assets to satisfy his forfeiture obligation.

This determination of ownership should have been decided years earlier when the trial jury rendered its forfeiture verdict. At the time, the prosecution had moved for a preliminary order of forfeiture, asking that Segal be required to forfeit his interest in Near North and any of its operating affiliates and subsidiaries named in the indictment.

Castillo had granted a broad motion allowing the government to seize Segal's assets.

At that time, subpoenas were issued for information relating to the assets of Near North and Segal's personal assets and a prosecution forfeiture department paralegal prepared a spreadsheet analysis reflecting ownership. Segal's lawyers were not allowed to see the documents obtained pursuant to the subpoenas which would have shown the date of acquisition. Segal believed the documents would have showed that the dates of acquisition would have been outside of the forfeiture period. The documents, Segal believed, would have reflected his ownership, not the corporation's.

Subsequently, Hogan brought in Thomas Moriarty, a retired Department of Justice investigator, who claimed to have assembled a list separate from the Forfeiture Department's subpoena returns. Segal believed Moriarty's account misrepresented which assets were owned by Segal personally, which assets were owned by his family, which assets were owned by Near North, which assets were owned by the family trust, and which were ERISA-protected assets. Under Seventh Circuit case law, ERISA qualified retirement accounts cannot be subject to forfeiture.[59] On December 7, 2012,[60, 61] Segal's attorney Joyce requested Hogan's acknowledgment of the protective status of the ERISA accounts, but was ignored.

Years later, even Judge Castillo would suggest that Moriarty was less than reliable, saying that Moriarty "has his pros and cons." Segal's lawyers believed Moriarty's analysis was flat wrong.

Segal's lawyers argued that Hogan was engaging in evidentiary sleight of hand and his claim that Near North owned certain assets was contradicted by several years of government filings claiming the assets were Segal's personal assets.

In January 2013, three days before the ownership hearing, Segal and the prosecution reached an agreement—subject to Castillo's ap-

---

59   U.S. v. Jack Hargrove, June 26, 2006, Seventh Circuit case law re ERISA).

60   Joyce to Hogan re: ERISA accounts, 12/07/12

61   Hogan's response letter to Joyce re: ERISA, 12/12/12

proval—to settle the forfeiture judgment. Segal's lawyers told him that Hogan had initially provided a range of settlement, but just before the scheduled evidentiary hearing, the parameters changed dramatically.

Segal was at a considerable disadvantage. His computers and records had been seized back in 2002 and were never returned. He had spent nearly eight years in prison and although he was no longer imprisoned, he still had no access to his records and no money to pay for lawyers, experts, or accountants. He was desperate and despondent. He had no funds for forensic accounting and lawyer representation. Segal was grateful that his lawyers had deferred payment of their fees over these many years, a reflection, he believed of their confidence in a positive financial outcome.

Hogan had ignored Segal's asset valuations and ownership during the years that the forfeiture proceedings had gone on. For all this time, there were no independent appraisals or updates made on the assets, except for the cash bank accounts. Notably, there was no increase in any of the valuations during this period. This, Segal believed, was Hogan's way of taking as much of Segal's assets as he could. For example, the government had valued a real estate partnership at $2.5 million and after the settlement agreement was reached, Segal would learn that his partnership interest had actually been sold for $10 million. What stuck out was the government's own records showed that up to the time of the settlement, they collected $7.9 million in distributions from the restrained assets and had other Segal cash in their possession which would have been sufficient to settle the $15 million forfeiture judgment. Had that been done, Segal's lawyers believed that that would require that Segal's other restrained assets be released.

Now, Hogan offered to settle by returning $8 million of the frozen assets. These included assets such as Segal's family's trust insurance (Segal didn't own them) and the ERISA retirement accounts (not subject to forfeiture under the law). Segal's attorney Joyce sent a letter to Hogan requesting more information on the several millions of dollars in the ERISA accounts and referenced a discussion with Moriarty. Hogan's responded that Moriarty was not in agreement because no evidence was furnished. The ERISA documents were in Hogan's possession and ERISA asset managers would not provide any information to Segal or his lawyers because of the restraining order. Segal's lawyers believed it was clear under the law that ERISA-protected accounts cannot be seized in a federal forfeiture. Later, when Segal's attorney challenged Hogan, at one point, he pointed to a restitution case as support for his position. Of course, restitution is different than forfeiture. IThe appellate court skirted the issue by basically saying that Segal waived his rights to the ERISA accounts under his settlement agreement.

Facing a take-it-or-leave-it-offer as well as massive legal bills, Segal wanted to help his family. Based on years of Judge Castillo's unfavorable rulings, in desperation, Segal agreed to the settlement.

But the case *still* was not over.

After the settlement was reached, Hogan immediately moved to grab funds to cover the false premium credits, claiming preposterously that there was interest to be collected for the period of Segal's incarceration. These were the credits that were supposedly owned to clients and not paid, even though not a single client said they were owed money.

Subsequently, Segal made repeated efforts to obtain information from the prosecution regarding restrained insurance policies, all without success, until the deadline for purchasing the policies from the government had lapsed. The policies could not be replaced. Segal also made numerous requests for the government to lift the restraint over the funds to which Segal was entitled, but Hogan refused to do so. Segal also exercised his right to purchase the remaining half interest in a sports partnership from the government (which was part of the settlement), but at the last minute, Hogan took steps to foil Segal's right to do that by forcing Segal to take another asset (which the government did not want to deal with) even though the settlement agreement said Segal could choose any asset he wished. Three days before the expiration date, when Segal executed his option, the government brought in someone else to submit an offer. As a result, the prosecution refused Segal's execution of his option. As far as Segal was concerned, this was all part of Hogan's vindictiveness.

Segal appealed and found a glimmer of hope when, during the oral argument in the appeals court, one of the judges said, in effect, that Segal seemed to be a man held hostage.

Although the case was on appeal, Dennis Burke, former U.S. Attorney for the District of Arizona, and John Sandweg, former Acting Director of U.S. Immigration and Customs Enforcement and former Acting General Counsel of the Department of Homeland Security, wrote a seven-page letter on Segal's behalf to Jay Macklin, General Counsel for the Executive Office of United States Attorneys, requesting that the forfeiture proceedings be removed from the U.S. Attorney's Office in Chicago.

"The inability of the [prosecution] to supervise this matter has led to questionable tactics and abuses in the forfeiture process, leading to the unjust enrichment of the government," the letter said. "Lacking appropriate supervision...the assigned Assistant United States Attorney, William R. Hogan, Jr., has been permitted to engage in a hyper-zealous and exceptionally unusual campaign that strains the boundaries of ethical conduct....For well over a decade, the prosecution of Mr. Segal has been handled almost exclusively by Mr. Hogan. This Assistant United States Attorney has appeared at every stage and a 2013 civil Tax Court matter where he interfered, multiple times, with the discovery process with the IRS General Counsel's Office in Chicago. It is [our] understanding that the insertion into the Tax Court matter led to complaints within the IRS regarding Mr. Hogan's behavior. Notably, despite being convicted of conspiring to defraud the IRS, the United States Tax

Court recently found in the IRS's civil tax fraud proceeding against Segal, which was based on the same facts as his criminal conviction, that 'there are no deficiencies in income tax due' from Segal and further ruled that there was no civil fraud penalty...an analysis of the forfeiture to date reveals that the [government] has received approximately three times the amount it was entitled to under the personal forfeiture of Mr. Segal. The [prosecution] has seized close to $40 million in actual assets to satisfy a $15 million forfeiture judgment."

Hogan, the letter declared, had tied up Segal's assets for seven years in forfeiture proceedings and essentially extracted a "forced settlement" by relying upon the depletion of Segal's resources and the prosecution's ability to wage a protracted legal battle.

The letter requested reassignment of the case in the hope that an independent fresh set of eyes "would help bring closure to this matter and remove any question that the Department's interests in justice were superseded by the motives of one Assistant United States Attorney."

Macklin's response was terse and, true to form, turned a blind eye toward the record. He said that "no further action is needed at this time" and that "In regards to your allegations concerning Assistant United States Attorney Bill Hogan, an attorney's zealous advocacy for the United States is not a basis for recusal." Segal saw the response as protective silence.

When Segal was choosing his settlement assets—as Hogan said he would be allowed to do—Segal said he did not want his investment in Lakeshore Entertainment. However, Hogan told Segal and his lawyers he had to take Lakeshore Entertainment, which the government valued at $1.5 million, because Hogan did not want to deal with the asset representative, Tom Rosenberg. So instead, Segal gave up half of his interest in a sports franchise, but was granted a right of first refusal on the purchase of the other half. Lakeshore, which once was a successful independent motion picture production company producing over thirty movies, ultimately went out of business due to business dynamics and was of no value to Segal. At the last minute, before the option was to expire, Hogan came up with a competing offer.

In January 2016, Segal's glimmer of hope became a reality when the Seventh Circuit agreed that he could exercise his right to purchase the minority interest in the sports partnership. The court held that Hogan's last-minute competing offer was not a commercial, reasonable one and wasn't even a firm offer. By that time, the prospective buyer had pulled out, saying to the media that when he found out what the government was trying to do to Segal, he no longer wanted to pursue the offer.

Segal's legal team filed a motion to modify the settlement supported by a sworn affidavit from Ron H. Braver,[62] a former special agent with the Internal Revenue Service criminal division. Braver reviewed thousands of documents and records and concluded the government had collected more than $32 million in personal assets belonging to Segal and his wife and still had $5.5 million assets that were not liquidated. The total would most likely be even more if future distributions or sales were included, Braver declared.

At the same time, the motion put Hogan squarely in the crosshairs as the cause of the many years of litigation. The defense accused Hogan of numerous vindictive post-trial actions, including claiming that Near North owned property that was actually owned by Segal, withholding documents and accounting evidence that showed Segal's ownership of assets,[63] undervaluing Segal's assets and running out Segal's option to purchase life insurance policies that could not be replaced. The motion outlined a litany of accusations that Hogan presented false evidence, made false misrepresentations, and shifted positions to rearrange facts.

"One may ask, why is Hogan now taking a position completely contrary to the position he took at trial and the forfeiture hearing?" the motion asked. "The most apparent answer is that since the inception of

---

62   Ron Braver affidavit.

63   DOJ Asset Forfeiture Policy Manual - Brady Obligations

this case, Hogan has been on a mission to punish Segal....[64] The less apparent answer...is that, in Hogan's crusade to punish Segal, Hogan got caught up in a web of his own lies—lies he made to Segal, to this Court and to the Seventh Circuit—regarding certain key facts concerning the ownership and valuation of the assets the government seized and some funds Segal put into his own company that would have reduced the forfeiture amount."

Judge Castillo, as he had in the past, did not ask the prosecution to respond to this latest motion to revisit the forfeiture settlement. He denied it as if he were scraping something off the bottom of his shoe, pausing to remark gratuitously that Segal, being a certified public accountant and lawyer, knew what he was doing and, being an intelligent man, should have known better.

As the case continued its Dickensian march into the early winter of 2017, Segal and his legal team prepared to appeal again.

Lawyers for Segal's wife, Joy, also were preparing to appeal a separate Castillo decision. At the time of the jury's forfeiture verdict, the government seized all of Joy's assets, including her marital assets that were acquired prior to any of the acts of racketeering alleged by the indictment. At the time, her assets purportedly were seized to make sure there were sufficient funds to satisfy Segal's $30 million forfeiture order even though Joy had never been charged with a crime or had any financial interest in Near North.

Joy had waited for years, despite the economic duress. Her lawyers twice filed motions for release of funds, but Judge Castillo denied them both—the first request in July 2008 and the second in September 2009.

Finally, in January 2010, with her assets still restricted, Joy signed a settlement agreement drafted by the government. Under the agreement, the prosecution agreed to immediately release to Joy financial accounts, including ERISA accounts and retirement accounts, partner-

---

64   Defendant's Reply Brief in Support of His Motion to Modify, 4/21/17, Pages 14-66.

ships owned by Joy, shares of stocks she received from her maternal grandmother, two properties she owned as a result of a marital settlement agreement, a Chicago condominium where she lived with her children and grandchildren and some personal effects, such as jewelry, which she had acquired over a period of three decades. Segal's lawyers believed that under forfeiture law, these assets arguably should not have been restrained at all.

In return, Joy agreed to give the government priority over other of her assets, but only to the extent needed to satisfy the $15 million modified forfeiture order if Segal's assets were not sufficient to do so.

Castillo had signed off on the agreement in November 2010.

Incredibly, after Segal agreed to his settlement in February 2013, the prosecution failed to account for the ownership, date of acquisition and independent valuation of Joy's confiscated assets. Her lawyers brought motions for an accounting in 2013 and 2014. Castillo denied both motions, saying that the motions were premature since the forfeiture proceedings were still ongoing.

Joy's lawyers noted that the government had seized more than $19 million of Joy's assets. After former IRS agent Braver filed his affidavit concluding that the prosecution had seized more than $32 million of Segal and Joy's assets, Joy's lawyers filed a third motion for accounting in December 2016.

At that time, Castillo was prompted to ask Hogan, "Is there ever going to be a time when Mrs. Segal…receives an accounting?"

It seemed a reasonable question. After all, a torrent of litigation had passed through his courtroom. And most forfeiture cases resulted in settlements, often for less than the ordered judgment, Even the most casual of observers, let alone the judge presiding over the case, would have sensed that something didn't smell right.

Nonetheless, Hogan's response was a master of vagueness and Judge Castillo let it slide.

"If there's anything left over at the end of the process," Hogan replied. "But I don't think there is going to be. I've been in the contact with the IRS. There's a $20 million or $22 million federal tax bill alone. Now a good chunk of that is interest and penalties, but there are also tax bills owed to Illinois, California—I believe New York. The Court is aware, because the trustee has filed reports ongoing, that there are claims that he intends to pay out pursuant to Court approval."

What Hogan didn't say was that since 1993, the position of the Department of Justice has been that states cannot tax entities owned by the federal government. And since Near North had been forfeited to the federal government and so had Segal's assets—it was preposterous to argue that there could be any state tax bill.

Moreover, Segal managed to obtain a copy of one of the trustee's letters to the state of Illinois written in 2010 that directly contradicted Hogan's statements in court and strongly suggested he was misleading Judge Castillo.

In the letter, the trustee, M. Scott Michel, informed the Revenue Litigation Bureau of the Illinois Attorney General's Office that he was precluded from paying any state tax claims by a Stay Order that had been entered in the case. Michel said, "I am not in a position to submit any payments to the Illinois Department of Revenue or any other state tax agencies on behalf of Near North at this time. I am aware of no statute requiring such payments to be made, and I will seek relief from the District Court to enforce the Stay Order if required."

At the same time, the trustee then went on to say that in the end, he would leave it up to the Department of Justice to make the final approval and decisions, despite the 1953 Department of Justice memorandum on tax issues.[65]

Although Joy's lawyers asked for an explanation, there was no re-

---

65   Liability of the United States for State and Local Taxes on Seized and Forfeited Property, DOJ
      Memorandum, 10/18/93.

sponse from the government as to how Near North tax liabilities would require satisfaction through the use of Joy's assets.[66, 67, 68]

Castillo asked, at one point, "Is there somewhere, Mr. Hogan, a document that the government has as to what the forfeiture has been, the amounts and proceeds so far?"

This also was a reasonable question. Hogan's response was a non-response. "Those schedules have been filed with this Court on a regular basis," he said.

In fact, the forfeiture trustee had stopped filing his reports in August 2011. Over the years, Segal's lawyers were never allowed to see the trustee's reports—some were filed directly with the judge, some were kept under seal and after 2011, the court record didn't even reflect that reports were being filed at all. Yet at the same time, the trustee and his lawyers had billed for at approximately $5 million. The reports, the defense believed, undoubtedly contained information favorable to Segal and should have been disclosed. The corporation's records, for example, would show whether Segal's investments were on Near North's books or not and whether the corporation had any control of Segal's investments, the defense believed. Before Segal's settlement, Segal's lawyers sent a letter to the trustee's lawyer requesting accounting information as to corporate or Segal assets. The trustee's lawyer responded that it was up to the Department of Justice to respond.

Segal saw this as essentially ceding control to and providing cover for Hogan because there was no accounting to expose the non-existent liabilities such as state and federal income tax and general creditor liabilities, which on their face would be precluded by the law.

"Do you know offhand what that shows in terms of total amount?" Castillo asked. "That have been actually forfeited, used to meet the $15

---

66   Douglas Bacon response email to Doherty, 1/28/13

67   Joyce letter to Douglas Bacon dated 4/14/14

68   Douglas Bacon response to Joyce, 4/17/14

million forfeiture judgment? I'm just wondering if such a document exists somewhere that is easy to access."

"It does," Hogan said, "but not in the form that you posed it."

Following that statement, Joy's lawyers asked for a list of all seized assets from Joy Segal and Michael Segal,[69] a list of all assets the government had designated as belonging to Near North and a list of Near North assets versus Segal assets. The government again did not comply with that request and Castillo did not order the government to do so. This in effect became a shield for deflection and delay. It seemed like Castillo was asking logical questions, but he accepted whatever Hogan said.

In October 2017, Castillo denied a third request by Joy's lawyers to intervene in the case. Castillo said once again that the motion was filed "too soon" because there was nothing showing that the government had claimed more than $15 million in forfeiture assets from Segal. Over five years, Castillo could have asked for a partial accounting or specific documentation, but that didn't happen. In essence, Hogan was attempting to make up for the reduction in the forfeiture judgment from $30 million to $15 million by not only relabeling Segal's assets as Near North assets, but by further asserting that because of alleged tax liabilities, Joy's assets still under government control would be required to foot the bill. This represented a continuing financial punishment inflicted on Segal and his family.

And so, in 2018, Joy's lawyers and Segal's lawyers appealed to the Seventh Circuit U.S. Court of Appeals[70] in the hope that the judges would recognize what a charade the proceedings had become.

The case was *still* not over.

In May 2019, following the oral arguments before the appeals court, Joy's lawyer, wrote a letter to Hogan (with a copy to the U.S. Attorney and a copy the chief of the criminal division) outlining several spe-

---

69   Joyce letter and follow up to Douglas Bacon re: Explanation of Seized assets, 10/21/10

70   Appellate Brief for Joy Segal, 03/06/18, Appellate Brief for Michael Segal, 03/06/18.

cific misstatements and misrepresentations Hogan made to the appeals court. Her lawyer requested that Hogan file a correction with the court.

On June 7, 2019, Hogan replied on behalf of himself, the U.S, Attorney and the head of the criminal division: "The government does not believe further response is warranted." The response was no surprise to Segal, but he felt that Hogan, in answering on behalf of his superiors as well as himself, showed a breakdown in the system of checks and balances.

In September 2019, the Seventh Circuit rejected Segal's appeal. The court held that his agreement to settle his personal forfeiture was definitive. "We agree with the district court that the four corners of the 2013 agreement control Mr. Segal's rights and interests. The district court denied Mr. Segal's effort to modify or rescind the settlement agreement," the court ruled.

The court also upheld Judge Castillo's refusal to permit Joy Segal to intervene. Although all Joy wanted was to enforce her settlement agreement, the court refused to allow it.

"Reaching the merits of Ms. Segal's appeal, we agree with the district court that Ms. Segal has no right to intervene at this time," the court said. "Ms. Segal can assert no further claims to forfeited property until forfeiture proceedings are completed—if any property remains."

"Mr. Segal's tactics are egregious," the court continued. "His sixty-eight-page reply in the district court relied mostly on 'gratuitous attacks on counsel,' with 'page after page of vitriol against one of the prosecutors,' a brief which that court 'would have been justified as striking as overlength and improper.' In his brief on appeal, Mr. Segal accuses the government of all sorts of serious wrongdoing—such as that it outright 'fabricated the record'—without offering any evidence. The legal arguments that Mr. Segal raised in the district court and in this court are baseless, hyperbolic, and conspiratorial. And they are diametrically opposed to arguments he has made successfully earlier in the case."

This response respectfully was extremely disappointing to Segal and his lawyers because their district court filing which was referenced in the appeal contained multiple pages of specific facts of misconduct.

The court threatened that if there were further proceedings, the parties and their lawyers could be liable "for excessive costs for unreasonable multiplication of proceedings."

Two days later and within ten days of Castillo's retirement from the bench, Hogan went back to court, presenting Castillo an order to transfer $11 million from the U.S. Marshal's fund to the trustee, bringing the amount under the trustee's control to $20 million. Hogan said that all debts and liabilities would be satisfied and that there would be no money for Joy to bother interceding about—the money left over—about $23 million—would be forfeited by Near North. Castillo again agreed and accepted the filing, although it was based on what Hogan said.

At that point, it became clear to Segal what was happening. Pursuant to a court order issued after Segal's conviction and forfeiture hearing, his and Joy's personal assets were frozen and placed in the U.S. Marshal's Seizure Asset fund. How, Segal now wondered, could his personal assets still in the U.S. Marshal's fund be used to satisfy the obligations of Near North's forfeiture?

This was, as far as Segal was concerned, Hogan's long-term scheme to take not just the $15 million that Segal agreed to in his settlement, but every last penny of Segal's and Joy's assets. Pursuant to Joy's settlement, which Judge Castillo approved, the prosecution agreed to return certain assets to her. As for the remaining seized assets, she had agreed to release her interest in those assets to the extent the prosecution needed them to satisfy Segal's personal forfeiture judgment. Joy's settlement did not have anything to do with the separate corporate forfeiture of Near North and it did not address any of Near North's corporate liabilities.

To the extent that the prosecution did not need the remaining assets in the U.S. Marshall's Seizure Asset Fund to satisfy Segal's $15 million personal forfeiture liability, Joy had retained the right to claim her interest in those remaining assets. The pertinent sentence in the agreement said: "In the event that the remaining property is released at any time and/or not otherwise ordered forfeit at the completion of all proceedings, including by any modifications to or revocation of the forfeiture judgment by the Court or any reviewing court, the claimants (Joy)…are not barred by the terms of this document from asserting an interest in that property if the United States asserts no further interest in or claim to the property."

On August 15, 2019, the prosecution and the forfeiture trustee filed motions acknowledging that the U.S. Marshal's Seized Asset Fund had $34 million until Segal's $15 million forfeiture liability was settled, leaving $19 million in cash and $5 million in unliquidated assets.

So, when Hogan presented the order to Judge Castillo to release $11 million from the remaining $19 million so that the trustee could pay Near North's (in some instances undisclosed) corporate liabilities, it became clear to Segal that the lines had blurred—actually had been erased—between the Near North forfeiture and his personal forfeiture.

There had never been a court finding or citation that any of the assets held in the U.S. Marshal's Seized Asset Fund belonged to Near North. So, to Segal, what was happening was obvious. Hogan was making sure that neither Segal or Joy would get any of the remaining $19 million. And Castillo was going along with it.

Segal's remaining assets—the assets that had been set aside to satisfy his forfeiture judgment—were being used to satisfy Near North obligations.

This was, as far as Segal was concerned, just more sleight of hand by the prosecution. The Seventh Circuit had agreed with Castillo's ruling to refuse to allow Joy to intervene, but at the same time it had tossed a bone in her direction—although it was a very small bone. The court said that "at the conclusion of the forfeiture proceedings, Ms. Segal will be notified of her right to participate and may choose to intervene at that time. But until 'the entire premise of that intervention' materializes, she must wait."

The parties returned to court on September 25, 2019, just two days before Castillo was to retire from active service as a federal judge. Hogan declared that "in a couple weeks, the trustee will submit a final report and final bill, and if there's any money left over from the eleven million that we transferred, then I'll file another motion with whomever inherits this case from you to transfer that back from the (U.S.) Marshal's fund, and that will be the conclusion of the case.

He added, "So, this motion and order seeks a discrete amount that's in the Marshal's fund that is the proceeds of forfeited assets. It has nothing to do with Joy Segal. There's nothing left for Joy Segal to attach or to make a claim to. This is money that's already been liquidated from the forfeited assets over the course of the last 15 years."

For five years—year after year after year—Hogan had repeatedly told Castillo there could be no accounting for what was left of Joy's assets until the forfeiture of both Segal and Near North was complete. And amazingly, Castillo bought into Hogan's argument. In fact, Castillo only questioned Hogan once about it and when Hogan gave a vague non-answer, Castillo let it go—he wasn't about to start digging in his heels now.

When Joy's lawyer sought seven days to review the matter, Castillo was abrupt.

"I'm going to enter the order that you're requesting," Castillo told Hogan. He added that if Joy's lawyer wanted to intervene, he could file a motion to intervene "before my successor judge and file a motion to reconsider the order that I'm entering today. But having presided over this case for seventeen-and-a-half years, I think the order is well taken and should be entered today posthaste. I'll enter it."

That left Joy's lawyers only one option—to go before U.S. District Court Judge John Lee, who inherited the case when Castillo retired and joined the firm of Akerman LLP.

One of the last things that Judge Castillo said before he closed out his involvement in the case would ever resonate with Segal.

"This has taken on a life of its own unfortunately," Castillo said. "But that's just the way it was."

That's just the way it was?

That's justice? Segal asked himself.

As far as he was concerned, this and the many decisions in his case in the prior years had little to with justice.

Before his eyes, the overwhelming power of the judicial system had been harnessed in his case for the sole purpose of protecting its own agents and prosecutors, whose misconduct was clearly and copiously documented. The appeals court essentially said that any further attempts to allege misconduct would be punished. *Where is the check and balance in that?*

So, Segal thought, the prosecutors were free to act with impunity. They knew—as Segal now realized—that the likelihood that they'd ever be held accountable for their actions was somewhere between slim and none.

Postscript

A Note from Michael Segal

*"The Department of Justice has an obligation
to its lawyers and to the public to prevent
prosecutorial misconduct. Prosecutors, as
servants of the law, are subject to constraints and
responsibilities that do not apply to other lawyers;
they must serve truth and justice first."*

— Attorney Sal Cognetti in a letter to
Chicago U.S. Attorney's office.

I AM HOPEFUL THAT THOSE who have read this far have come to recognize, as I have, the consequences, at times, when the federal justice system fails. Over the years, I have not only had the time and strength to fully explore the far reaches of my case, but also to reflect on the personal and professional impact on me, my family, my friends, and my company.

Mine is a complicated story, difficult to put to paper in a fashion that can be easily grasped. I want to thank Rob Warden, Executive Director emeritus of the Center on Wrongful Convictions at Northwestern

University Pritzker School of Law for introducing me to Maurice Possley, who wrote my story. Collaborating on this book and reconnecting with the pain, embarrassment and anger that the events described herein caused has been a most difficult experience. However, I feel this is important because what happened to me can happen to others. Some people may believe that the government does not prosecute someone for no reason and that if government parties do engage in misconduct, the end justifies the means. I now understand that this is not true.

We are in a time in the United States when at times, misconduct by prosecutors is increasingly unchecked by courts, Congress, and the state and federal agencies responsible for policing such claims. But despite news about misconduct allegations, the issue doesn't seem to resonate for most people because they tend to believe that the government will not treat its citizens unfairly. In my case, this belief was perpetuated by some of members of the media who essentially accepted the government's narrative on its face. Being the first high profile case of the new U.S. Attorney Patrick Fitzgerald presented red meat for all concerned.

I believe I am in a unique position to expose my prosecution for what it was: an alleged accounting irregularity case dependent on finite accounting evidence that could only result in one clear answer. This book documents numerous examples of the presentation of false evidence that the prosecution never corrected. It also details the exposure of and failure to prosecute the eight months of cybercrimes involving government witnesses who passed on and used the information by government parties as well as the surreptitious taping of my defense attorney.

My arrest was highly unusual in a federal prosecution for under the McCarran-Ferguson Act, a congressional mandate federal jurisdiction and regulations are preempted as to the 50 state insurance departments and it came after I filed my civil lawsuit against the Takeover Group. The lawsuit threatened to expose improper activities in the federal investigation. My arrest was a tactic designed to coerce me to become an undercover informant. When I declined to become a tool of the government, my legal nightmare began. And once my lawyers and I began exposing the cybercrimes committed in connection with my case, the prosecution took on a life of its own. Ultimately, the government would ignore the hacking and other misconduct perpetrated against me, and ratchet up the pressure on both my company and me by filing four superseding indictments which included my corporation which was not in accordance with the Department of Justice regulations after the indictment of Arthur Andersen in the Enron case, but also had the effect of emotional delays, extensive media coverage and increased legal expenses.

If I had known at the outset what I now know about how a racketeering conviction drains your assets and deprives one of the ability to fight wrongful charges, I probably would have backed off my civil lawsuit against the Takeover Group. I say that even though I had the strongest possible case against those former employees who were acting unlawfully and with hostility first from within Near North and later from their positions at a competing Fortune 500 company to destroy me and my company.

Additionally, I probably would not have allowed my company's lawyers to file pre-trial motions asserting prosecutorial misconduct in violation of constitutional protections, which, although well-documented, triggered the filing of the RICO charge as well as the threat (which the government ultimately carried out) to indict Near North which destroyed 45 years of my life's work and passion.

Challenging the violations of my due process rights was, in hindsight, perhaps a mistake because I simply did not understand the power of the government, the tactics it would engage in, and the lengths to which it would go to protect itself and punish me. As a result, I was the target of a vindictive prosecution that destroyed a $250 million company, cost me $50 million in forfeitures, and denied me bail, unlike virtually every other person convicted of a white-collar crime, while I awaited sentencing. My ten-year sentence was more severe than those imposed for virtually all but the most violent crimes. The jobs of 1,000 employees evaporated. And all of it caused untold emotional damage to my family.

It is my hope to expose the truth in a case riddled with falsehoods. I had hoped that once the real facts were aired in court, the government would relent and cease pursuing its incomplete and inaccurate narrative. Instead, the prosecution doubled down. This case was U.S. Attorney Patrick Fitzgerald's first high profile prosecution, there would be no backing down.

At the same time, I have never doubted for one second my decision to refuse to wear a wire and to work undercover. I knew then that I'd done nothing wrong and I realized immediately what they were trying to do. I refused to participate in framing people I had no relationship with, much less my friends. It's interesting to note as stated in Maurice Possley's book, the government had taped me for over 600 hours which included my lawyer and not one minute was introduced into evidence.

Financial crimes invariably create victims. Yet in my case, prosecutors never found or produced a single victim to put on the witness stand nor did they present any evidence of any unlawful transaction. That's because there weren't any. Judge Castillo acknowledged that no client suffered a loss and that there was no fraudulent intent and no misrepresentation. So, it is my belief that in the end, the victims in the case were myself, my family, and the 1,000 employees of Near North. I admit that to this day, in the dark of night, I awaken and replay and repeat what transpired and am still mystified by how one can be convicted of a crime and punished based on no victims and no loss and a final court ruling of no criminal intent or non-disclosure and misrepresentation.

Years later, the public statements made by President Barack Obama and Attorney General Eric Holder about the importance of protecting cyber-security ring hollow, given the involvement of Aon—a Fortune

500 corporation employees and their legal support—in the cyberhacking and delivery into the hands of the government thousands of documents, many covered by the attorney-client privilege. Not only does the inaction by the FBI make a mockery of any official statements about cyber security, it raised a question of whether we are truly safe when government parties themselves may be the violators or protectors of the violators.

In today's world, the large-scale cyberhacking in my case would be considered particularly outrageous especially in today's current business and political high-profile intrusions and media focus. The collaboration of the Takeover Group and subsequent protection by the government enabled them to operate with impunity. I believe they were no better than a burglary ring—they stole documents, records, files and business from Near North, the company that employed them, nurtured their careers, and promoted them to executive positions.

My case illustrates that a code of silence—the refusal to acknowledge misconduct —at times runs deep among agents, prosecutors, trial judges, and the very top levels of the U.S. Department of Justice. The result is a subversion of the system of checks and balances that is fundamental to our federal justice system and the protection of prosecutors and government agents. Article VI of our Constitution mandates that both federal and state officers of all three branches of government take an oath to support the Constitution. In my case, I believe these oaths were broken by a number of individuals.

Very often, the excuse or justification is used to protect the reputation of prosecutors and the Department of Justice and particularly under the landscape where a high percentage of judges were U.S. prosecutors. As we know, prosecutors have more experience with guilty people than those who are innocent.

In my case, challenging the misconduct resulted in Draconian punishment that still continues. In a September 2019 ruling, the Seventh

Circuit U.S. Court of Appeals denied the latest request for relief. In addition to the denial of relief, the court chastised me for "gratuitous attacks on counsel," with "page after page of vitriol against one of the prosecutors." The court, respectfully in my opinion, simply ignored our evidence that was supported by the government's own records, trial transcripts and our forensic accounting. Not to mention the long history of the case with the cyberhacking of emails and the taping of my attorney. And so, my punishment continues. Should I continue to fight to the misconduct, I am threatened with further adverse action from the courts. All for attempting to exercise my Constitutional rights.

Frankly, when my grandchildren were in middle school, studying the government and our Constitution, I had to restrain myself from undercutting their understanding of the value of the Bill of Rights and the due process elements of our Constitution by oversharing my own tale. I am hoping that someday in the future, they may read this book and understand there are frailties and hopefully, in time, their faith in the system of checks and balances will be well-placed.

How skewed have things become?

Look no further than the day that a former FBI agent who was working on my behalf chanced to cross paths on a Chicago street with an FBI supervisor who had become aware of the former agent's effort to prompt the Bureau to turn over evidence that FBI Agent Murphy had received stolen emails from the Takeover Group. Even though when Agent Murphy was confronted and shown a stolen email sent by the Takeover Group to his home email account, he stated he didn't remember receiving it. The supervisor bragged that the former agent would never prove that the Takeover Group had any connection to the cybercrimes. He ended by pointedly asking, "When did you go over to the dark side?" The meaning was clear—only the government's "truth" mattered.

I believe that's exactly what happened in my case as the prosecutors, FBI agents, and, yes, the judge at times acted in self-aggrandizing ways to put their own careers and reputations ahead of truth, justice, and the life of a man and a company.

Even today people who have observed my prosecution and sentencing issues continue to ask me why I thought the judge disliked me so much - was it personal? I do not believe it was personal yet it's hard to accept the clear rulings that simply denied me of any ability at times to present the facts and my innocence. No bail before sentencing and what many feel was a Draconian sentencing for a victimless crime. These facts and unexplained rulings and a lack of imposing government's response to misrepresented trial records and filings was hard to accept and to understand.

Some including one of my lawyers expressed their opinion that the judge as an ex-prosecutor was reluctant to rule against the government when the serious misconduct involving exculpatory issues were presented.

Similarly of concern is when Professor Albert Alschuler presented his brief and argument before the Appellate court that my conviction of dishonest services was unconstitutional in the absence of a bribe or a kickback as ruled by the Supreme Court in June 2010. Judge Evans of the Appellate court stated to the effect that Segal was looking for a get out of jail card and then ruled that Segal's trial instructions and crime was predicated on dishonest services was now harmless error, even though the District Court's judgment and the Appellate court's first judgment was based on dishonest services. Judge Evans bought Hogan's argument that it was harmless error.

As this book went to press, some of the major players were still attempting to profit from their involvement in my cases. No one had suffered any sanction.

Prosecutor Dean Polales, the originator of the targeted prosecution who was looking for a way to enhance his curriculum vitae which some would say was lackluster, was an attorney in private practice and touted himself to clients as the prosecutor who "took Segal down." Recently, one of the senior partners in the firm that hired Dean Polales related that when he asked as to the background of Segal's prosecution for it was hard to understand the actual crime, he stated that Segal lied to him. My retort was simple by my silence for it was not worth reliving at this point.

One of my lawyers told me that when moving to a new law firm, the Takeover Group's attorney Eric Brandfonbrener stated that he had helped take down "one of the most powerful men in the city."

Former prosecutor Virginia Kendall, who, among other things, fought to keep me in the Metropolitan Correctional Center for 18 months prior to my sentencing, became a federal judge, touting her involvement in my prosecution as getting the support from a U.S. Senator.

Prosecutor Hogan who was brought in as the hired gun, continues to receive accolades for tormenting me and my family with his use of false facts in the forfeiture proceedings. Even today as my civil forfeiture proceedings continue on after 15 years Hogan is somehow allowed to insert himself into all the processes of my civil forfeiture. He continues to work for the U.S. Attorney's office raising questions as to why he has not retired or seek alternative careers. In the early weeks of the publication of my indictment I received a letter from a Northbrook-based consulting firm who flatly warned me as to Assistant U.S. Attorney Hogan's behavior stating as to his accounting case prosecution, exculpatory evidence was destroyed and interfered with by Hogan. Unfortunately, I ignored this information at that time.

FBI Agents Patrick Murphy and Kendall submitted their narrative of my prosecution in support of various government awards. Murphy subsequently joined the firm of Grant Thornton to head a fraud detection department. Grant Thornton's website and press releases heralded Murphy's handling of the Segal prosecution.

Others beyond the prosecution team benefited as well. It is my firm belief that this is part of a playbook used by the government to manipulate facts in its favor, to provide benefits to others and to protect themselves. Confessed hacker David Cheley, for example, faced no prosecution and was protected by government parties as to standard investigation and indictment procedures. The government also provided benefits to AON, USI and their Takeover Group employees, including advance knowledge of court filings and my arrest, which allowed them to seek competitive business advantage. Their signing and stock bonuses were not touched.

In return, the Takeover Group provided benefits to the government including a prepackaged false regulatory and accounting prosecution of me and Near North, access to confidential and privileged documents, and the leak of government-supportive case information to the media. In addition, Hogan arranged for the four Takeover Group members to each receive a whistleblower fee of $250,000.

They also all got what was important to them in addition to their common goal—the destruction of me and my company.

Judge Castillo's grand pronouncements contained in media soundbites from the bench and his harsh sentence undoubtedly raised his profile. Ironically, when he became Chief U.S. District Judge in 2013, he took the seat previously by U.S. District Judges Marvin Aspen and James Holderman, both highly respected jurists with no tolerance for misconduct.

Prosecutors enjoy immunity for what they do in the course of prosecuting a case. Thanks to my lawyer, Sal Cognetti, legislation was passed requiring federal prosecutors to adhere to state canons of ethics. But state bar associations rarely punish prosecutors for ethic breaches. The fact is that no one or no institution hardly ever acts and if they do, serious punishment is rarely imposed. Although my lawyers documented violations of the ABA canon of ethics, sadly I was advised that it would be unlikely that the Illinois Attorney Registration and Disciplinary Commission (ARDC) would review federal prosecutors. In my mind it's not illogical to think that prosecutor Hogan will leave no stone unturned to protect his exposure and results of any misconduct which explains his ongoing control for 15 years of all the processes, let alone the motivation of the vindictive financial punishment and questionable length of incarceration.

Exhibiting the extreme of Hogan's conduct was his involvement in instigating a civil IRS proceeding as to the incomplete and inaccurate Klein Tax Conspiracy to further punish me. Additionally, he attempted interference of my pro se defense before the IRS and when I was successful in having the Tax Court rule that there was no civil fraud based upon a lesser legal standard than the government tax conspiracy which resulted in two extra years of incarceration, Hogan went after the Senior IRS prosecutor and alleged that I had bribed him. After the prosecutor was cleared, his functions were marginalized by the department as a silent punishment for him following the law which was rarely found in my prosecution.

What I have found most frustrating, however, is an astonishing lack of action on all fronts—even though James Cole, who represented me before he became the First Deputy to former Attorney General Eric Holder, called my prosecution "one of the worst cases" he had ever seen. Attorney Cole and Will Olsen worked for five months and prepared a document of over 100 pages setting forth the various issues of misconduct as to the evidence presented in my case including the cybercrimes, attorney client privileges and evidentiary attachments. I was encouraged for he and other national criminal lawyers raised their opinion that with the new administration in Washington, that main justice, the DOJ, would be more inclined to look into these issues and basically would not tolerate such conduct. A week before presenting the filing, I was informed that Jim Cole was nominated to be the First Deputy under AG Holder and it would not be appropriate for him to represent these compulations. Another attorney of national criminal stature continued on and made the filing to the DOJ. The compulation was addressed to Lanny Breuer and a letter was sent by an assistant several weeks later that basically said that I had my chance in court. These abuses never have been specifically directly addressed by the Department of Justice—not by Lanny Breuer, former head of the Criminal Division who once said that one case of misconduct is too many; and not by Holder, who was on the record as having promised "prompt action" against any misconduct by federal prosecutors under his supervision. Worst of all, Gary Shapiro, First Assistant U.S. Attorney in Chicago and Hogan's immediate boss, did nothing. Some people speculate any review of misconduct in my prosecution could interfered with the continuation of Patrick Fitzgerald as U.S. Attorney who was on track with other sensitive local investigations. Of course, he continued on and became the first U.S. prosecutor to indict and convict two governors Rod Blagojevich and George Ryan.

Yet, despite my experience and the devastating adversity over these years, I still do believe in the Constitution and federal system of criminal justice. There were days, weeks, even months when I didn't think so. In the darkest time, while I was incarcerated in the Metropolitan Correctional Center, I felt cut off from my family, my lawyers, my friends—the world. The process of getting to visit me was so onerous I did not encourage friends and family to try to see me. All visits by my lawyers were tracked by the government. I realized that I could not be consumed by self-pity and I chose to fight back. It's unfortunate and devastating that at times, human nature or the lack of discipline takes over people's actions. Nothing becomes perfect in our lives, but it's hopeful there will be more understanding as to the need for checks and balances and the need for more deterrents to curb this conduct or happenstance.

When I walked into the federal prison in Oxford, I almost felt relieved—that's how onerous the MCC was. I was able to slow down and work in an atmosphere where I could rationally go back and assemble facts. I still had hope that our system would work, and I tried to figure out how to make it work for me. There were many times when facing the false testimony and false evidence was extraordinarily painful. I would work myself into a frenzy and blame myself and inabilities for both fighting back and the absence of presenting evidence by one of my trial lawyers and vetting my evidence as to both my innocence and the misconduct. There were days that I had to virtually shut down to recuperate and restore my drive. I could barely accept the trauma of my surreal experiences. Anger, determination, and hope kept me going. I felt as if I were putting a giant puzzle together. And so, I doubled and then redoubled my efforts. At one point, I had accumulated seventeen boxes of documents in my cell. I was driven by the thought that I could bring the truth to light. When a new warden tried to cite me for having more than the maximum of three boxes, I persevered, and convinced him to allow me to keep them. And then I continued on, keeping my focus and refusing to give up. This continued to take a toll on me for I had the personal drive of outrage and having the proof of innocence to continue on but at times, I became paralyzed and blamed myself as to not managing my attorneys and not thinking out that presenting the constitutional misconduct issues which directly lead to the Rico count and perhaps not listening to others that you cannot win with the government under my circumstances.

When I came back from my incarceration, I was very concerned about how I would be received. After all, more than 200 articles featuring the most vicious type of mischaracterization and political smears had been published portraying me as a thief who had stolen $30 million dollars. I was greeted warmly. Even strangers approached me to express their belief that I was treated unfairly and unjustly. Some of these encounters brought tears to my eyes. Some have expressed their admiration for resisting the government's pressure. Most see my punishment as outrageously severe, although not everyone was so kind—my country club forced me out and refused me readmission upon my return.

I am hoping that this book will help people understand how a crime can be manufactured and that there was no crime deserving of such excessive punishment. And how, in the end, our system of checks and balances utterly failed.

In the past several years, I have been asked repeatedly what I did to prompt such relentless pursuit—a pursuit that continues more than fifteen years later in ongoing forfeiture hearings. Surely, I must have done *something* to generate that level of enmity and condemnation as well as an unusually harsh sentence. Although it is difficult to reduce it to a soundbite, when I explain what happened, they are perplexed and confounded. I thank them for their interest and concern and move on. It is now my hope that this book provides a deeper understanding of what happened and that readers will perhaps become more knowledgeable and come to their own conclusions.

My deepest regret, looking back at all that has happened, is the havoc that was wrought on my family and my loyal and hard-working business associates, whom I truly respect for helping me build my business. They genuinely suffered.

I have emerged from the darkness a calmer person. I am no longer awakened by nightmares of what I have lost and the trauma that myself and my family went through. I realize that there was a time when I spent too much time on every little issue, sometimes to the detriment of other, perhaps more important, issues. I was so dedicated to growing my business that I moved too quickly at times and did not pay attention to the back of the house. In my single-mindedness, I was hurtful to some along the way. I blame myself for not quite seeing what was happening before my eyes—several trusted employees conspiring to take my business from me. And when I did see it, albeit later on, I was not good at handling the conflict.

When I finally was released, I was fearful that the mischaracterizations and lies would define me—that I would be ever judged by the prosecution's case and the media's account of it. I have come face to face with the reality that for too long in my life, I was too focused on work. I am trying to make up for that now. I have been warmly embraced by friends and family. I am becoming the grandfather to my grandchildren that I could not be while I was in prison. For all of these things, I am very grateful.

My motivation for cooperating in the writing of this book was not self-pity nor was it an attempt to retry my case. Let me be clear my purpose is not to imply that two wrongs don't make a right. I am sincerely hopeful that this book may prevent other instances of prosecutorial overreach. No justice system can function effectively if there are components within it that disregard the rules and mechanisms of check and balance to be relied upon. Myself and many others still cannot fathom how one federal prosecutor could be so embolden with no supervision allowing a repetitive pattern of misconduct, but equally perplexed how other government parties of supervision and judicial review become aligned and at times ignore and become silent. A glaring example was when the government filed before my trial a motion in limine to prevent testimony relating to government misconduct and the destruction of my company, unfortunately as my trial lawyer stood by and without furciferous objection, which was granted by Judge Castillo.

Equally concerning is when Professor Albert Alschuler presented his brief and argument before the Appellate court that my conviction of dishonest services was unconstitutional in the absence of a bribe or a kickback as ruled by the Supreme Court in June 2010. Judge Evans of the Appellate court stated to the effect that Segal was looking for a get out of jail card and then ruled that Segal's trial instructions and crime was predicated on dishonest services was now harmless error, even though the District Court's judgment and the Appellate court's first judgment was based on dishonest services. Judge Evans bought

Hogan's argument that it was harmless error.

I truly believe what I experienced, devastating as it was, is not universal, but instead a perfect storm of circumstances that I hope are not the rule in our judicial system, but the exception.

In the end, the judicial system was harnessed against me for the sole purpose of protecting its own agents and prosecutors, whose misconduct was clearly documented. I am reminded of a comment made to me when I was starting my career: "Kid, nothing is on the square." An old-school sentiment, to be sure, and something I didn't want to embrace, but it turned out to be a real-life lesson.

Until there are unassailable checks and balances in our system of justice and principled individuals willing to uphold them without exception, there will be prosecutors and agents willing to pursue convictions by any means possible, without regard for their oaths. The public, the legislature, the defense bar, prosecutors and their superiors and the courts must act responsibly and with integrity. There must be no tolerance for misconduct. The alternative is continuing injustice.

About that there is no doubt.

Cast of Characters

Dana Berry. Berry, now deceased, was the co-leader and master strategist of the Takeover Group's effort to gain control of Near North Insurance by making false claims about its accounting. He participated in the theft of thousands of Near North documents, some of which were provided to his new employer, the Aon Corporation. He was the author of the document that laid out the group's plan to take over Near North. Berry had the personal number of Patrick Ryan, CEO of Aon, and made calls to him long before he joined Ryan's company. When Berry found out he had cancer, before all of the treachery went down, Segal made numerous calls to find him the best physician and extended many other kindnesses. Berry paid him back by destroying the company.

Judge Ruben Castillo. A former prosecutor, Judge Castillo repeatedly rejected defense efforts to hold prosecutors accountable for improprieties including collaborating with the Takeover Group's hacking of documents, the taping of Segal's defense attorney Harvey Silets, and the hiding of exculpatory evidence. Judge Castillo granted a government motion to bar Segal's defense lawyers from presenting any evidence as to government misconduct and destruction of Segal's company, Near North, which Segal believed materially interfered with his defense. For 17 months, he repeatedly denied bail prior to sentencing, something unheard of in white collar criminal cases. The judge was a member of the United States Sentencing Commission, whose mission is to standardize guidelines for sentencing. Somehow, he worked within those guidelines to pronounce a 10-year sentence on a victimless conviction that was ruled non-fraudulent.

David Cheley. Cheley hacked thousands of documents from Near North for the Takeover Group starting four months before he left Near North, and continuing for another four months after he joined Kemper Insurance. Some of these documents ended up on a computer server at Aon Corp. and in the personal email of FBI Agent Patrick Murphy. Cheley avoided state prosecution on the directions of Assistant U.S. Attorney Virginia Kendall. At the time of the cybercrimes public exposure Cheley programmed his own website to automatically link to the FBI's website. Cheley was never subjected to a complete investigation or prosecution as to the proven and confessed cybercrimes.

Tim Gallagher. A Takeover Group member, Gallagher, under the pretense of working out differences between the group and Segal, lured Segal to a meeting at a hotel lobby where Segal was arrested. Gallagher was a major player in an effort, which began long before Segal's arrest, to mischaracterize and smear Segal in calls to members of the media, particularly *Chicago Tribune* columnist John Kass. Gallagher went on to work for Aon Corp and left sometime after receiving a sign-on bonus. Segal believed Gallagher obtained confidential Near North's sales prospect records and data before leaving as a Near North employee.

Devra Gerber. A Takeover Group member, Gerber told Segal she didn't want to be part of an extortion, but in fact, was involved anyway. She subsequently joined Aon. Segal hired her through her family relationship and personally mentored her. Several months before the Takeover Group left Segal's company, Gerber told Segal she wanted to take some time off and never disclosed the ongoing conspiracy of the Takeover Group and her participation.

William Hogan. A career federal prosecutor, Hogan has been accused several times of prosecutorial misconduct. He was fired and later reinstated after engaging in improper behavior in the prosecution of a Chicago street gang—failing to disclose that he permitted his witnesses to use the prosecutor's office for telephone conversations to buy drugs and to have sex with women. He acted to punish Segal each time Segal tried to expose Hogan's use of false evidence and misrepresentation of false testimony by government witnesses. Hogan made clear his vindictive punishment for he told Segal's lawyer at a forfeiture hearing that Segal made a mistake as to his filing at the Department of Justice. He threatened and obtained superseding RICO charges that destroyed Near North. Though Hogan was a line prosecutor, he nevertheless was involved in Segal's appeals process as well as the forfeiture proceedings—which continue even today.

Edward Joyce. Joyce is a prominent Chicago attorney who represented Segal in U.S. District Court and the Seventh Circuit U.S. Court of Appeals and filed numerous motions of misrepresentation of evidence and presenting facts of misconduct accusing prosecutor Hogan of misconduct.

Virginia Kendall. An Assistant U.S. Attorney who prosecuted Segal and Near North, Kendall became a U.S. District judge after Segal's trial. Segal maintained that because she was being vetted to be a federal judge after the trial, she insisted on Segal being confined to the Metropolitan Correctional Center instead of being allowed to remain free on bond, as to other white collar convicted parties, crippling Segal's ability to communicate with his attorneys. Segal believed Kendall took actions to delay Segal's sentencing for the same reason. Kendall used her role in Segal's prosecution in support of her vetting to be considered for a federal judge appointment.

Andrew Lotts. Lotts performed an extensive forensic reconstruction of Near North accounting records that exposed as baseless the government estimates used to convict Segal. Using the only methodology approved by the Illinois insurance statute, Lotts showed a positive reconciliation balance in the Premium Fund Trust Account, not the negative balance that the government claimed. Andrew Lotts and his associate Jill Skidmore went beyond their professional relationship and were personally committed and outraged as to the misrepresentation of the accounting data at Near North and attempted to meet with Segal's defense attorneys and showed up at Segal's sentencing hearing hoping to be called as witnesses.

Jeff Ludwig. A member of the Takeover Group, Ludwig conspired with government witness Ron Heitzman, who falsely testified that his firm, McGladrey & Pullen, had created the government accounting exhibit used against Segal. Ludwig asked the firm to change their invoice to buttress the false claim. Ludwig went to USI after leaving Near North. During the day of Segal's arrest Ludwig called Near North executives suggesting they abandon ship and join USI. Additionally, Ludwig conspired with another Near North employee to remove a proprietary database of Near North's association business customer records and database.

Michael Mackey. Mackey arranged for the hiring of Tom McNichols, who created most of the false accounting reconciliations used by prosecutors to convict Segal. Mackey attempted to hide his involvement with the Takeover Group for he had worked at Aon at one time and had no interest of going back.

His strategy after the others created the issues to indict Segal and Near North was to help engineer a sale of Near North's business and bringing other employees to Mesirow Insurance. Segal believes Mackey was a double-agent sharing information on both sides between the Takeover Group and Segal. Mackey inserted his lawyer to represent Near North employees who Segal believed carried information to government parties.

Mackey went to work for Mesirow Insurance and he insisted that his new employer, Mesirow hire Pat Muldowney who was Segal's legal corporate counsel's assistant and who Segal also believed would pass information on to Mackey, in particularly the progress being made as to the apprehension of Cheley's cybercrimes.

Tom McNichols. Hired by the Takeover Group, McNichols helped them in their plan to extort control of Near North using phony accounting documents. When that failed, he fabricated documents that became government exhibits at the trial. Among other things, McNichols created emails supposedly notifying Segal that the Premium Fund Trust Account was out of balance, but forensic records showed these emails were never sent. McNichols was the only Takeover Group member to testify in court and he repeatedly contradicted his own testimony.

Patrick Murphy. The FBI agent who arrested Michael Segal was deeply aware of, if not involved in, misconduct. He recorded a conversation during which he advised confessed embezzler Daniel Watkins how to change a sworn affidavit so that it falsely implicated Segal. Murphy also denied receiving stolen emails provided by the Takeover Group, though these were discovered by the defense. Patrick Murphy signed his initials on three separate documents to provide credibility that the documents be considered as a group exhibit that would include integrated accounting data that was impossible from the face of the documents.

Dean Polales. Prosecutor Polales, who left the U.S. Attorney's Office after Segal's trial for private practice, accompanied FBI Agent Murphy to arrest Segal. Polales asked Segal to wear a wire to entrap others. Polales was the head of the corruption unit, not the financial crimes unit that would normally be involved in investigating charges of the sort brought against Segal.

Daniel Reidy. A former top prosecutor in the U.S. Attorney's Office in Chicago who became a partner at the prestigious law firm of Jones Day, Reidy was the leader of Segal's defense team. Reidy was good at pretrial constitutional motions and the cross-examination of witnesses, but he did not present any accounting witnesses at the trial, although Segal had paid for an extensive forensic reconstruction of the accounting at Near North.

Pat Ryan. CEO of Aon Corporation, a Fortune 500 company that competed with Segal's Near North Insurance Brokerage and received and benefitted from stolen documents taken by Takeover Group members (who were later hired by Aon). Ryan was a major fundraiser for former U.S. Senator Peter Fitzgerald who recommended Patrick Fitzgerald for U.S. Attorney. Within days of taking office, Patrick Fitzgerald began an investigation of Segal and Near North. Ryan denied knowing the new Takeover Group employees at Aon indifference to a phone call by Takeover Berry while employed at Near North to Ryan's unlisted home phone number.

Michael Segal. Over the course of four decades, Segal, the CEO of Near North Insurance Brokerage, expanded a three-person office into a powerhouse company with 1,000 employees in seven states. In 2002, he was arrested six days after filing a lawsuit against former employees who had been stealing documents and proprietary information for a rival company, the Aon Corporation. At the time of his arrest, Segal was unaware that former employees were working with prosecutors to take down him and his company. Convicted and sentenced to ten years in prison, Segal sought to expose the misconduct and other questionable conduct by prosecutors that interfered with his proof of innocence and when his lawyers filed the pre-constitutional trial motions as to the right to amend its existing filing in civil court, was given a superseding Rico indictment destroying his $250M company.

Jeffrey Steinback. Steinback became one of Segal's sentencing attorneys on the recommendation of another attorney. Segal believed that Steinback utterly failed him, refusing to return his phone calls, interfering with Segal's ability to present a defendant's version of the issues, and breaking a promise to present Segal's accountant Andrew Lotts at the sentencing hearing. Segal also believed Steinbeck had conversations which were not disclosed with Segal's prosecutors.

Matt Walsh. Takeover Group member Walsh worked closely and was led by Dana Berry and was one of the links to cyberhacker David Cheley, who stole thousands of documents from Near North and shared them with Segal's competitors at Aon and with the prosecutors. Walsh was known for making threats against Near North Employees who supported Segal. Walsh went to Aon. Today Walsh is under a court restraining order from Aon for he left Aon helping a group of other employees to a competing insurance brokerage

Daniel Watkins. Watkins embezzled as much as $250,000 from Near North over more than a decade. After Segal discovered the theft, Watkins agreed to provide a sworn affidavit acknowledging his actions and stating that he had acted on his own. Before this was finalized, McNichols persuaded him to work with the FBI and to change his story to claim

Segal had participated with him in stealing petty cash from Near North which was the sole predicate for Segal's Klein Tax Conspiracy conviction. Years later, Watkins admitted in U.S. Tax Court that he acted alone. but this had no effect on approximately three additional years of incarceration for Segal for the same trier of facts that the government used to support his criminal conviction.

The footnotes in this book are the actual
supporting documents and court filings in
the Segal prosecution case for law students and
lawyers who have more interest. The purpose is
not only to provide support, but also provides
additional legal education for legal topics.
These documents can be found online at
www.convictionatanycost.com.

The Prosecution of
Michael Segal – A Timeline

January 20, 2002 – Michael Segal and Near North Insurance Brokerage act to protect the company by filing a lawsuit against members of the Takeover Group who were stealing confidential documents. The Takeover Group had unsuccessfully attempted to extort $40 million in stock that would give them control of the company in return for fixing accounting issues they created. Segal was unaware that some members of the Takeover Group were secretly working with federal prosecutors.

January 26, 2002 – Former Near North employee Tim Gallagher lured Segal to a surprise meeting with federal prosecutor Dean Polales and FBI Agent Patrick Murphy at the Westin Hotel in Chicago. Segal was asked to wear a wire to record unidentified individuals targeted by the prosecution. Segal refused to wear a wire and was arrested. Simultaneously, FBI agents raided Near North's offices and Segal's residences, carting off 6,000 boxes of records as well as computers and hard drives containing thousands of pages of attorney-client privileged documents.

February 14, 2002 – A one-count indictment is returned against Segal charging him with making a false statement to the Illinois Department of Insurance by asserting on a renewal application for his insurance producer's license that he properly maintained a Premium Fund Trust Account. The charge was based solely on the false claims of the Takeover

Group and came after Segal sued the Takeover Group and ultimately was among several such counts that were dismissed by Judge Ruben Castillo after the jury verdict.

February 25, 2002 – At Segal's arraignment, after his attorneys subpoenaed the Takeover Group, rather than allow those witnesses to be questioned in court, the prosecution dismissed the indictment. However, the prosecution continued the grand jury investigation of Segal and Near North.

April 24, 2002 – David Cheley, a former temporary employee of Near North, is confronted with the evidence of his cyber-hacking of Near North computers. The confrontation occurs during a meeting at Kemper Insurance where Cheley then worked following an investigation by former FBI agent David Grossman that uncovered the theft of hundreds of documents from Near North. The investigation showed that Cheley passed stolen confidential and attorney client privileged documents to members of the Takeover Group. The investigation also showed that FBI Agent Patrick Murphy received documents at his personal home email and that copies of confidential Near North documents were on the server of the Aon Corporation, a Near North competitor that hired some of the Takeover Group members.

September 17, 2002 – Near North attorney Joshua Buchman met with the prosecution team to inform them that Near North was filing an amended complaint in its civil lawsuit to include the cyber-crimes that included attorney-client privilege documents. Prosecutor William Hogan responded by asserting that the government witnesses had nothing to do with the cybercrimes and threatened to file a RICO indictment against Segal if Near North filed the amended complaint.

September 23, 2002 – Despite denials from FBI Agent Murphy and the prosecution that no such records existed, the prosecution disclosed a file that allegedly had been missing for 18 months that confirmed not only the cyber-hacking, but also the wiretapping of Segal's defense attorney Harvey Silets.

October 31, 2002 –The first superseding indictment was returned against Segal and—as threatened by Hogan—it contains a RICO count. The 16-count indictment charged Segal with using millions of dollars in insurance premiums to pay his own personal and business expenses. The indictment also contained charges of mail and wire fraud and making false statements to the Illinois Department of Insurance.

November 1, 2002 – Segal appeared before U.S. District Judge Ruben Castillo and entered a plea of not guilty to the charges. He remained free on a $750,000 bond secured by his signature.

November 22, 2002 – Segal defense files a motion seeking the return of all privileged information and to bar the prosecution from using any of that information in preparation for trial or during the trial itself. This includes more than 11,000 emails to and from Segal, at least 1,300 emails between Segal and a number of his attorneys and approximately 9,400 emails and faxes that had been seized from the office of Segal's legal counsel at Near North.

February 2, 2003 – Judge Ruben Castillo expressed misgivings about the government's failure to establish a "taint team" to review privileged documents. "I'm concerned that that doesn't seem to have happened in this case," the judge declared. "(T) he Court is going to order the government to return all privileged information."

May 13, 2003 – After the prosecution for the first time claimed that it had treated potentially privileged material with "extreme caution," despite not having a taint team in place, Castillo reversed himself. Without an explanation, Castillo denied the defense motion to return the documents.

June 10, 2003 – The defense filed a motion requesting an evidentiary hearing to consider evidence that the prosecution witnesses—David Cheley and the Takeover Group—were acting as government agents and thereby violating Segal's Fourth Amendment right to freedom from illegal searches.

June 13, 2003 – Another superseding indictment was returned against Segal and Near North, which was further part of prosecutor Hogan's threat of retaliation for Near North proceeding with its civil suit against the Takeover Group. This indictment, based on the same charge cited in the previous indictment, would put Near North out of business. One count charged former Near North employee Daniel Watkins, who admitted stealing from Near North, with embezzlement.

July 3, 2003 – Prosecution files opposition to the motion for evidentiary hearing saying that "Cheley was completely unknown to the government, and nothing caused the agents to believe that any information being provided was a result of stolen or improper access to this corporation's computer network....Cheley was completely independent of the government and unknown to the government. There is not the slightest indication that any government agent knew of unauthorized intrusions into the Near North system let alone an illegal hacking of the system by Cheley or anyone else."

July 10, 2003 – The prosecution admitted that Cheley was in fact known and claimed that it had learned "for the first time" that FBI

Agent Jane Higgins had suddenly remembered that she had a set of notes from a January 14, 2002, conversation with members of the Takeover Group. To Segal, this was ample proof that the government was hiding evidence and attempting to cover up improper conduct.

August 1, 2003 –The defense responded: "Before its amended filing, the government unequivocally stated that it knew nothing about the hacking activity and that it never received any hacked information from its witnesses. The Court and the defense now know that both of these statements were 100 percent false."

August 7, 2003 – Judge Castillo denied the defense motion for an evidentiary hearing. The judge did concede that there were "many detailed and specific facts" showing that the Takeover Group members were acting as agents of the prosecution. However, Castillo ruled the facts were "too conjectural, speculative, and attenuated to warrant what is presently framed as an extensive, invasive, and far-reaching inquiry."

February 4, 2004 – Near North attorney Sal Cognetti, Jr., filed a motion asking Judge Castillo to reconsider his denial of a hearing. The motion noted that Segal and Near North "were the victims of thousands of unlawful hacking intrusions; that the hacker specifically targeted and accessed confidential attorney-client privileged communications, many of which relate to the subject matter of the criminal charges; that least one of the cooperating witnesses affirmatively solicited information from the hacker; that the Government was aware of the unlawful computer access; and that there were frequent (approximately 400) undocumented contacts between the cooperating witnesses and the Government during the relevant period." That motion was denied.

March 17, 2004 –A fourth superseding indictment is filed against Segal and Near North.

March 23, 2004 – Admitted embezzler Daniel Watkins pleaded guilty to charges that he stole between $70,000 and $120,000 from Near North. In a signed plea agreement, Watkins said he withdrew money for Segal and recorded the withdrawals as postage expenses. Years later, he would admit he chose to record the money in that fashion without any direction from Segal.

April 19, 2004 – Jury selection begins in the trial of Michael Segal and Near North Insurance.

June 21, 2004 – Jury returns verdicts of guilty against Segal and Near North. The charge of making a false statement when he said he was unaware that Watkins had been embezzling was dismissed by the prosecution prior to the jury's deliberation. One charge had been dismissed at the conclusion of the evidence. Judge Castillo would later dismiss seven of the counts relating to making misrepresentations to the Illinois Department of Insurance.

June 22, 2004 – Forfeiture hearing concludes with the jury ordering Near North to be forfeited and Segal to forfeit $30 million. Segal is taken into custody and transferred to the Metropolitan Correctional Center.

July 1, 2004 – On the prosecution's motion, Judge Castillo appointed a trustee and attorneys for the trustee to operate Near North. The trustee would be ordered by prosecutor Hogan to withdraw Near North's civil lawsuit against the Takeover Group, although one law firm had estimated the suit could have generated around $50 million in damages. At Hogan's direction, the trustee rejected offers by qualified buyers for Near North's insurance business which, if accepted, could have hundreds of jobs and generated $100 million for the prosecution. The trustee and attorneys were still in place in 2017 even though Near North was long gone.

November 30, 2005 –Judge Castillo sentenced Segal to 121 months in prison—10 years and one month—and ordered him to make restitution of $841,527. Segal is designated for the Federal Correctional Institution in Oxford, Wisconsin.

December 13, 2005 – Judge Castillo sentenced Watkins to two years of supervised release with six months spent in home confinement. Watkins also was ordered to pay $109,000 in restitution (although it likely was never paid) and a $5,000 fine. Judge Castillo also imposed a $1.4 million fine on Near North.

February 16, 2006 – Joy Segal filed a claim to certain property subject to forfeiture relying in part on a marital property settlement entered in the Circuit Court.

August 2, 2007 –The U.S. Court of Appeals for the Seventh Circuit upholds the convictions of Segal and Near North. The appeals court vacated the $30 million forfeiture order and remanded the case back to Judge Castillo to make sure there was no double-counting and that Segal was not unfairly penalized.

August 31, 2009 – Judge Castillo cut the forfeiture to $15 million. The prosecution had claimed the proper amount was $18 million. Segal's lawyers presented evidence it should be at most $1.5 million and that perhaps the prosecution actually owed Segal money.

June 8, 2010 – Segal attorneys James Cole and Will Olson co-authored a 122-page filing with Lanny Breuer, then head of the Criminal Division of the US Attorney's office that detailed egregious and unlawful misconduct before and after the Segal grand jury proceedings, the trial and appeal, as well as post-trial forfeiture proceedings. The filing ultimately was ignored.

June 24, 2010 – U. S. Supreme Court issues ruling in U.S. v. Skilling finding that honest services fraud—which the prosecution had accused Segal of committing—was listed to bribery or kickback schemes. Segal appeals his convictions arguing there was no bribery or kickback scheme involved in his case.

November 2010 – The Court approved Joy Segal's settlement relating to her marital dissolution claims (filed in 2006) for interests in certain property as follows: Joy Segal entered into a settlement where the US released to Joy Segal certain property subject to forfeiture (i.e. Segal's interests in certain property) in exchange, Joy Segal released any claims she had to any and all remaining property, proceeds from the sale of properties, etc. not specifically identified in her Settlement Agreement which the US previously identified as being otherwise subject to forfeiture. Joy agreed that by her agreement, the US shall seek forfeiture of any and all remaining property so it may be applied to satisfy the forfeiture judgment entered against Segal. Unless the property is specifically identified as property that will be returned or released to Joy Segal, any remaining property, **jointly owned with or individually owned by Segal** except as specified, shall be subject to further forfeiture proceedings until such time as a final order not subject to appeal is entered.

December 2010 – After the Justice Department responded to the filing from Cole and Olson by asserting that the misconduct had been dealt with by the courts, Segal lawyer Stanley Brand responded, "That is incorrect. The issues we have raised regard prosecutorial misconduct by the U.S. Attorney's Office in Chicago that has caused a grave injustice to Mr. Segal. We request that our concerns be submitted to the Office of Professional Responsibility for consideration." At a subsequent court hearing, Hogan approached members of Segal's legal team and essentially said Segal "would be sorry" for filing his complaint (including more than 150 pages of evidentiary support) with the Justice Dept. and OPR.

May 3, 2011 –The U.S. Court of Appeals for the Seventh Circuit remands the case back to Judge Castillo for a hearing to determine whether Segal should be resentenced in the event any honest services conviction affected his 10-year prison term. The appeals court also upheld Castillo's decision that the forfeiture amount was $15 million.

May 2011 – Nearly a year after Segal's complaint was filed with Breuer, an attorney for the Office of Professional Responsibility, replied to Brand with a two-page letter saying that no action would be taken.

May 29, 2012 – One year and 26 days after the appeals court ruling remanded the case for resentencing, Judge Castillo finally reduced Segal's sentence to allow him to be released from prison immediately, approximately four months early.

August 21, 2012 – Judge Castillo orders a two-step hearing for January 5, 2013 to determine which of Segal's restrained assets would be used to satisfy the $15 million judgment. The first hearing was to determine ownership of the restrained assets; the second was to determine the value of all assets owned by Segal. Segal would then use $15 million of his assets to satisfy his forfeiture obligation.

January 2, 2013 –As the hearing approached, Prosecutor Hogan offered to settle by returning $8 million of the Segal's frozen assets. Segal had been fighting for years for the return of his financial records and computers to no avail. Asset holders were restrained from talking to Segal and there were no independent appraisals. Under economic duress with the only apparent alternative even more years of litigation, a desperate Segal accepted the deal.

February 2014—Admitted embezzler Daniel Watkins testified under oath in a civil tax proceeding brought against Segal that he never conspired with Segal to defraud the IRS and had no knowledge of Segal ever cheating on his taxes. When Segal rejected an IRS offer to end the case and insisted on questioning Hogan, The IRS dismissed the case on its own. As a result, a $1.1 million tax lien was vacated and Segal received a refund of more than $25,000.

August 2015 – Dennis Burke, former U.S. Attorney for the District of Arizona, and John Sandweg, former Acting Director of U.S. Immigration and Customs Enforcement and former Acting General Counsel of the Dept. of Homeland Security, send a seven-page letter to Jay Macklin, General Counsel for the Executive Office of United States Attorneys, requesting that the forfeiture proceedings be removed from the U.S. Attorney's Office in Chicago. The letter accused Hogan of engaging in a "hyper-zealous and exceptionally unusual campaign that strains the boundaries of ethical conduct."

October 5, 2016 – Segal filed a motion to modify the settlement agreement. After three years of fighting false evidence filed by Hogan, the motion said that the government had taken more than $40 million in personal assets from Segal—$32 million more than the $8 million settlement agreement and $25 million more than the $15 million that Castillo had ruled was owed. The defense accused Hogan of numerous vindictive post-trial actions including falsely claiming that Near North owned property that was in fact owned by Segal, withholding documents and accounting evidence that showed Segal's ownership of assets, undervaluing Segal's assets and deliberately running out Segal's option to purchase life insurance policies that could not be replaced. Hogan ignored the court records and court ruling showing that Segal had put more money in than any benefit he received from his company.

July 12, 2017 – Judge Castillo denied Segal's motion to modify the settlement agreement.

August 9, 2017 – Segal filed a Motion to Amend the July 12, 2017 Order. The motion said that the court erred concerning the $8 million in immediate benefits it found Segal received as a result of the settlement agreement. Specifically, the government valued two insurance policies that it claimed Near North had a right to release to Segal as part of the settlement as being worth $2,043,780. As part of the settlement, Segal elected to receive those two policies in lieu of cash or some other asset. However, neither Near North, nor the government, ever had ownership over those two insurance policies that were to go to Segal, and therefore, the government could not transfer those policies to Segal and Segal never received those two policies for which he negotiated. In other words, Segal did not receive $2 million of the $8 million the court found he received. Segal's motion also said the court made an error when it disregarded Segal's $15 million forfeiture order and its obligations under Federal Rule of Criminal Procedure 32.2 by ignoring the economic underpinnings of *Contempo Design Inc. v. Chicago and Northern Illinois District Counsel of Carpenters*, 226 F. 3d 535. The government had coerced Segal into agreeing to pay the government millions more than the $15 million he was obligated to pay, and further, there was no consideration for the amounts the government received.

August 16, 2017 – The District Court denied Segal's Motion to Amend the July 12, 2017 Order.

September 6, 2017 – Segal filed a timely Notice of Appeal.

September 16, 2019 - The Seventh Circuit issued its Opinion and Final Order and rejected Segal's appeal. The Court held that his agreement to settle his personal forfeiture was definitive. "We agree with the

District Court that the four corners of the 2013 agreement control Mr. Segal's rights and interests. The District Court denied Mr. Segal's effort to modify or rescind the settlement agreement," the Court ruled.

The Court also upheld Judge Castillo's refusal to permit Joy Segal to intervene. Although all Joy wanted was to enforce her settlement agreement, the Court refused to allow it. The Court went on to state, "Mr. Segal's tactics are egregious. His sixty-eight-page reply in the District Court relied mostly on 'gratuitous attacks on counsel'". In his brief on appeal, Mr. Segal accuses the government of all sorts of serious wrongdoing—such as that it outright 'fabricated the record'—without offering any evidence. The legal arguments that Mr. Segal raised in the District Court and in this court are baseless, hyperbolic, and conspiratorial.

The Court's response was extremely disappointing to Segal and his lawyers because their District Court filing which was referenced in the appeal contained multiple pages of specific facts of misconduct. The court threatened that if there were further proceedings, the parties and their lawyers could be liable "for excessive costs for unreasonable multiplication of proceedings."

It seems that Hogan's long-term scheme to take not just the $15 million that Segal agreed to in his settlement, but every last penny of Segal's and Joy's assets.

Two days later after the Appellate Court's opinion came down and within 10 days of Judge Castillo's retirement from the federal bench, Hogan went back to court presenting Judge Castillo with an incomplete and inaccurate order that stated, with little or no justification based on his own self-serving affidavit, that the forfeiture issue was settled.

About Michael Segal

MICHAEL SEGAL WAS BORN AND raised on the north side of Chicago. The son of a furrier, he received an undergraduate degree from Loyola University of Chicago. He began working full-time as a certified public accountant and at the same time attending DePaul University Law School where he obtained a law degree.

After several years of providing outside financial services to a small brokerage, Near North Insurance, he was invited to join the firm as a business manager. Later, he became a partner there and ultimately assumed full ownership. Early on, Segal was an early pioneer in recognizing that insurance services were a non-tangible commodity that could be delivered and marketed through cyber-technology deliveries and services. Near North National Group's culture was known for a diverse and youthful work force.

Under Segal's leadership, Near North Insurance grew from a small, storefront office into the nation's fifth largest independent insurance brokerage including wholesale distribution, facultative reinsurance, structured settlements and a motion picture guarantee company under its holding company, Near North National Group. The firm reported annual sales in excess of one hundred billion dollars, supported more than 1,000 employees in eight U.S. cities and London, included numerous Fortune 500 companies as clients, and developed numerous specialized market segments.

CPSIA information can be obtained
at www.ICGtesting.com
Printed in the USA
FSHW011907030520
69795FS

9 781733 155427